Development Under Adversity:

The Palestinian Economy in Transition

Edited by Ishac Diwan and Radwan A. Shaban

Palestine Economic Policy Research Institute (MAS) and the World Bank

M A S

The findings, interpretations, and conclusions expressed in this paper are entirely those of the author(s) and should not be attributed in any manner to the World Bank, to its affiliated organizations, or to members of its Board of Executive Directors or the countries they represent. The World Bank does not guarantee the accuracy of the data included in this publication and accepts no responsibility for any consequence of their use.

The material in this publication is copyrighted. The World Bank encourages dissemination of its work and will normally grant permission to reproduce portions of the work promptly.

Permission to photocopy items for internal or personal use, for the internal or personal use of specific clients, or for educational classroom use is granted by the World Bank, provided that the appropriate fee is paid directly to the Copyright Clearance Center, Inc., 222 Rosewood Drive, Danvers, MA 01923, U.S.A.; telephone 978-750-8400, fax 978-750-4470. Please contact the Copyright Clearance Center before photocopying items.

For permission to reprint individual articles or chapters, please fax your request with complete information to the Republication Department, Copyright Clearance Center, fax 978-750-4470.

All other queries on rights and licenses should be addressed to the World Bank Office of the Publisher or faxed to 202-522-2422.

Cover photographs by Miriam Sushman: students at Al Rafiden primary school in Sheik Radwan, Gaza City; and workers passing through the Erez checkpoint.

Ishac Diwan is Manager of the Macroeconomic Management and Policy Division of the Economic Development Institute of the World Bank.

Radwan Ali Shaban is Senior Research Fellow at the Palestine Economic Policy Research Institute (MAS) and Associate Professor of Economics at Georgia Institute of Technology.

Library of Congress Cataloging-in-Publication Data

Development under adversity : the Palestinian economy in transition /
    edited by Ishac Diwan and Radwan A. Shaban.
            p.   cm.
    Includes bibliographic references and index (p.).
    ISBN 0-8213-4418-8
    1. Palestine--Economic conditions. 2. Palestine--Economic policy
I. Diwan, Ishac. II. Shaban, Radwan Ali.
    HC415.25.D48   1999
    333.95694--dc21   99-12532
                                                        CIP

Contents

List of Figures, Tables and Boxes

Figures

Tables

Boxes

Foreword

Nabeel Kassis, MAS Director

The Declaration of Principles (DOP) signed by the Palestine Liberation Organization and Israel in 1993 was seen by many Palestinians as an important cornerstone in the process of nation-building and achieving a just and lasting peace. Raising the standards of living and laying the foundations for sustainable economic development in the West Bank and Gaza Strip are regarded as key for cementing a just political solution and ensuring the success of the peace process. Building Palestinian institutions of governance is another vital element in the success of this process. The Palestine Economic Policy Research Institute, or Ma'had Abhath As-Siyasat Al-Iqtisadiyeh Al-Filistini (MAS), is an autonomous national research institute that was established in May 1994 to utilize Palestinian expertise to provide policy makers with quality analysis of policies and strategies critical to the development of the Palestinian economy.

Over a short time period, MAS has actively contributed to the understanding of Palestinian economic development and to shaping economic policies. MAS's research has resulted in numerous publications in the areas of banking and monetary policy, fiscal policy, trade policy, poverty, social security, industrial development, and overall economic development strategies. MAS has organized several workshops on economic policy issues that have been summarized in *MAS Policy Notes* and in the local media. MAS's Monitoring Unit publishes the semi-annual *MAS Economic Monitor* and the annual *Social Monitor*.

This book is a product of joint effort by MAS and the World Bank. It builds on the extensive research output of MAS, the World Bank, and other researchers. The project was conceived from the beginning as an equal partnership between the two institutions. Its aim was to provide a comprehensive study of Palestinian economic development since the signing of the DOP and to present analysis on strategies and policies most conducive to sustainable economic development. This project was perceived from the outset to be a sequel to the influential 1993 six-volume report, *Developing the Occupied Territories: An Investment in Peace*, which was produced by the World Bank with the support of a Palestinian team appointed by the Palestine Liberation Organization.

The production of this book has entailed several iterations of reviewing the manuscript both by MAS and the World Bank; workshops at MAS involving policy makers and researchers on various background papers or chapters, with summaries published in the local media; and a review by various Palestinian ministries dealing with economic matters. The findings of this manuscript were presented and discussed in November 1997 at two conferences in Nablus and Gaza City. These conferences were well attended by the research and policy-making communities, and included high-ranking officials from several ministries. These thorough reviews have enriched and sharpened the discussion and presentation of the manuscript. We trust the book will have the intended impact of providing a better understanding of the difficulties facing both Palestinian economic development and policy-making.

Foreword

Joseph Stiglitz
Senior Vice President and Chief Economist
World Bank

The Palestinian economy has been operating far below its enormous potential. The situation has continued to deteriorate since the 1993 signing of the Declaration of Principles. Ultimately, a mutually advantageous resolution of political uncertainties is necessary for the economy to embark on a path of strong and sustained growth. However, an important message emerging from this book is that there are economic policies which the Palestinians and the donors can implement immediately to generate noticeable economic improvements.

The Palestinian economy began to weaken after 1988 with the *Intifada* and declined further after the Gulf War in 1990-91. Per capita expenditure has continued to fall during the interim peace process. At the end of 1995, approximately one-fifth of the population of the West Bank and Gaza Strip were living in poverty, and today the number is probably higher. The unemployment rate averages roughly 20 percent when the border is open and increases to 30 percent when it is closed.

Development Under Adversity documents the degree to which the permit and closure policies implemented by Israel since 1993 have led to a decline in employment for Palestinians in Israel. In 1992, an average of 116,000 Palestinians worked in Israel; in 1996 the number dwindled to 28,100. This was the result of a reduced number of permits issued by Israel to Palestinians plus the sharp increase in border closures, which were in effect for more than one-third of 1996. Closures are only the most obvious manifestation of Israeli policies. An example of a less visible hindrance to Palestinian development is the delay from inspection procedures which make it virtually impossible for Palestinians to export perishable goods, like flowers and strawberries. Consequently, many promising export industries have been shut down and farmers have reverted to low-value crops, such as potatoes and onions, grown for local consumption.

Despite these obstacles and setbacks, the Palestinian economy has enormous potential. The most important asset any country has is its people. It takes much more time to build a high-quality work force than it does to build infrastructure and factories. The Palestinian economy is blessed with excellent people. Its general development indicators—including life expectancy, literacy, and child mortality rates—are among the best in the Middle East and North Africa region. The average adult in the West Bank and Gaza Strip has spent eight years in school. Given the average relation between schooling and per capita income, one would expect a per capita GNP level of a little more than $10,000, adjusted for purchasing power parity. The Palestinian economy is operating at less than half of that level.

The book identifies other promising factors for economic growth, including a vibrant and well-organized civil society, the potential for significant tourism, an extensive international network of skilled and wealthy expatriates, a location at the trade intersection of East and West, no government debt, a good tax system, and widespread international sympathy.

Taken together, and given the right environment and an effective development strategy, the Palestinian economy could generate substantial growth rates in the near future. Some of the most important elements of the development strategy identified in the book are: opening up markets abroad through new trade channels and diversifying away from a disproportionate reliance on Israel in trade and delivery of services; creating a governance system with an efficient civil service, an investment-oriented public expenditure program, and suitable tools for stabilizing the economy; and taking advantage of the dynamic civil society and the resourceful non-governmental organizations in the delivery of health, education, welfare, and infrastructure services.

The book finds that donors can also make a big difference in stabilizing the economy, alleviating poverty, and laying the foundations for sustained growth. As the initial five-year pledge period draws to a close, donors need to review their role and, hopefully, renew their funding commitments into the future. The next round of support should focus less on mitigating short-term financial crises and more on investment—particularly long-term finance to support infrastructure reconstruction and sustainable delivery of social services.

Development Under Adversity is the outcome of a collaborative effort by a Palestinian think tank—the Palestine Economic Policy Research Institute (MAS)—and the World Bank. The process of writing the book was as important as any specific finding. At every stage there has been consultation and dialogue within Palestinian society, including a series of MAS-sponsored seminars and background papers contributed by experts and policy-makers. The World Bank has benefited from being able to assist in this Palestinian-led process of self-discovery and civic participation. The book not only embodies the conclusions of these wide-ranging discussions, but also attempts to reflect the uncertainties and debates. We see this as the beginning of an ongoing process that focuses on the vital economic development issues facing the Palestinian economy.

Acknowledgments

The book has been produced jointly by the Palestine Economic Policy Research Institute (MAS) and the World Bank. It was written by a core team, including Radwan A. Shaban, Task Manager for MAS; Ishac Diwan, Task Manager for the World Bank; Osama Hamed, MAS; and Ali Khadr, the World Bank.

The book has relied extensively on studies carried out by MAS and the World Bank. The core team was assisted by specialists in the West Bank and Gaza Strip and abroad, many of whom prepared background papers for this book. The background papers are listed in the bibliography. Research has relied extensively on analysis of raw data sets of labor force, expenditure, and demographic surveys carried out and made available to us by the Palestinian Central Bureau of Statistics. Martha Sipple was the editor for the book, and Isabelle Schnadig provided data support.

Definitions and Terms

Abbreviations and Acronyms

AHLC	Ad Hoc Liaison Committee
CG	Consultative Group on the West Bank and Gaza
CPRS	Center for Palestine Research and Studies
CU	customs union
DOP	Declaration of Principles
EAP	Emergency Assistance Program
EGS	employment generation scheme
EIP	export insurance program
EU	European Union
FTAs	free trade agreements
GIE	Gaza Industrial Estate
GCC	Gulf Cooperation Council
GDP	gross domestic product
GNP	gross national product
ICA	Israeli Central Administration
ICBS	Israeli Central Bureau of Statistics
IEC	Israel Electric Company
IFC	International Finance Corporation
ILO	International Labor Organization
IMF	International Monetary Fund
JEDCo	Jerusalem Electricity Distribution Company
JLC	Joint Liaison Committee
LACC	Local Aid Coordination Committee
LDC	less developed country
LMICs	lower middle-income countries
MENA	Middle East and North Africa
MIGA	Multilateral Investment Guarantee Agency
MEHE	Ministry of Education and Higher Education
MHE	Ministry of Higher Education
MIP	mortgage insurance program
MOE	Ministry of Education
MOF	Ministry of Finance
MOH	Ministry of Health
NGO	non-governmental organization
O&M	operation and maintenance
OECD	Organization for Economic Co-operation and Development
OPIC	Overseas Private Investment Corporation
PA	Palestinian National Authority

PADICO   Palestinian Development International Company
Paltel   Palestinian Telecommunications Company
PCBS   Palestinian Central Bureau of Statistics
PEA   Palestinian Electricity Authority
PECDAR   Palestinian Economic Council for Development and Reconstruction
PLO   Palestinian Liberation Organization
PMA   Palestinian Monetary Authority
PPP   purchasing power parity
PRCS   Palestine Red Crescent Societies
PWA   Palestinian Water Authority
REDWG   Regional Economic Development Working Group
RWB   West Bank exclusive of East Jerusalem
RWBGS   West Bank and Gaza Strip exclusive of East Jerusalem
RWG   Refugee Working Group
SACU   Southern African Customs Union
SMF   secondary mortgage facility
SWG   Sectoral Working Groups
TAP   Tripartite Action Plan on Revenues, Expenditures and
          Donor Funding for the Palestinian Authority
VAT   value-added tax
UIP   unemployment insurance program
UNDP   United Nations Development Programme
UNRWA   United Nations Relief and Works Agency
UNSCO   United Nations Special Coordinator Office
US   United States
WBGS   West Bank and Gaza Strip
WTO   World Trade Organization

Agreements

Annex 5   Economic Annex to the Interim Agreement

Declaration of Principles Israeli-Palestinian Declaration of Principles on
                           Interim Self-Government Arrangements

Cairo Agreement   Agreement on the Gaza Strip and the Jericho Area

Early Empowerment   Agreement on Preparatory Transfer of Powers
Agreement   and Responsibilities

Economic Protocol   Protocol of Economic Relations

Gaza-Jericho Agreement   Agreement on the Gaza Strip and the Jericho Area

Hebron Protocol   Protocol Concerning the Redeployment in Hebron

Interim Agreement	Israeli-Palestinian Interim Agreement on the West Bank and Gaza Strip
Oslo Agreement	Israeli-Palestinian Declaration of Principles on Interim Self-Government Arrangements
Oslo II Agreement	Israeli-Palestinian Interim Agreement on the West Bank and Gaza Strip
Paris Protocol	Protocol of Economic Relations
Taba Agreement	Israeli-Palestinian Interim Agreement on the West Bank and Gaza Strip

Weights and measures

BCM	billion cubic meters
DWT	deadweight tonnage
kg	kilogram
km	kilometer
kW	kilowatt
MCM	million cubic meters
Mw	megawatt

Currency

JD	Jordanian dinar
NIS	New Israeli shekel
US$	United States dollar

All dollar figures presented in the book are expressed in current US dollars unless otherwise specified.

Chapter 1

Introduction and Background

Ishac Diwan and Radwan A. Shaban

This book analyzes some key strategic choices facing the emerging Palestinian economy in the short and medium term. It reviews economic developments since the 1993 signing of the Declaration of Principles on Interim Self-Government Arrangements (Declaration of Principles or Oslo Agreement), identifies the underlying structural assets and liabilities of the economy, and explores options that would allow the economy to capitalize on its potential assets and reduce the impact of its weaknesses.

Since the signing of the Oslo Agreement, the economic situation has continued to deteriorate. The decline in household incomes, a sharp increase in unemployment, and the general broadening of poverty pose serious challenges to economic sustainability. Given the loss of jobs abroad, the most pressing economic challenges are to remove constraints to domestic production. Ultimately, advantageous resolution of political uncertainties—control of borders, access to natural resources, and management of territory—is necessary for strong and sustained growth of the economy, but there are policies that can be implemented immediately which would generate noticeable economic improvements in the short and medium term.

This book outlines three specific areas of policy change to foster stabilization and encourage growth in the Palestinian economy in spite of existing political difficulties:

- freeing access to external markets, opening new trade channels to the world, and reducing disproportionate reliance on Israel in trade and delivery of services;
- creating a governance system with an efficient civil service, minimal fiscal deficits, and suitable tools for stabilizing the economy; and
- taking advantage of a dynamic private sector and resourceful nongovernmental organizations (NGOs) in the delivery of health, education, welfare, and infrastructure services.

The donor community can help greatly to implement development with support for investment projects, especially those that facilitate free and diversified access to outside markets; by supporting the move toward lean and efficient government; and by encouraging all interested parties to overcome the obstacles to development.

The peace process based on the Oslo Accords has created new political and economic forces which have had a fundamental impact on the Palestinian economy. Yet, the initial conditions of the Palestinian economy have also played a key role in the recent economic record. This chapter reviews the historical development of the Palestinian economy over the past two decades and demonstrates how the economy is operating substantially below its capacity. Favorable political and policy conditions would permit rapid economic growth driven by a greater and more efficient use of existing resources.

Historical Overview

The West Bank and Gaza Strip (WBGS) has followed a skewed pattern of economic development since the Israeli occupation of 1967. This pattern is examined in terms of the evolution of per capita gross national product (GNP) and gross domestic product (GDP), structural changes in the labor market, and a policy framework that has depressed economic activity.

Per Capita GNP and GDP

As illustrated in Figure 1.1, the pattern of economic growth and stagnation since 1967 can be broken into four phases:

- *Phase I—1967 through mid-1970s.* Rapid growth was driven by integration with Israel and the start of the Gulf oil boom. The opening of the Israeli market to manual Palestinian labor, new trade, and technological opportunities brought rapid growth in domestic production. From a regional context, WBGS growth in GNP per capita in the 1970s was more than double Israel's growth rate, but was only slightly greater than rates in neighboring Arab countries.
- *Phase II—mid-1970s through early 1980s.* Slightly less rapid growth continued to be fueled by migrant worker wage remittances from the Gulf and by foreign transfers. Per capita income reached a peak in 1980 at $1400 (in 1986 prices).

Figure 1.1 Evolution of the GDP and GNP per capita in WBGS (in 1986 prices)

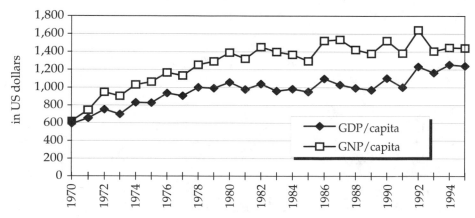

Sources: ICBS and World Bank.

The WBGS overall growth rate exceeded Israel's, but this is not unusual when integrating with a larger, richer, and more technologically advanced neighbor. While growth in Israel slowed in the mid-1970s, income and output in the WBGS continued to increase.

- *Phase III—early 1980s until Intifada in 1987.* This phase is characterized by stagnation and declining employment opportunities. The collapse of the regional oil boom prompted a decline in worker remittances from the Gulf. While continued growth in Israel provided a cushion from the regional slowdown, employment in Israel was virtually flat in the mid-1980s. Beginning with the *Intifada*, employment for Palestinians in manufacturing and services declined. This decline was offset by a rise in construction employment in response to an Israeli housing boom, resulting from a surge in immigration. However, recession and near hyperinflation in Israel had a serious impact on the 35 percent of the Palestinian labor force employed in Israel, and on the majority of Palestinian trade with Israel. Once work opportunities abroad declined, there was increased pressure to employ workers at home.
- *Phase IV—late 1980s until 1993.* Output declined as the *Intifada* continued due to strikes and repression of economic activity. Political and economic uncertainty prevailed. A recovery in 1992, apparently fueled by drawdowns of savings and expectations of peace, was followed by a renewed decline in 1993.

Structural Dislocation of the Labor Market

The phases of growth and stagnation of the Palestinian economy are largely driven by developments of the labor market. Reflecting the economy's dependence on exported labor, the number of Palestinians working within the WBGS was roughly equal in the mid-1980s to the number in the late 1960s, despite very high growth rates of population and labor force.

According to Palestinian Central Bureau of Statistics (PCBS) estimates, the WBGS population was estimated at 2.5 million in 1996, and is projected to reach 3 million people by the year 2000. The natural rate of population growth is the highest rate in the world, due to high fertility and low and declining mortality. The overall natural rate of population increase was estimated at 3.9 percent per annum in 1994. The total fertility rate (number of children born to a woman through her reproductive cycle) was 5.61 in the West Bank and 7.44 in the Gaza Strip in 1994, for an average of 6.24. Fertility rates continue to be high despite a sharp decline in mortality rates. Infant mortality rates were halved during the period 1980-95, declining to a rate of 28 per 1000.

High population growth rates are matched by high growth rates of the labor force. The WBGS labor force was estimated at one-half million workers in 1996, and will increase at an average rate of 30,000 workers annually through the remainder of the century. For about two decades after the 1967 occupation, growth in the Palestinian labor force was largely absorbed by external labor markets.

Skilled workers found employment in Jordan and the Gulf countries, and the unskilled workers found employment in Israel.

Recently, the WBGS labor market faced two major shocks: (i) the elimination of
Gulf countries market for newly educated Palestinian workers (a trend which started
in the mid-1980s and became more pronounced following the 1990-91 Gulf War);
and (ii) the rapid drop in demand for existing unskilled Palestinian workers in Israel, and its increased riskiness beginning with the interim period of the peace process. These shocks have affected various segments of the labor market differently.
Elimination of the Gulf demand reduced new opportunities for educated and skilled
workers, but its impact on the existing Palestinian workers in the Gulf was fairly
limited. The drop in Israeli demand for Palestinian workers is more serious, and is
exacerbated by large numbers of unemployed workers in Israel seeking employment in the WBGS. The two shocks have been difficult for the Palestinian economy
to absorb, and their magnitude in relation to the total labor market is compounded
by a legacy of constrained development, and by the difficulties arising from strategic uncertainty of the peace process and closure-related constraints. The result has
been high Palestinian unemployment in the WBGS and under-utilization of labor
resources.

Elimination of the Gulf Market as a Potential Source of Demand

Since the Gulf War, the possibility of employment in the Gulf countries for new
Palestinian graduates has basically disappeared. This shock followed a decade of
declining demand for new graduates in Jordan and the Gulf Cooperation Council (GCC) countries. This shock has seriously affected better-educated Palestinians, who have traditionally sought employment there.

Jordan and GCC countries slowly absorbed a large number of Palestinian workers in the 1970s and, to a lesser extent, in the 1980s. Palestinian migrants to these
countries are usually dropped from labor force computations. By the early 1990s,
the cumulative number of migrant workers living abroad was estimated at more
than 100,000 workers. The recent PCBS demographic survey lends support to this
estimate. Palestinian migration into GCC countries slowed from the mid-1980s on-
ward, due to increasingly restrictive policies in GCC countries that attempted to
limit the number of expatriates, particularly Arab workers, and also due to increasing competition from cheaper labor from Southern Asia.

While a more favorable political arrangement could permit absorbing some Palestinian workers in the GCC countries, the pressures facing GCC labor markets
make this an insignificant and unreliable possibility from the Palestinian labor market perspective. GCC labor markets are experiencing increasing unemployment among
nationals, as well as policy changes that limit the amount of expatriate employment.

Permanent Reduction in Employment in Israel and its Increased Riskiness

The average number of Palestinian workers in Israel increased in stages from the
late 1960s until it peaked in 1992 at 116,000 workers. Since then, Palestinian em-

ployment in Israel dropped successively but rapidly to 28,000 workers in 1996 (Figure 1.2). The current employment rate is about one-third of the 100,000-worker level that Israel implicitly committed to maintain in the Economic Protocol. In a four-year period, Israel reduced its employment of Palestinian workers by 88,000, more than one-fifth of the Palestinian labor force.

Reduced Israeli demand for Palestinian employment reflects three policy changes. First, since 1991 (when work permits were introduced), the number of permits issued to Palestinians has declined (see Figure 4.4 in Chapter 4). Second, the strictness of permit policy has increased since March 1993, reducing the number of workers with permits. While the actual number of workers exceeded the number of permits by a substantial margin in 1991-92, the reverse was true in 1996. Work permits were often invalidated by border closure, which was applied during more than one-third of 1996. Third, employment in Israel has become more risky because the incidence and duration of closures cannot be predicted.

Figure 1.2 Substitution of Palestinian Workers with Foreign Workers in Israel

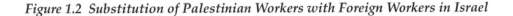

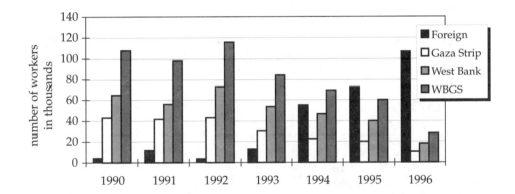

Sources: ICBS for Palestinian employment up to 1994, and PCBS for Palestinian employment in 1995-96. Number of foreign workers refers to permits issued, with data obtained from the Israeli Ministry of Labor.

Palestinian jobs in Israel may have been lost permanently. The Israeli economy has been adjusting by substituting Palestinian workers with workers from Eastern European and Southern Asian countries. Employment of foreign workers has increased at a faster rate than the decline of Palestinian workers: from 1992 to 1996, work permits for foreigners increased from 4,000 to 107,000. Foreign workers can be found in the very same jobs in which Palestinians used to work.

While the initial impetus for reducing Palestinian employment in Israel was political in nature, the loss may be permanent for both political and economic factors. Politically, violence is unlikely to disappear in the region in the near future, and restricting Palestinian access to employment in Israel has become a knee-jerk political response by the Israeli government, regardless of its political philosophy. Economically, Israeli employers have adjusted by substituting foreign workers for Palestinian workers. Employment of Palestinians has become more costly because workers might not be able to reach their jobs on any given day.

The Legacy of Long Occupation

The economic record of the WBGS prior to implementing the peace process is best understood in the context of structural weaknesses that are associated with the history of long occupation, as well as a policy framework that has resulted in weak domestic productive activity. These structural weaknesses in the Palestinian economy arose from four key factors that remain serious constraints to growth and job creation.

- *Asymmetric market relations with Israel.* Manual labor and manufacturers from WBGS had fairly free access to Israel, as did skilled labor from elsewhere; but the domestic expansion of WBGS agriculture and manufacturing was restricted. All Palestinian goods had limited access to much of the region due to restrictions on trade with Jordan, practical difficulties in trading across Israeli borders, and inadequate infrastructure. There were no restrictions on imports from Israel; but for imports from the rest of the world, the economy operated under the Israeli trade regime that was extremely protectionist until the mid-1980s.
- *Regulatory restrictions.* Expansion of the private sector, particularly medium and large firms, has been held back by regulatory restrictions (especially investment approvals required by the Israeli Civil Administration (ICA), an uncertain legal and tax framework, and political risks. The formal financial system was literally shut down until 1993. These conditions caused a bias toward the export of labor.
- *Fiscal compression and institutional under-development.* Fiscal compression and institutional under-development have led to the under-provision of public goods. Spending on public goods has suffered due to low tax receipts, a close-to-balanced budget practice by the ICA and municipalities, and the inability of utilities to borrow for investment (in contrast to international practice). Public sector revenues were low at 16 percent of GDP—partly because a portion of Palestinian tax payments, perhaps as much as 10 percent of GDP, accrued to the Israeli treasury.
- *Restricted access to natural resources.* Administrative limitations on surface and aquifer water harvesting have meant stagnation in water usage for Palestinian agriculture. During the 1980s and early 1990s, agricultural production was also hampered by the loss of land to settlements and to urbanization in the Jordan Valley—land traditionally and currently irrigated. The lack of clear zoning regulations and restrictive public land utilization policy have created barriers to industrial expansion.

The Infrastructure Gap

A key outcome of the policy framework is little investment in public infrastructure for two and half decades following the 1967 occupation. Compared to other countries with similar levels of income, infrastructure in the WBGS is seriously deficient (Table 1.1), due to years of neglect and lack of investment.

Table 1.1. Comparing Infrastructure Services in the WBGS

Country	Population (million)	Per capita income (US$)	Electric supply (kW per) 100 people)	Electric power system losses (%)	Households with sanitation (%)	Number of phones (per 100 people)	Meters of paved roads (per 100 people)
Egypt	55.0	650	21.0	14.0	50	4.3	59
Jordan	3.9	1,120	25.0	19.0	100	7.0	170
WBGS	2.4	1,450	13.0	30.0	25	3.1	80
Lebanon	4.0	2,500	32.0	N.A.	N.A.	9.3	N.A.
Syria	13.0	2,800	30.0	N.A.	63	4.1	180
Israel	5.1	13,500	82.0	4.0	100	37.1	266
Mauritius	1.1	2,700	33.0	14.0	100	9.6	190
LMICs*	1,152.6	1,620	21.5	12.4	N.A.	7.9	N.A.
OECD**	N.A.	19,710	82.6	7.3	N.A.	45.1	N.A.

Note: Data are for the years 1992-94.
* Lower middle income countries.
** Organization for Economic Co-operation and Development.
Sources: World Bank (1994c); International Yearbooks of Telecommunications Statistics, Electricity Statistics; Road Statistics; KPMG report on telecommunications, and internal World Bank reports.

- *Transport.* Virtually all the major roads were constructed before 1967 and have received minimal or no maintenance. International transportation (ports and airports) are entirely under Israeli control.
- *Electricity.* Per capita supply is significantly lower than other countries in the region. Supply is almost entirely supplied by the Israel Electric Company and there are very large system losses as assets have been allowed to depreciate.
- *Telecommunications.* There are just over three fixed phones and one mobile phone for every 100 persons. All neighboring countries, including Egypt, have a higher phone penetration ratio.
- *Water.* Water consumption per person is much lower than in neighboring countries, and water quality has been deteriorating. Depleted aquifers and sea water seepage has rendered water in the Gaza Strip brackish. Water supply is substantially dependent upon the Israeli company, Mekoroth.

• *Sanitation.* Only 25 percent of households are connected to sewage networks. Collection, treatment, and disposal of sewage are growing problems. The networks, where they exist, are under great strain and a major health hazard.

Underutilized Potential

Despite the long occupation and the structural weaknesses facing the WBGS economy, there are distinctive assets that could lead to rapid growth if utilized properly. In the right environment and with the right mix of strategies and policies, the WBGS economy could thrive and become a leader in the region.

• *The people.* The WBGS has high-quality human resources, as implied by the average years of schooling of the adult population (Table 1.2). There is no shortage of entrepreneurial talent or professional skills. The private sector is highly resourceful with a demonstrated ability to operate under challenging conditions.

Table 1.2. General Development Indicators

	West Bank*	Gaza Strip	WBGS Total
Male life expectancy	70	70	70
Female life expectancy	73.5	73.5	73.5
Average years of schooling for 15+ years	8.0	8.3	8.1
Literacy rate for 15+ years (%)	83.4	84.9	83.9
Female literacy rate 15+ years (%)	75.3	78.7	76.4
Male enrollment rate for 6-15 years (%)	91	89	90
Female enrollment rate for 6-15 years (%)	92	90	91
Infant mortality rate (per 1000) in 1995	25	32	28
Infant mortality rate (per 1000) in 1980	50	59	54
Child mortality rate (per 1000) in 1995	32	41	36
Child mortality rate (per 1000) in 1980	67	81	73
Total fertility rate (children per woman)	5.61	7.44	6.24
Family size	6.7	7.81	7.06
Refugees (% of total)	27.0	64.0	40.0
Female-headed households (%)	7.8	6.3	7.0

* Figures for the West Bank in this table do not include Jerusalem.
Source: Extracted and computed from various tables in PCBS (1996a).

- *Financial capital.* There are plenty of private capital resources ready to be invested in the WBGS if the business environment and policy framework are conducive. The emergent banking industry attracted deposits in excess of $1.7 billion by the end of 1996, much of which is yet to be invested domestically. Many of the successful businessmen in the Arab world are Palestinians who have already demonstrated great interest in investing in the WBGS.
- *Social capital.* There is a vibrant and well-organized civil society. Many institutions were formed during occupation to deliver public services, which were not adequately provided by the ICA. NGOs, universities, and hospitals

---

Box 1.1 *The Palestinian Diaspora*

Diaspora Palestinians are estimated to number 4.5 million—nearly twice the population of the WBGS. There are an additional 0.8 million Palestinian citizens in Israel. Two waves of refugees and their descendants largely constitute the Palestinian Diaspora. The first wave occurred in 1948 with the establishment of the state of Israel, and the second with the 1967 occupation of the WBGS. While there are large concentrations of Diaspora Palestinians in Jordan, Lebanon, and Syria, the community is widespread, extending to Europe, North and South America, and Australia.

The Diaspora Palestinian community has come to be recognized for its entrepreneurial spirit and strong work ethic, as well as leadership, managerial, and vocational skills in business, banking, engineering, medicine, and government planning. Expatriate Palestinian entrepreneurs include a wealthy elite that forms an international network operating out of such business centers as London, Athens, Cyprus, Riyadh, Qatar, Amman, Brooklyn, Detroit, and Boston.

Estimates of this wealthy elite's combined assets are between $40 and $80 billion. The elders of the overseas community, now mostly in their 60s and 70s, command the greatest personal wealth, much of it built on petrodollars in the Gulf region and on construction and property development in Europe and the US. The younger expatriates, mostly in their 40s and 50s, include a large number of highly educated professionals, such as academics, doctors, engineers, and managers, who hold top positions in corporations and are prominent in banking, both in Europe and the Middle East.

Well before the beginning of the peace process, wealthy Palestinian expatriates were channeling funds into the WBGS. A lot of the funds went to educational and humanitarian organizations, such as to universities and hospitals. The biggest conduit for private aid was the Geneva-based Welfare Association, of which more than 100 of the richest Diaspora Palestinian businessmen are members.

Source: Abu-Ghaida (1996).

have played a major role in delivering health services, education, agricultural assistance, and welfare aid to poor families.

- *International networks*. Successful Palestinian entrepreneurs in Europe and the United States (US) can help the Palestinian economy through networks and international contacts, whether for markets, expertise, technical know-how, or capital. The expatriate Palestinian community will be key in developing the tourist and construction sectors (Box 1.1).
- *Culture*. The unique religious and cultural heritage of the WBGS has the potential to revitalize tourism in the region. The tourism industry was the mainstay of the West Bank economy in 1967, but suffered serious setbacks due to the unsettled political and security situation. With peace and the normalization of relations in the region, tourism and related industries can again become a major source of employment for Palestinians, especially if cooperative arrangements can be developed with neighboring countries to promote tourism on a regional basis.
- *Newcomer's advantage*. As Palestinian economic management is a newcomer to the world of development policy, it can learn from the mistakes and successes of others in policy formulation and implementation. This should save the economy setbacks from the failed policies adopted by other developing countries, such as expanding public sector employment to reduce unemployment, using price controls to keep the cost of food low for urban consumers, or using state agencies to deliver private goods.
- *East-West link*. Given the WBGS' geographic location and Palestinian experience in trading with both the Israeli and Arab economies, the WBGS could become a significant transit point for future trade within the region. The free trade agreements (FTAs) signed with the European Union (EU) and the US should also make the WBGS an attractive economy to export-oriented industries.
- *No debts, good tax system*. Unlike most other developing economies, the Palestinian economy has not had to deal with the burden of a crushing external debt. It has succeeded in establishing a fiscal base that is relatively large by regional and even international standards (20 percent of GDP in revenues). Sound macroeconomic conditions can, however, be swiftly lost by imprudent policies, especially if the public sector expands too much as a way of reducing unemployment.
- *International sympathy*. Because of strong international interest in resolving the Palestinian-Israeli conflict, there are good prospects for attracting international assistance to help overcome infrastructure bottlenecks and deficiencies. While much of the aid disbursed so far has gone toward ameliorating deteriorating conditions in the short-term, the international community would most likely continue to support long-term infrastructure needs in the interest of improving overall conditions.

In view of these strong structural assets, the Palestinian economy is operating below its potential both quantitatively and qualitatively. To assess the quantitative underutilization of labor, we constructed an index of the average weekly

Figure 1.3 Index of Average Weekly Hours of the Labor Force (1980-96)

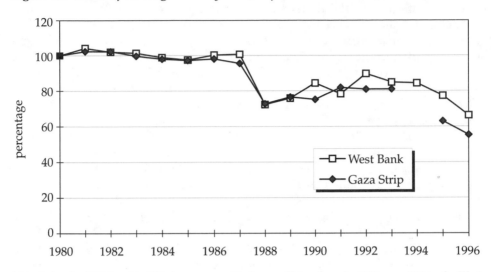

Note: Index for 1980 is set to 100. Average weekly hours of labor force in 1980 were 43.3 in the West Bank and 43.7 in Gaza Strip.
Sources: 1980-94 data are based on ICBS; 1994 data were not collected in Gaza Strip; and 1995-96 data refer to fall and spring of these years, respectively, and are based on PCBS.

Figure 1.4 Per Capita GNP Increases with Education Level: 102 Countries in 1990, but WBGS Income Level Is Far Below Potential

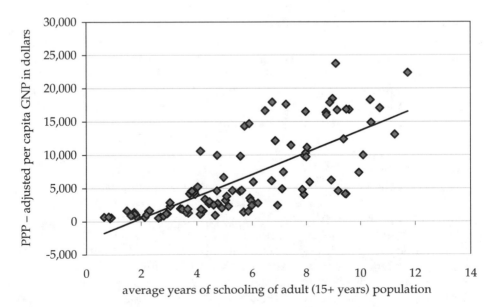

Note: WBGS average years of adult schooling was 8.1 years in 1995.
Source: Data from Barro and Lee (1996).

hours worked by the average person in the labor force. The index captures both open unemployment and underemployment of the existing labor force. Due to the predominance of part-time jobs and disruptions to employment during the *Intifada* years and during border closures, the index turns out to be much more revealing than the straight unemployment figures. This index is set at 100 for 1980 (corresponding to 43.3 hours in the West Bank and 43.7 hours in Gaza Strip). Figure 1.3 illustrates the decline in average hours worked for the 1980-96 period. The economy was operating close to full employment in the early 1980s, exporting workers to Israel and GCC countries. Then, an unstable environment during the *Intifada* led to a drop of the index to 72 in 1988, implying that 28 percent of existing labor force potential was not utilized. The index improved in the early 1990s but then dropped unambiguously over 1992-96. By spring 1996, only 63 percent of the West Bank and a mere 55 percent of Gaza Strip's available labor force potential was utilized.

Figure 1.4 clearly illustrates the continued deterioration of underutilizing the labor force over one and a half decades. Also illustrating the WBGS underutilized potential is the fact that per capita incomes are very low given the high quality of the potential workforce. This can be illustrated by comparing the WBGS levels of skills and income with other countries. Figure 1.4 shows for 102 countries how increasing educational levels are associated with higher levels of income. The average amount of education for the WBGS adult population was 8.1 years in 1995. Given the average relation between schooling and per capita income, one would expect a per capita GNP level of a little more than $10,000, adjusted for purchasing power parity (PPP). Even with very conservative PPP adjustments, the Palestinian economy is operating at one-third to one-half of its potential, considering its excellent human resources.

With the right economic environment and political climate, the WBGS economy could quickly generate substantial growth and not experience shortages of labor quantity or quality. The removal of regulatory constraints, the establishment of supporting institutions and infrastructure, and reduced political uncertainty should, therefore, allow the economy to grow. Once free of the legacy of high debts, inefficient public enterprises, and a revenue base too small to meet needed public expenditures, public policy can focus on creating the framework conducive for development. Direct foreign investment is likely to follow once profitable opportunities and a stable environment are established.

Analysis of the Palestinian economy's recent record and strategic policy options is carried out in three parts. Part I of the book analyzes the recent economic (Chapter 2) and political (Chapter 3) developments associated with the peace process. The special impact of border closures is addressed in Chapter 4.

Part II analyzes policies for growth and job creation under adverse conditions of the uncertain interim period. This section identifies policies that could enhance economic development in the interim period, while broader political uncertainty remains unresolved. Though mindful of the somewhat limited potential for economic growth in this environment, the analysis identifies key areas where policy improvements can have an impact on economic outcomes. This analysis first examines investment (Chapter 5), trade and free access to outside markets (Chapter 6), and the financial sector (Chapter 7). The potential improvement of public sector operations is analyzed in the context of improving fiscal management (Chapter 8); and instruments that could mitigate the impact of the large shocks influencing the WBGS economy are discussed in Chapter 9. The impact of donor aid is addressed in Chapter 10.

Part III analyzes human resources and public infrastructure, and tackles policies and issues that have both an immediate impact on economic outcomes and a long-term influence on economic growth once the political conditions become more conducive and supportive of economic development. Chapter 11 focuses on policies to improve the outcome of the educational system for a rapidly growing population, while Chapter 12 addresses the challenge of managing growth in the health sector. Improving infrastructure and finding ways to encourage the private sector to contribute to such improvement is discussed in Chapter 13.

Bibliographic note: This chapter draws on Shaban (1993, 1996), World Bank (1993a), ICBS (1995), PCBS (1996a, 1996d, 1996e), and Shabaneh (1996).

Part I

Recent Developments: New Constraints and Frustrated Developments

With the signing of the Declaration of Principles in September 1993, there were high hopes for a quick resumption of economic growth. These expectations were based both on the presence of strong structural advantages in the Palestinian society and economy, and on the fact that for a variety of reasons, growth had remained below potential prior to the onset of the peace process.

Yet, in spite of a significant donor effort, the economic situation has deteriorated markedly since the beginning of the peace process in 1993. Unemployment and poverty have emerged as major problems, amid a rapidly growing public sector, the slowing of private investment, and a collapse in trade flows. Palestinian policy makers have had to operate under a constraining framework in implementing the Palestinian-Israeli agreements—beginning with the Palestinian Authority's (PA) inception in 1994 and extending through a series of enlargements of its spheres of influence. Much more constraining has been the day-to-day reality of closures, the diminishing porosity of the WBGS borders, and the reduced ability to travel to, work in, and trade with Israel. Increased difficulties in business operations and heightened uncertainty regarding the feasibility of a permanent settlement have stifled private investment.

These difficulties are taxing economic development, and require all efforts to concentrate on stabilization, institutional growth, and the donor process. In light of the recent experience of ongoing cycles of closure, economic decline, and violence, Palestinian policy makers will not be able to foster the kind of ambitious economic vision to which the population aspires unless the prevailing political, policy, and institutional frameworks undergo deep transformations.

Chapter 2

Worsening Economic Outcomes Since 1994 Despite Elements of Improvement

Radwan A. Shaban

Introduction

With the signing of the Declaration of Principles in September 1993, there were high expectations of rapid economic growth that would improve living conditions in the WBGS. There were several reasons for optimism. It was anticipated that the PA would adopt policies more favorable toward local economic development than the policies of the ICA. The financial sector would be permitted to develop and play a key role in facilitating investment and transactions. Legal and regulatory obstacles to development would be eliminated, inducements for private enterprise would be introduced, and public sector services and infrastructure would be improved and expanded. These developments would take place with the generous support of donor countries. Moreover, the Palestinian-Israeli partnership for peace was expected to generate friendlier Israeli policies toward Palestinian economic development.

In September 1993, about two-thirds of the WBGS population believed that the peace process would improve their economic conditions (Box 2.1). These expectations were somewhat tempered in the first year after the Declaration of Principles due to (i) difficulties encountered in negotiating the May 1994 Agreement on the Gaza Strip and Jericho Area (Cairo Agreement or Gaza-Jericho Agreement); (ii) challenges to creating Palestinian capacity for economic management and institutions of governance; and (iii) slow initial disbursement of foreign aid. In June 1994, approximately 31 percent of the West Bank and 45 percent of the Gaza Strip population believed that their economic conditions would improve as a result of the peace process. Only 15 percent of the West Bank and 8 percent of the Gaza Strip population believed that the peace process would leave them economically worse off.

Between October 1994 and March 1995, 40 to 52 percent of the respondents reported that their economic situation and standard of living had deteriorated in the aftermath of the implementation of peace process. The dashing of economic expectations is particularly frustrating to Palestinians given the solid economic performance of the Israeli economy (Box 2.2). While emphasis was placed on improving Palestinian economic conditions at the signing the Declaration of Principles, the Israeli economy benefited significantly from the peace dividend as the Palestinian economy was allowed to collapse.

This chapter documents the frustration of these expectations in the period since the September 1993 Declaration of Principles. This period has been accompanied by deteriorating living conditions as reflected in increased and high rates of poverty, and in extremely high and widely fluctuating unemployment rates. The chapter analyzes the decline in economic indicators that contributed directly to the deteriorating living conditions, as well as the few areas where improvements were achieved despite all odds.

Box 2.1 *Palestinian Public Opinion on Economic Improvements*

The Center for Palestine Research and Studies (CPRS) in Nablus, the West Bank, has been carrying out opinion polls on the political and socio-economic conditions in the WBGS since September 1993. Twenty-six public opinion polls were conducted between September 1993 and March 1996.

The opinion polls illustrate that around the time of signing the Declaration of Principles, about two-thirds of the population of the West Bank (65.6 percent) and the Gaza Strip (65.4 percent) expected implementation of the Declaration of Principles to improve Palestinian economic conditions. The fraction of people believing that their economic situation would improve was much less in June 1994 after signing the Cairo Agreement (31.4 percent in the West Bank and 45.1 percent in the Gaza Strip). The fraction of people who reported that their economic condition improved since the implementation of the peace process ranged between 3.9 and 13.3 percent in the West Bank and between 10.8 and 15.7 percent in the Gaza Strip.

Despite early high expectations for improvement, the fraction of people reporting their economic situation to have worsened since the Declaration of Principles ranged between 35 and 52 percent in the West Bank and between 48 and 57 percent in the Gaza Strip. In comparison with the West Bank, the Gaza Strip has higher portions of people whose economic situation has either improved or worsened.

In repeated public opinion polls, unemployment and job availability were recorded as the most critical concern among a host of socio-economic and cultural factors, such as violence, repression, moral decay, and religious abandonment. This primary concern for employment was repeated in the October 1993, May 1994, and December 1995 polls. The shocks that influence the region are reflected in the optimism and pessimism regarding future economic and political developments.

Source: CPRS, public opinion polls, various, 1993-97.

(box continues on next page)

(Box 2.1 continues)

Selected Survey Results

Below are the survey results concerning economic development taken from various CPRS public opinion polls. All figures are represented in percentage of respondents.

Expectations and Reality of Economic Improvements

Q.: Will the proposed Palestinian-Israeli agreement improve economic conditions in the WBGS?

(September 10-11, 1993)
answering yes: 65.4 in Gaza Strip; 65.6 in West Bank; 65.5 in WBGS

Q.: With the implementation of self-government, do you believe that your standard of living ____?

	Total	West Bank	Gaza Strip
(June 30, 1994)			
Will improve	36.0	31.4	45.1
Will worsen	13.0	15.5	8.1
Other	51.0	53.1	46.8

Q.: Following the peace process and implementation of autonomy in the Gaza Strip and Jericho, my economic situation and standard of living has

	Total	West Bank	Gaza Strip
(September 29-October 1, 1994)			
Improved	9.2	7.5	11.8
Worsened	40.8	35.6	48.5
Other	50.0	56.9	39.7
(March 16-18, 1995)			
Improved	8.4	3.9	15.7
Worsened	52.7	52.0	53.8
Other	38.9	44.1	30.5
(August-September 1995)			
Improved	9.8	9.2	10.8
Worsened	43.5	35.9	57.0
Other	46.7	54.8	32.2
(March 1997)			
Improved	12.6	13.3	11.3
Worsened	51.9	49.3	56.5
Other	35.5	37.4	32.2

(box continues on next page)

Deteriorating Living Conditions

Declining Standard of Living: Real Per Capita Consumption Expenditure Declined by 15 Percent

Perceptions of a deteriorating standard of living are borne out by statistical evidence. National accounts have been compiled by the Israeli Central Bureau of Statistics (ICBS) up to 1993 and by the PCBS for 1994 (data are not yet available for more recent years). However, nationally representative household surveys conducted by the PCBS can be utilized to make credible measurements of the evolution of the WBGS standard of living. The following conclusions are based on analysis of the Palestinian Expenditure Consumption Survey that was carried out in 12 rounds from October 1995 to September 1996 (Box 2.3).

- The average per capita consumption expenditure in the WBGS was $1,431 annually ($1,519 in the West Bank and $1,214 in the Gaza Strip) during the October 1995-September 1996 period.
- In comparison to private consumption expenditure figures obtained from Israeli national accounts, real per capita expenditure in the 1995-96 survey

---

(Box 2.1 continues)

Pessimism/Optimism about Political and Economic Conditions

Q.: Taking into consideration the political and economic conditions facing the occupied territories and the current Palestinian-Israeli negotiations, are you optimistic or pessimistic about the future?

Percentage of Respondents in WBGS

	Optimistic	Pessimistic	Not Sure
February 19, 1994:	39.0	36.7	24.3
March 20, 1994:	20.5	51.2	28.3
May 31, 1994:[a]	66.4	21.4	12.2
March 16-18, 1995:	49.1	31.9	19.0
August-September 1995:	49.5	28.8	21.7
June 28-30, 1996:[b]	34.4	27.6	38.0
March 6-9, 1997:	64.5	29.7	5.8

a. "Optimistic" category includes "optimistic to a limited degree." Question is slightly different in May 1994 poll.
b. Question is modified to state "following the success of Likud party and its leader, Netanyahu, in the Israeli elections." The "not sure" category includes those stating "no change has taken place in the peace process."

period declined by about 15 percent from its 1992-93 average in the WBGS. Coming on the heels of the large shock cause by the *Intifada* after 1988, real per capita expenditure is now at its lowest level for any year since 1980.

- The decline in real per capita consumption expenditure has been much steeper for the West Bank, which witnessed a decline of 26 percent from the 1992-93 average to the 1995-96 survey period. In contrast, real per capita expenditure has not changed very much in the Gaza Strip.
- The sharp decline in average consumption expenditure would have been much greater if it were not for economic aid cushioning the shocks. By March 1997, $2.714 billion had been committed to specific forms of expenditure by the donor countries and $1.527 billion had been disbursed.

Greater decline in the standard of living in the West Bank compared to Gaza Strip can be explained by the fact that the majority of Palestinian civil service institutions, including the police force, were set up in Gaza Strip. In addition, the expansion of PA powers over urban centers of the West Bank started in 1995, following the Oslo II Accords. Thus, the Gaza Strip had a greater proportion of government expenditure and donor money than the West Bank, which cushioned the decline in consumption expenditure. Nevertheless, inequality in the Gaza Strip remains higher than the West Bank (Box 2.4).

While the analysis indicates a disturbing trend of income reduction, it also points to moderate levels of inequality. The overall Gini coefficient of per capita expenditure for the WBGS is 0.378, which is relatively low by international standards. However, inequality in the Gaza Strip is unambiguously higher than in the West Bank and trends indicate that inequality in the entire WBGS is on the rise (Box 2.4).

High and Increasing Levels of Poverty

One of the disturbing economic outcomes in the WBGS since 1993 is the high level of poverty. Mostly, this has occurred as a result of worsening labor market conditions. Given a poverty level of $650 per capita annually (less than $2 per day), approximately one-fifth (19.1 percent) of the population was poor at end-1995. This implies that about one-half million of the estimated 2.5 million Palestinians are poor. The incidence of poverty is greater in the Gaza Strip, where more than one-third (36.3 percent) of the population was poor at end-1995, amounting to about 350,000 people. In the West Bank, roughly one out of ten people were poor, approximately 150,000 people. Since 1995, the situation seems to have deteriorated much more.

The profile of poverty reveals the nature of hardship. An average family with a regularly employed person at the going wage rate should be able to avoid poverty. The incidence of poverty is very much tied to the softness in the labor market and the repeated and severe shocks from border closures. Closures prevent workers from reaching their jobs and inhibit private sector expansion and job creation. Poverty is more widespread among those living in refugee camps. The refugee camp rate of poverty at end-1995 was 31 percent compared to 17 percent for urban and rural households. Refugee camp households rely on labor earnings as the major source of their livelihood, and thus are more severely affected by economic shocks that stem from labor market downturns.

Excessively High and Widely Fluctuating Unemployment Rates

The working hypothesis of the policy makers in Palestinian economic development in the peace era is that domestic job creation by the export-oriented private sector would improve employment. These jobs would gradually attract Palestinian workers from Israel, thus transforming the Palestinian economy from labor-exporting to commodity-exporting. However, political considerations in the post-

---

Box 2.2 Impressive Economic Performance in Israel

The Israeli economy has enjoyed rapid growth since the late 1980s. GDP has risen 42 percent since 1990, at an annual average of 6 percent. The growth rate of real GDP reached 6.5 percent in 1994 and 7.1 percent in 1995; per capita GDP growth rate reached 4.0 and 4.3 percent in these two years, respectively. A wave of immigrants, increasing the population by about 12 percent, has contributed to this growth. Also, the prospects for a political settlement of the Arab-Israeli conflict contributed to a rise in investment.

The Israeli economy has reaped substantial economic benefits from the peace process. It has experienced improved trade relations with countries that were boycotting Israel in the past, improved creditworthiness that lowers the international cost of borrowing, and a substantial inflow of private capital.

The Israeli unemployment rate declined from over 11 percent in 1992 to less than 6 percent in 1995. This was due to a sharp rise in employment in both private and public sectors. The total number of employed persons rose from 1,610,000 in 1990 to 2,094,000 in 1995. New immigrants accounted for about 235,000 and Israeli veterans accounted for about 245,000 of this increase. At the same time, the employment of Palestinians decreased sharply while the employment of foreign workers increased.

The stock of capital increased by 35 percent and labor input increased by 43 percent. Rapidly increasing investment and sustained growth were accompanied by a rise in the deficit in the balance of payments. The financing of the deficit was carried out through loans guaranteed by the US government and through private capital inflows. The latter constituted about $6.5 billion in 1995.

Sources: Arnon (1996) and ICBS.

Oslo period have created an environment that is suffocating export-oriented private sector development. This environment, where Palestinians are suddenly shut out of their jobs in Israel, has generated high and widely fluctuating unemployment rates. Employment is considered the most important socio-economic concern by WBGS residents polled in the surveys (Box 2.1).

Box 2.3 Palestinian Central Bureau of Statistics

The Palestinian Central Bureau of Statistics (PCBS) is the official central agency responsible for compilation and production of data on the Palestinian economy and society. PCBS has published numerous reports on demography, education, labor force, expenditure patterns, and consumer price indices, and plans to conduct a census of the population soon. PCBS publications are used extensively in this report. Summaries of PCBS publications are on the agency website at www.pcbs.org.

In 1994, the PCBS conducted a comprehensive census of business establishments, which became the basis for economic surveys in construction, manufacturing, services, and internal trade. These surveys, along with proper estimation of the value added in agriculture, provide the basis for computation of national accounts. These surveys are collected annually, starting in 1994. Until the PCBS publishes official statistics on national accounts, the estimation of GNP and GDP will include much guesswork. Rough estimates of GNP and GDP over the 1994-96 period have been conducted by the World Bank, the International Monetary Fund (IMF), and the United Nations Special Coordinator Office (UNSCO). The generated figures have a substantial margin of error attached to them, and should be treated with extreme caution.

A more fruitful analysis of recent economic development would rely on household surveys. The PCBS has completed three nationally representative types of surveys. A large demographic survey of about 15,000 households was conducted in mid-1995. Two rounds of labor force sample surveys were conducted in September-October 1995 and April-May 1996, each consisting of more than 7,000 households. Beginning in summer 1996, labor force sample surveys were collected on a quarterly basis. A detailed household expenditure survey of around 4,800 households was collected between October 1995 and September 1996.

This book relies on detailed analysis of the raw data of the demographic survey along with the first two rounds of the labor force sample survey and the first three months of the expenditure survey. The analysis provides an interesting perspective on the impact and adjustment of economic shocks at the household and individual levels.

The measurement of the rate of unemployment in the WBGS is controversial. The most reliable (and probably lowest) estimates are those reported by PCBS, which uses nationally representative household surveys and follows the rigorous definition of (and receives technical advice from) the International Labor Organization (ILO). According to this definition, someone is unemployed if he or she has not worked at all (not even one hour), was available for work, and sought employment during the reference week. In many countries, surveys use the simpler method of self-declaration of the respondent, resulting in higher rates than would be implied by the ILO definition. The method used by PCBS was stricter, and thus explains the discrepancy between popularly reported unemployment figures and those reported by PCBS.

Using the two labor force sample surveys, the PCBS estimate of the unemployment rate was 18.2 percent in September-October 1995 and 28.4 percent in April-May 1996. These rates are high by any standard, but are more significant in this case given the strict definition of unemployment and the absence of any unemployment insurance. Even with the PCBS's strict definition, the WBGS unemployment rate is higher than that of all 57 economies analyzed in the World Bank's *World Development Report: 1995*.

Figure 2.1 shows how the unemployment rate fluctuates widely over a short time period. Out of roughly one-half million workers in the labor force, the unemployed numbered 92,000 in September-October 1995 and 149,000 in April-May 1996. The magnitude of unemployment fluctuates widely over a short time, as reflected in the 10-point increase over a six-month period. The difference between the two periods is the strictness with which the borders were closed to Palestin-

Figure 2.1 Unemployment Rate Fluctuates Widely in the WBGS

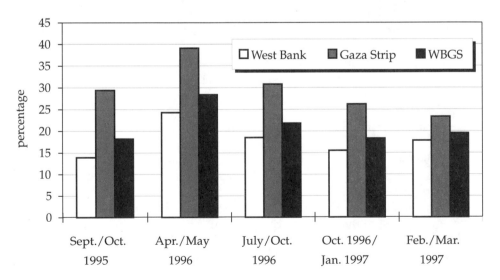

Source: PCBS various labor force surveys.

ian workers and goods by the Israeli-imposed closures. These wide short-run fluctuations have placed many workers into a risky employment situation.

Sharp Deterioration in Employment in Israel and Low Absorption of Returning Labor

Palestinian employment in Israel declined from an average of 116,000 workers in 1992 to 28,100 in the spring of 1996. The number of permits issued by Israel to Palestinians has declined, and workers are often unable to use these permits during closure periods (see Chapter 4). The Israeli economy has adjusted by importing workers from Eastern European and Southern Asian countries in such numbers as to substantially replace Palestinian workers. This could imply a permanent loss of employment opportunities in Israel even if the political situation allows a larger number of Palestinians to seek employment. As a result, Palestinian earnings from work in Israel collapsed from an estimated 25 percent of GNP in 1992 to 8 percent in 1995, and to 6 percent in 1996 (Figure 2.2).

Simultaneously, about 50,000 jobs were created in 1993-96 in the public sector (30,000 in the police force and 20,000 in central ministries and education). Private employment, on the other hand, did not appear to have grown much. Industry fared poorly, mainly as a result of border closure and the low investment rate. The growing sectors of the economy were agriculture (a traditional shock absorber, especially in the West Bank), with low productivity at the margin; and construction, a relatively capital-intensive activity. New entrants to the job market amounted to about 80,000 and at least 20,000 returnees in the 1993-96 period. In the same period, approximately 100,000 jobs were lost. These combined figures reflect a loss of 150,00 jobs.

Figure 2.2 Evolution of the Percentage of Palestinian Labor Force Employed in Israel and Net Worker Remittances as Percentage of GNP

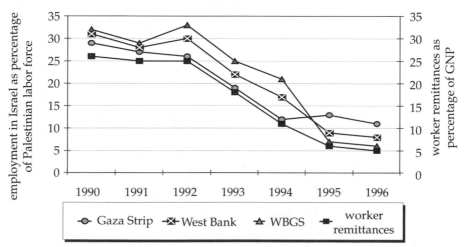

Sources: ICBS and World Bank.

Decline in Per Capita Incomes

Although the PCBS (which took over the ICBS data collection in the WBGS in 1994) recently started publishing reports on various aspects of the economy, available data on the national economy since 1994 are preliminary. There have been numerous "guesstimates" of GDP and GNP, all of which have to be treated with caution. Analysis of preliminary PCBS data suggests that real GDP per capita fell by 12 percent in 1995 and by another 6 percent in 1996. Real GNP per capita (which, in addition to domestic output takes account of income earned abroad, notably in Israel) fell sharply as well, by 10 percent in 1995, and an additional 7 percent in 1996 (Table 2.1).

Table 2.1 GDP and GNP Growth Rates (percentage)

	1993	1994	1995	1996
Real GDP per capita	- 5.6	4.0	-12.0	-6.0
Real GNP per capita	-14.4	2.0	-10.0	-7.0

Sources: World Bank analysis of preliminary PCBS national accounts for 1994-96 and ICBS for 1993.

Dramatic Fall in Trade

As a result of repeated closures and high transaction costs at the border (such as delays and the use of convoys for transport of merchandise to Israel), trade seems to have dipped since the beginning of Palestinian self-government. Rough estimates indicate that merchandise imports fell from 61 to 48 percent of GDP between 1992 and 1995 (by nearly 21 percent). Similarly, exports seem to have fallen from 14 to 12 percent over the same period (by 14 percent of GDP).

Though the fiscal situation recently improved in terms of revenue performance and expenditure restraints, the budget deficit remains important. Since 1994, the PA has given priority to establishing fiscal and economic institutions that have taken charge of key ICA functions. Under the ICA, fiscal expenditures were relatively low by international standards (12-14 percent of GDP). Under the PA, however, central administration expenditures have risen rapidly with the rising wage bill. In contrast, PA revenue collection has been efficiently managed, is probably close to its potential level, and is unlikely to appreciably increase in relation to GDP.

Fiscal developments in 1995 were more favorable than anticipated, due to strong revenue performance and expenditure restraint. As a result, the recurrent deficit for 1995-96 was about $100 million per year (3 percent of GDP). Recurrent expenditure grew as a result of emergency programs related to prolonged border closures and the continuous rapid growth in the civil service.

Box 2.4 Should Policy Makers Worry about Inequality?

High levels of poverty in the WBGS do not stem from extreme inequities in the distribution of income and wealth, and are mostly a reflection of the soft labor market. Analysis of the October-December 1995 expenditure survey suggests that inequality is relatively low in comparison to other developing countries. The Gini index of per capita consumption expenditure is 0.378 and the coefficient of variation is 87 percent.

While these figures suggest that inequality should not necessarily be a top concern for Palestinian policy makers, trends in the land and labor markets are likely to generate increasing inequality over time. Land price speculation, inequality in land ownership, and difficult access to land due to zoning regulations and the breakup of the West Bank into several jurisdictions, are factors likely leading to greater inequality in wealth over time. In addition, the trend of Palestinians increasingly returning to school is creating greater inequities in the labor market.

The Lorenz curves of expenditure inequality illustrate that the Gaza Strip economy has a greater level of inequality than the West Bank. The Gini index of inequality is 0.355 in the West Bank and 0.395 in Gaza Strip.

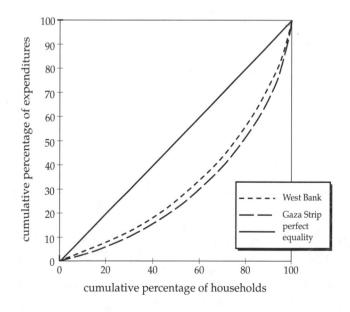

Sources: Shaban (1997) and based on PCBS expenditure data.

Areas of Relative Economic Improvement

While overall performance of the Palestinian economy recently has been dismal, there are areas of relative progress. Hopes for and expectations of an improved economy and political situation have stimulated interest from the private sector in possible investments—particularly from local and Diaspora Palestinians. The financial sector has expanded rapidly in recent years, albeit from a negligible base, in the number of banks and in total deposits. The housing sector witnessed a boom (tapering off in 1996-97), concentrated in the Gaza Strip and the larger cities of the West Bank, especially Ramallah. Institutions of administration and economic management have been established, albeit with difficulties, and should be ready to create the environment needed for private sector development.

Strong Private Sector Interest Demonstrated by Large Number of Newly Registered Companies but No Investment Yet

Only a few new firms were registered throughout the 1980s and early 1990s, due mostly to the repressive regulatory environment under the ICA. Since 1994, there has been an increase in registered establishments. The number of firms registered in 1994 to mid-1995 (3,028 in the Gaza Strip and 5,442 in the West Bank) is much larger than the total for the entire 1980s decade (1,745 in the Gaza Strip and 4,846 in the West Bank) (see Figure 2.3). Reflecting the potential interest in private sector development, several large shareholding companies have been set-up to invest in various sectors. These companies have leveraged their capital to establish a number of specialized companies, in conjunction with the public and with support from the banks. Several companies have already been financed by wealthy local and Diaspora Palestinians. A stock exchange opened in Nablus in 1997 to help mobilize resources and improve the efficiency of financial intermediation.

The Banking Sector is Ready for the Next Take-off

Since 1993, the banking sector has had an impressive record of expansion. The Arab banking sector largely was regulated out of existence during most of the Israeli occupation years. At end-1993, following a period of regulatory liberalizationtion, two Arab banks were operating. The Bank of Palestine had five branches in the Gaza Strip and the Cairo-Amman Bank had eight branches in the West Bank. By end 1996, there were 17 banks with 71 operating branches. Figure 2.4 demonstrates the growth in bank deposits. Total deposits grew from a very low level of $219 million at end-1993 by more than sevenfold, to a little more than $1.7 billion at end-1996. The average growth rate of bank deposits during this period was 6 percent per month. The fraction of bank deposits to GDP increased from approximately 7 percent at end-1993 to a little more than half of GDP at end-1996. Clearly, these rapid growth rates are not sustain-

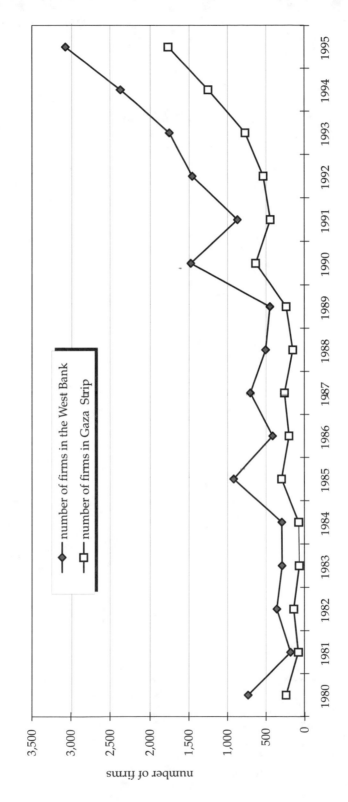

Figure 2.3 Number of Firms Registered by Year in the WBGS (1980–95)

number of firms

3,500
3,000
2,500
2,000
1,500
1,000
500
0

1980 1981 1982 1983 1984 1985 1986 1987 1988 1989 1990 1991 1992 1993 1994 1995

◆ number of firms in the West Bank
□ number of firms in Gaza Strip

Source: Shaban (1996).

Figure 2.4 Growth in Bank Deposits

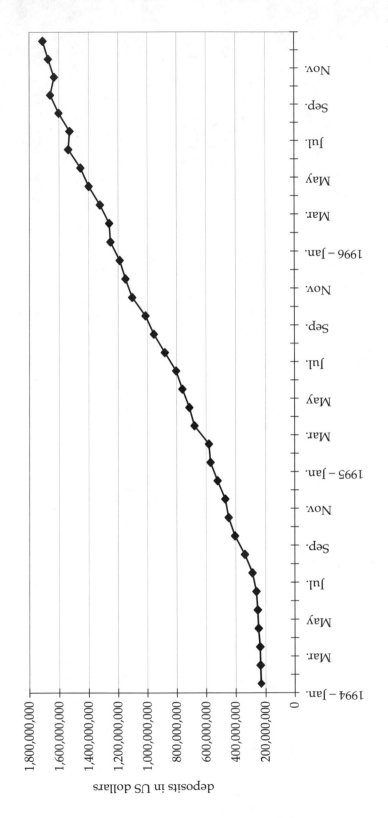

Sources: MAS and PMA data files.

able in the long run, and they have begun to slow down as the deposit base approaches its normal size in relation to the economy's size. While lending is still low, the banking sector has matured during this short period and is well positioned to play a key role in Palestinian economic development once the demand for credit picks up.

The Construction Boom

The construction sector also experienced rapid growth in the past few years, fueled by optimism about political and economic development. However, during periods of strict and prolonged border closure construction has been affected negatively by the lack of supplies (such as cement and steel) that are imported from or through Israel. By 1997, the boom in construction had tapered off.

Establishment of Institutions of Governance

Palestinian economic management has come a long way in the past three years. Authority has been transferred in several areas, and institutions of governance have been set up. However, the nascent Palestinian public administration has faced numerous difficulties. These difficulties emerge from the need to integrate Palestine Liberation Organization (PLO) cadres who moved back to the WBGS, lower-level Palestinian staff inherited from the ICA, and local activists and intellectuals, many of whom previously operated within the NGO sector. Difficulties remain, particularly in terms of definition and application of the exact role of the public and private sectors, decentralization, and coordination among the public sector entities. The tax authority has managed to increase revenue collection. The Palestinian Economic Council for Development and Reconstruction (PECDAR) has supervised the disbursement of significant funds and set up an effective works program. The security forces have improved public safety and the general maintenance of law and order. The courts are working better since the Palestinian police have begun to enforce the laws. Palestinians do not have to be home by sunset as was the practice before the transfer of authority to the PA. There is a renewed sense of freedom that encourages people to go out to Gaza's beaches or Ramallah's parks and restaurants late into the evening.

* * *

The signing of the Declaration of Principles was accompanied by high hopes for improvement and reconstruction of the Palestinian economy. Some segments of the economy have experienced improvement, but in general, the WBGS has been a casualty of the peace process. Economic activity has stagnated, with a substantial decline of per capita incomes. Private investment has not materialized, trade has been interrupted, and Palestinian employment in Israel has been sharply cut. These conditions have been responsible for the prevalence of very high poverty and unemployment rates. Undoubtedly, these poor economic conditions would have been worse if it were not for the donor aid that cushioned their impact.

The state of the Palestinian economy is particularly disappointing when compared to the performance of the Israeli economy, which has improved throughout the 1990s. As the Israeli economy has benefited from a large peace dividend, the peace process has heavily taxed the Palestinian economy. Economic activity in the WBGS is struggling in spite of the political process, rather than being assisted by it. If economic deterioration continues, it could lead to greater dissatisfaction with and opposition to the peace process.

Bibliographical Note: This chapter is based on the background papers of Shaban (1997), Al-Qudsi and Shaban (1996), Arnon (1996), and Shaban (1996). Other references include CPRS (1997), Gotlieb (1996), PCBS (1996c), Shaban and Al-Botmeh (1995), UNSCO (1996a), and World Bank (1995b).

Chapter 3

Recent Political Developments

Rex Brynen

Introduction

On September 13, 1993, the PLO and Israel signed an undertaking to "put an end to decades of confrontation and conflict, recognize their mutual legitimate and political rights, and strive to live in peaceful coexistence and mutual dignity and security to achieve a just, lasting and comprehensive peace settlement and historic reconciliation." By any measure, the changes worked out between the two parties in the Declaration of Principles (Oslo Agreement) and subsequent agreements have been both historic and far-reaching. Israel has withdrawn its military forces from most of Gaza Strip and from major population centers in the West Bank, with the exception of East Jerusalem and parts of Hebron. A democratically elected Palestinian Legislative Council and duly appointed PA have assumed the tasks of government in these areas. Progress in Palestinian-Israeli peacemaking has helped to spur the pace of regional political reconciliation, evident—until the 1996 change in the Israeli government—in growing political and economic interaction among countries of the region.

However, success of the interim phase depends very much on it being a transitory one. Throughout the region, and especially between Palestinians and Israelis, expectations have been substantially raised by the prospect of peace. Failure to satisfy these expectations could result in a political backlash. Opponents of peace—who have shown themselves willing to use violence to derail the process—stand ready to manipulate and mobilize such discontent. In turn, the collapse of the peace process would almost inevitably fuel more extremism and incite even greater violence.

This chapter will discuss how the political process has moved forward with successive agreements as envisioned under the Declaration of Principles. Reviewing the main events, phases, and arrangements, the chapter presents the impact of political progress on development efforts, the economic benefits emerging from the expansion of Palestinian territorial and functional authority, and the effect that postponement of targeted phases has on private sector confidence and foreign investment.

The Peace Process

The peace process began with the convening of the Madrid Peace Conference in October 1991, co-chaired by the US and Soviet Union and based on United Nations Security Council Resolutions 242 and 338. Direct bilateral discussions followed between Israel and the Palestinians, Jordan, Syria, and Lebanon. With very substantial issues between them, the ten rounds of Palestinian-Israeli negotiations from 1991 to 1993 proved slow and difficult.

Multilateral working groups were initiated in Moscow in January 1992 on key issues of regional concern: regional economic development, refugees, water, environment, arms control, and regional security. The multilateral track of the peace process brought regional parties together and fostered some modest new forms of cooperation. The Regional Economic Development Working Group (REDWG), sponsored by the EU, organized a series of international activities and established a monitoring committee and a permanent secretariat in Amman. Table 3.1 summarizes the various peace process agreements.

Perhaps the most visible manifestation of increased economic contact across the region, among governments and private sectors, has been the Middle East and North Africa (MENA) economic summits, held in Casablanca in October-November 1994, in Amman in October 1995, and in Cairo in November 1996. At the Casablanca meeting, participants agreed to establish the Middle East Development Bank for the region, and discussions are still continuing. The Refugee Working Group (RWG), sponsored by Canada, addressed the issue of Palestinian refugees and worked on databases, child welfare, public health, human resource development, economic infrastructure, and family reunification. Groups on water and the environment were chaired by the United States and Japan. These efforts included the 1994 multilateral Bahrain Environmental Code of Conduct for the Middle East, and the Declaration on Principles for Cooperation on Water-Related Matters, signed by Israel, Jordan and the PLO in February 1996. In general, progress in the multilateral groups has been slow, incremental, and very much tied to the pace of bilateral political negotiations.

The Declaration of Principles

In this context, the PLO and Israel embarked, with Norwegian facilitation, on parallel but less public discussions. These discussions ultimately bore fruit in the form of the Declaration of Principles, which was formally signed by the PLO and Israel on September 13, 1993 in Washington.

Central to the Oslo Agreement was mutual recognition between the PLO and Israel. The two parties pledged to begin permanent status negotiations in 1996, which would include the most difficult and important issues between them: borders, Israeli settlements (Box 3.1), security arrangements, refugees, and Jerusalem (Box 3.2). In the meantime, they agreed to negotiate transitional arrangements for Palestinian elections and interim self-government. These arrangements would begin with the withdrawal of Israeli forces from the Gaza Strip and the West Bank town of Jericho and surrounding areas, and the establishment of a Palestinian authority in these areas. Additional Israeli redeployments would occur at a later date, prior to Palestinian elections.

By securing mutual political recognition between the PLO and Israel, the agreement represented a breakthrough, setting the stage for more direct and intensive negotiations. The Oslo Agreement was a careful experiment in forward-looking constructive ambiguity. It sought to create a productive political process (focused on immediately achievable objectives) without prejudicing the political ambitions of either party or predetermining the ultimate outcome of negotiations. It was hoped that through such interim confidence-building measures and a growing volume of cooperative interaction, new possibilities would emerge for a comprehensive and mutually acceptable resolution of the Palestinian-Israeli conflict.

Implementing the Declaration of Principles: Gaza-Jericho Agreement, Economic Protocol, and Early Empowerment

The first of these transitional arrangements, the Agreement on the Gaza Strip and the Jericho Area (Cairo Agreement or Gaza-Jericho Agreement) of May 1994, established the framework for both Israel's withdrawal from Gaza Strip and Jericho and the creation of the PA. Annex IV of this agreement, the Protocol of Economic Relations, was signed a few days earlier in Paris. Referred to as the Paris Protocol (or Economic Protocol), it codified the economic relations between the PA and Israel during the interim period in the fields of monetary, fiscal, and trade relations.

Under the agreement's terms, the Palestinian Monetary Authority (PMA) was mandated to oversee the local banking system and manage official foreign currency reserves. However, the PA was not authorized to establish its own cur-

Table 3.1 Peace Process Agreements

Date Signed	Title	Key Provisions and Target Dates
October 1991	**Madrid Peace Conference**	• Inaugurated two separate yet parallel tracks of negotiations (bilateral and multilateral) to achieve just, lasting and comprehensive peace settlement, based on UN Security Council Resolutions 242 and 338 • Ten rounds of negotiations follow from 1991-93
September 13, 1993	**Declaration of Principles on Interim Self-Government Arrangements** (Declaration of Principles, Oslo Agrement, DOP)	• Set out overall framework for interim period and Palestinian self-government in WBGS • Mutual recognition of the PLO and Israel • Pledge to begin permanent status negotiations • Hold Palestinian elections by June 1994 • Sign Early Empowerment in July 1994
April 29, 1994	**Protocol on Economic Relations** (Economic Protocol, Paris Protocol)	• Codified economic relations between WBGS and Israel for the interim period in monetary, fiscal, and trade relations • Later incorporated as Annex IV of Gaza-Jericho Agreement and still later as Annex V of the Interim Agreement

(table continued on next page)

rency. The main result of the Economic Protocol was that taxes paid by Palestinians, formerly accruing to the Israeli treasury, would be remitted to the Palestinian treasury. The protocol also formalized the existing trade regime as a customs union with some exceptions. Specific procedures were outlined

(Table 3.1 continues)

Date Signed	Title	Key Provisions and Target Dates
May 4, 1994	**Agreement on the Gaza Strip and the Jericho Area** (Cairo Agreement, Gaza-Jericho Agreement)	• Established framework for transfer of power and responsibilities to PA • Agreed on Israeli withdrawal from Gaza Strip and Jericho • PA to assume authority in Gaza Strip and Jericho in all spheres except those related to final status issues
August 29, 1994	**Agreement on Preparatory Transfer of Powers and Responsibilities** (Early Empowerment Agreement)	• Israel transferred authority in the West Bank to PA in education and culture, health, social welfare, tourism, direct taxation and VAT on local production in December 1994 • Parties to explore possible expansion of transfer of powers to other spheres
October 30–November 1, 1994	**Middle East and North Africa Economic Summit,** Casablanca	• Agreed to establish Middle East development bank for the region • Agreed to establish regional tourist board
August 27, 1995	**Protocol on Further Transfer of Powers and Responsibilities**	• Israel transferred authority in the West Bank in agriculture, census and statistics, energy, insurance, labor, local government, postal services, and trade and industry
September 28, 1995	**Israeli-Palestinian Interim Agreement on the West Bank and Gaza Strip** (Interim Agreement, Oslo II Agreement, Taba Agreement)	• Confirmed expanding territorial and functional control of PA, including police • Detailed composition of Palestinian Legislative Council • Hold Palestinian elections in January 1996 • Additional Israeli redeployments to occur in intervals of six months (September 1996), 12 months (March 1997) and 18 months (September 1997) • Signed protocol for redeployment in Hebron in March 1996 • Recognition of Palestinian water rights • Provided for coordinating mechanisms in security, legal, judicial, and economic fields • Did not contain provisions for a "safe passage" between the West Bank and Gaza Strip, as provided in Oslo Agreement • Commence permanent status negotiations no later than May 1996

(table continues on next page)

for remitted tax revenues to be returned to the Palestinians for value-added tax (VAT), customs revenues, and other levies raised on goods coming from third countries.

VAT clearances provided the largest single source of revenue for the PA in 1995 and 1996. In 1996, VAT clearances amounted to $223 million. The VAT operates on a destination basis (VAT on imports from Israel is remitted by the Israeli treasury to the PA). VAT and other revenue clearances remitted to the PA in 1996 were $423 million—and may grow further in the future as remaining difficulties with tariff revenues and excise taxes on imports from Israel are resolved. There is no customs border between the WBGS and Israel and, subject to Israeli quality

(Table 3.1 continues)

Date Signed	Title Target Dates	Key Provisions and
October 23-31, 1995	**Second MENA Economic Summit,** Amman	• Agreed to establish Bank for Economic Cooperation and Development, based in Cairo, to promote private sector development and infrastructure projects • Established the Middle East-Mediterranean Travel and Tourism Association • Established the Regional Business Council
February 1996	**Declaration on Principles for Cooperation on Water-related Matters**	
April 22, 1996	**Amendment of PLO Charter**	• Palestinian National Council voted to amend Charter and delete clauses that contradict the agreements signed
November 1996	**Third MENA Economic Summit,** Cairo	• Discuss, among other things, permanent status negotiations
January 17, 1997	**Protocol Concerning the Redeployment in Hebron** (Hebron Protocol)	• Pushed back timetable of Interim Agreement redeployments, with the first to occur in March 1997 and the third by mid-1998 • Permanent status negotiations to resume within two months after signing Hebron Protocol
May 5, 1996- March 1997	**Permanent Status Negotiations**	• Address borders, settlements, security arrangements, refugees, Jerusalem, water, and sovereignty • Scheduled to start in May 1996; interim period originally intended to end in May 1999 • Despite formal opening in May 1996, substantive negotiations postponed to March 1997 under Hebron Protocol

Source: Israeli Ministry of Foreign Affairs.

standards, trade between the WBGS and Israel is presumably free. The only exceptions are five agricultural goods with declining quotas over a five-year period. As it turned out, however, the border remained mostly closed for Palestinian exports to Israel. Trade relations with third countries—tariffs, standards, quotas—are largely determined by Israeli policies, albeit with some limited exemptions. FTAs have since been negotiated with the EU and the US, and with ten other countries, including Arab countries in the Gulf.

The parties committed themselves to attempt to maintain normal labor movement between their territories (consisting almost entirely of Palestinian workers traveling to Israel). The Economic Protocol states: "Both sides will attempt to maintain the normality of movement of labor between them, subject to each side's right to determine from time to time the extent and conditions of labor movement into its area." In practice, this provision has not prevented periodic closure of the WBGS.

Israel's withdrawal from Gaza Strip and Jericho, and the establishment of the PA occurred in May 1994. New negotiations followed on the immediate transfer of additional areas of responsibility to the PA ("early empowerment") as well

---

Box 3.1 Israeli Settlements in the WBGS

According to unofficial Israeli sources, in 1992 there were 136 settlements in the West Bank with 130,000 inhabitants and 17 settlements in Gaza Strip with 4,000 to 5,000 inhabitants. The United Nations has taken the position that Israeli settlements in the WBGS have no legal validity and should be dismantled. Under the Declaration of Principles, settlements are one of the final status items to be negotiated.

To attract settlers, the Israeli government has offered a number of incentives, such as direct housing subsidies, land at discounted prices, mortgages at reduced rates, free hookups to utilities and municipal services, and higher schooling subsidies than in Israel. Israeli budgetary allocations for building settlements are not clear, but several sources report allocations to be as much as $20 billion over the past 25 years.

Infrastructure in the settlements (telecommunications, water, and electricity grids) is fully integrated into Israeli national systems and operated by the national agencies. Over the past 25 years transport systems were built to link settlements to Israeli metropolitan areas. With implementation of the Interim Agreement, the Israeli government built numerous roads for settlers to by-pass PA-controlled areas while traveling to other settlements or Israel. This road-building process led to a loss of additional Palestinian land. While the settlement issue is to be resolved during the final status phase, intensified settlement activity has been threatening progress in Palestinian-Israeli negotiations.

as the eventual redeployment of additional Israeli forces from areas in the West Bank. In August 1994, the parties signed the Agreement on Preparatory Transfer of Powers and Responsibilities (Early Empowerment Agreement), whereby Israel undertook to transfer authority in the West Bank over education and culture, health, social welfare, tourism, direct taxation, and VAT on local production. In August 1995, a subsequent Protocol on Further Transfer of Powers and Responsibilities brought about the transfer of authority in eight additional areas (agriculture, census and statistics, energy, insurance, labor, local government, postal services, and trade and industry).

Israeli-Palestinian Interim Agreement: Oslo II

These measures set the stage for a political landmark—the Israeli-Palestinian Interim Agreement on the West Bank and Gaza Strip (Oslo II Agreement, Interim Agreement, or Taba Agreement), signed in Washington in September 1995. The lengthy and detailed agreement confirmed the process of expanding the territorial and functional control of the PA. It contained a number of core elements related to redeployment, transfer of jurisdictional and functional control, governance, water rights, taxation, and coordinating mechanisms.

Israel agreed to withdraw its military forces from the six Palestinian cities (defined as zone A), which include Tulkarem, Qalqilya, Jenin, Nablus, Ramallah, and Bethlehem. In addition, special arrangements would be negotiated for the city of Hebron, followed by Israeli redeployment from that city. Israel further agreed to redeployment from other populated areas of the West Bank (zone B), including some 450 Palestinian towns and villages. Together, zone A (3 percent of the territory of the West Bank) and zone B (27 percent of the West Bank) contain the majority of the Palestinian population. The remaining areas which cover most of the territory (including agricultural land, the Jordan Valley, nature reserves, areas with lower population density, Israeli settlements, and designated military areas) were assigned to zone C.

It was further agreed that "in order to maintain the territorial integrity of the West Bank and the Gaza Strip as a single territorial unit, and to promote their economic growth and the demographic and geographical links between them," the parties would protect the "normal and smooth movement of people, vehicles, and goods within the West Bank, and between the West Bank and the Gaza Strip." The agreement did not address territorial control of Jerusalem, as that issue was reserved for final status negotiations (Box 3.2).

Simultaneous with the initial redeployment, all civil powers and responsibilities in zones A and B (about 40 spheres, including those covered by the previous early empowerment agreements) were transferred to the PA. In zone C, the PA was granted functional civil jurisdiction in areas not relating to territory. Powers and responsibilities relating to territory gradually would be transferred to Palestinian jurisdiction, except for areas that were reserved for final status negotiation, such as settlements.

The Oslo II Agreement detailed the composition of an elected Palestinian Legislative Council and its executive authority, including a directly and popularly elected president. Subsequent to the initial redeployment of Israeli forces, Palestinian elections were to be held under international supervision throughout the WBGS. Under special arrangements, it was agreed to allow Palestinians of Jerusalem to vote in the elections. The president and Palestinian Legislative Council were to hold office for an interim period of up to five years.

The PA also assumed responsibility for internal security and public order (civil policing) in zone A. In zone B, the Palestinian police are responsible for public order, with Israel retaining "overriding responsibility for security." Under the Oslo II Agreement, Israel retains full security control of zone C, and committed itself to additional military redeployments over 18 months and the transfer of additional powers and responsibilities to the Palestinian police. It was agreed that the maximum number of Palestinian police would be 18,000 in Gaza Strip and 12,000 in the West Bank.

The Oslo II Agreement explicitly recognized Palestinian water rights in the West Bank—subject to definition in final status negotiations—and included water issues related solely to Palestinians in areas where civil jurisdiction was transferred to the PA. It was agreed that the Palestinians would be permitted to develop additional water resources in specified areas to meet the shortfall in water requirements.

The Economic Annex to the Interim Agreement (Annex 5) comprised the earlier 1994 Economic Protocol that was part of the Cairo Agreement, and added more detailed clauses regarding the clearance of import tax revenues from Israel to the PA and the implementation of direct and indirect taxation. It contained a number of specific confidence-building measures, as well as an annex devoted to cooperation programs.

The Oslo II Agreement provided for a host of coordinating mechanisms. Chief among these was Joint Liaison Committee, previously established under Article X of the Declaration of Principles. A Joint Security Coordination and Cooperation Committee was established, along with the Joint Regional Security Committee and Joint District Coordination Offices. The Legal Committee addressed legal and judicial cooperation, and provided a vehicle for Israel to raise concerns arising from Palestinian legislation. Unlike a similar committee established under the Gaza-Jericho Agreement, the Legal Committee had no power to delay or veto contentious Palestinian legislation. The Joint Civil Affairs Coordination and Cooperation Committee (which brings together Joint Regional Civil Affairs Subcommittees for each of the West Bank and Gaza Strip, and District Civil Liaison Offices in the West Bank) is responsible for facilitating cooperation in civil areas. The Gaza-Jericho Agreement continued the Joint Economic Committee originally established by the Economic Protocol.

Following Israeli redeployment, Palestinian elections were held in January 1996 throughout the WBGS for the president of the PA and the 88-member Legislative Council. International observers judged the elections to have been "an accurate expression of the will of the voters." The overwhelming majority of elected candidates supported the peace process, signaling Palestinian hopes for an end to decades of conflict. In April, the Palestine National Council (the political arm of the PLO), met in Gaza Strip to formally amend the PLO Charter, eliminating those clauses contrary to the spirit of Oslo. A month later in May 1996, final status talks were formally opened. However, the onset of substantive negotiations was delayed by forthcoming Israeli general elections. Prior to the elections, the Labor Party revised its electoral platform so as to eliminate its previous opposition to Palestinian statehood.

Despite the successful implementation of the initial stages of Oslo II, serious challenges continued to confront the peace process. In November 1995, Prime Minister Yitzhak Rabin was assassinated by an Israeli extremist opposed to the peace process. In February and March 1996, during the run-up to Israel's general elections, the Palestinian Islamist group Hamas launched four suicide bombings in Jerusalem and Tel Aviv, following the assassination of one of its leaders. Israel responded by imposing its most severe closure ever on the WBGS, including restrictions on travel between areas of the West Bank (see "internal closure" in Chapter 4). This resulted in substantial Palestinian economic losses through foregone wages and exports, price increases, a steep rise in local unemployment, and shortages. International development projects were severely disrupted. For its part, the PA responded to these events with stepped-up security measures against militant groups.

In May 1996, a new government under Prime Minister Benjamin Netanyahu and a Likud-led coalition was elected in Israel. Netanyahu voiced opposition to any future establishment of Palestinian sovereignty and expressed support for additional Israeli settlement activity in the West Bank. Following the elections, these elements were reflected in government policy. However, the Israeli government did declare its commitment to previously signed Palestinian-Israeli agreements, and expressed its hope for achieving peace and security in cooperation with the PA.

The Hebron Redeployment

One immediate test of the peace process came over the issue of Hebron. Under Oslo II, Israeli redeployment from much of the city had been slated to occur in March 1996. Implementation was delayed by the Peres government. Subsequently, the Netanyahu government insisted on renegotiating its agreement with the PA. This delayed the process further, until a new accord was reached in January 1997.

Appended to the new Protocol Concerning the Redeployment in Hebron (Hebron Protocol) were a number of agreed minutes and notes. These included several mutual undertakings by the parties, including commitments by Israel to negotiate the establishment of a Gaza port and airport, as well as "safe passage" between the West Bank and Gaza Strip, already over two years behind schedule. Final status negotiations were to restart in March 1997. Furthermore, the Oslo II timetable for additional Israeli redeployments was relaxed considerably. A letter from US Secretary of State Warren Christopher to Prime Minister Netanyahu suggested that "the first phase of further redeployments should take place as soon as possible, and that all three phases of the further

redeployments should be completed within twelve months from the implementation of the first phase of the further redeployments, but not later than
mid-1998." This was a delay of approximately one year. Israel argued that
the scope of such redeployments should be at its sole discretion, a view apparently endorsed by the US. The Palestinian position is that the specifics of
redeployment are to be agreed between the two parties and not determined
unilaterally by Israel.

Some argued that the Hebron Protocol demonstrated the commitment of
the Netanyahu government to the Oslo process. Others pointed to the postponement of redeployment, Israel's ability to determine and sharply limit
the scope of future withdrawal, Israeli unilateral measures in and around
Jerusalem, and intensification of settlement activity, as suggesting a continued drift away from the Oslo process. The Hebron Protocol identified some
of the constraints hampering socio-economic development (mobility and
transportation links), but not others (divided control and existing economic
agreements). While the agreement pledged continued negotiations on the
former, it contained no guarantees that progress would be forthcoming.

Looking Ahead: The Political Economy of Transition

In anticipating the progress of the Palestinian-Israeli peace process, two essential
points should be taken into account. First, the development community must

---

Box 3.2 *The Issue of East Jerusalem*

The 1948 war led to the partition of Jerusalem into eastern and western parts.
At the end of the 1967 war, East Jerusalem was occupied by Israeli forces.
Under occupation, the Jerusalem city limits were expanded by Israel to include some surrounding areas of the West Bank. Israel annexed the expanded
city in July 1980. Palestinian residents of Jerusalem were given the option of
obtaining Israeli citizenship, although very few have chosen to do so.

Actions taken by Israel were considered invalid by the United Nations,
which called upon Israel to refrain from taking any action that would alter
the status of Jerusalem. Although the international community has not recognized Israeli annexation of East Jerusalem, Israel continues to exercise
authority over the area. Palestinians insist that East Jerusalem is part of the
West Bank in accordance with the 1967 borders and that Israel should
withdraw from all areas occupied during the 1967 war in compliance
with UN resolutions. In the Declaration of Principles, the PLO and Israel
agreed that the future of Jerusalem was an issue to negotiate during the
permanent status phase.

(box continues on next page)

expect the unexpected. Unanticipated acts of political violence, border closures, and major changes in government policy all have affected development programs to date, and are likely to do so in the future. Thus, it is essential to build flexibility and responsiveness into development programs from the outset.

A second point concerns the deliberately phased nature of the peace process. The granting of interim Palestinian autonomy in areas of the WBGS was intended to set the stage and improve the climate for the final status negotiations. Certainly, the extended duration of the transition and its yet undetermined outcome has created political vulnerabilities. Protracted transition increases the risk that unforeseen events—whether accidental or deliberate expressions of political rejection by opponents of the peace process—could stall negotiations. Indeed, the unforeseen has often interceded. However, the Oslo process did manage to significantly increase interaction between Palestinian and Israeli political leadership, as well as between the Palestinian and Israeli peoples.

Progress in the peace process is crucial to economic development. Neither the Declaration of Principles nor the current pattern of limited Palestinian autonomy was designed to serve as the outline of a final settlement. The specific provisions of the Oslo II Agreement allow the PA to manage the main government-controlled sectors of the economy. However, it provides for only partial control over policy instruments. The agreements do not secure the full ability to make important strategic choices, particularly with respect to the type of fiscal instruments or the choice of external economic relations. The current territorial arrangements—

(Box 3.2 continues)

Because important economic links exist between the rest of the WBGS (RWBGS) and Jerusalem, decisions concerning Jerusalem have critical implications for WBGS economic prospects and priorities. The following are among the most significant.

- •The West Bank's tourism potential is critically dependent on Jerusalem's ancient religious sites.
- • Major north-south transportation links in the West Bank pass through Jerusalem.
- • The only tertiary-care hospital and some of the best secondary-care hospitals available to Palestinians are located in East Jerusalem.
- • East Jerusalem houses most Palestinian marketing facilities as well as social and cultural infrastructure.
- • Qalandia Airport, a potential outlet for linking the West Bank with regional airports, is within annexed Jerusalem.
- • Parts of East Jerusalem are an integral part of the power network covering the region from Ramallah to Bethlehem.

the patchwork quilt of zones A, B and C, arranged in declining degrees of Palestinian authority—are complex and unwieldy. Such dimensions severely complicate Palestinian institution-building and administrative development and hinder the implementation of infrastructure projects. The spring 1996 "super closure" aggravated this further by restricting movement within the West Bank and further isolating the West Bank from Gaza Strip.

* * *

Against this backdrop, the danger is that negotiations will become stuck in the transitional phase. For Palestinians, the "interim" may come to seem "interminable." Current territorial and political arrangements increasingly resemble a Bantustan-like form of political containment, rather than a waypoint on the road to a just and lasting peace. Should this containment trend continue, violence is likely to grow, with perilous effects on Palestinian-Israeli relations. An example of the strife threatening to erupt followed Israel's September 1996 opening of a tunnel adjacent to Al-Haram Al-Sharif in Jerusalem, when clashes between the Israeli army and Palestinian demonstrators and police left more than 100 persons dead. In the regional sphere, existing multilateral initiatives would be imperiled.

A more promising route would involve continued improvement upon, and expansion of, the existing Interim Agreement, coupled with progress toward resolving final status issues. Palestinian support for the peace process would be consolidated by the assumption of a growing degree of self-determination and a sense that core issues are being addressed. Regionally, progress in the peace process would serve to facilitate multilateral initiatives and promote general improvement in the quality and quantity of Israel's relations with other Arab countries.

Bibliographic Note: The overall framework for Palestinian self-government is set out in the Declaration of Principles. Provisions for the first step in the transfer of powers and responsibilities are detailed in the Gaza-Jericho Agreement and the Economic Protocol. Provisions for partial, pre-Interim Agreement transfer of powers and responsibilities in the West Bank outside of Jericho are specified in the Agreement on the Preparatory Transfer of Powers and Responsibilities. The framework for Palestinian assumption of remaining powers and responsibilities in the West Bank (Gaza-Jericho blueprint) is laid out in the Interim Agreement. The special arrangements governing Hebron are detailed in the Hebron Protocol.

Chapter 4

The Harsh Reality of Closure

Radwan A. Shaban

Introduction

With the beginning of the peace process, it was natural for the Palestinian economy to start reducing its overwhelming dependence on Israel in the areas of trade and labor. It was hoped that this would be achieved gradually as trade links with new markets supplemented commerce with Israel and led to expanded domestic production. Reconstruction of the Palestinian economy would, in turn, increase the demand for local labor and reduce Palestinian dependence on the export of labor to Israel.

However, a forced separation between the two economies has been driven by political considerations, and has created serious dislocation in the Palestinian economy. This chapter documents the phenomenon of border closure, provides estimates on resulting aggregate losses, and analyzes its impact on households, firms, private investment, and government operations.

Permit and Border Closure Policies

The 1967-87 period is characterized by effectively open access for Palestinians and Israelis to each other's towns. Beginning with the *Intifada* in late 1987, Israeli civilians have largely shied away from Palestinian urban centers to avoid the prospect of hostility. Palestinian access to Israeli territories was limited for the first time during the Gulf War, and since 1991 Palestinians laborers are required to obtain work permits to enter Israel. Since March 1993, Palestinians of the RWBGS have been denied entry to Israel and Jerusalem unless they have an Israeli-issued permit. Fixed roadblocks have been set up by the Israeli army at the major crossing points between the RWBGS and Israel and Jerusalem to enforce these restrictions. While the permit policy has prevented the majority of Palestinians from casual entry into Jerusalem and Israel, it was not an insurmountable obstacle—at least initially—to the entry of workers seeking jobs, particularly from the West Bank, where the borders with Israel are long and porous. There is no effective enforcement for compliance of private Israeli establishments (for example, a construction site or farm). The actual number of Palestinians working in Israel has often deviated substantially from the number of work permits issued. In 1992, 70,000 work permits were issued, while 116,000 Palestinians were working in Israel. However, with the increased intensity and policing of border closures, the situation has reversed.

Introduced in March 1993, permit policy heralded a new era of controlling Palestinian access to Jerusalem and the Israeli labor market. Subsequently, border closure policy was imposed for specified or unspecified periods after violent events in Israel. During closures, even Palestinians with valid work permits are denied entry into Israel. Each episode of closure has usually been accompanied by increasingly stiffer conditions, such as longer delays at crossing points, more thorough searches, and increased patrols for random checks on potential violators. Under these conditions, actual Palestinian employment in Israel is substantially less than the number of work permits issued. In 1996, the average actual employment estimate (10,300 from the Gaza Strip and 18,700 from the West Bank) accounted for only two-thirds of the average number of issued work permits (18,700 for the Gaza Strip and 23,600 for West Bank).

Figure 4.1 traces the frequency of border closures. The days of closure applied to the West Bank were 17 in 1993, 58 in 1994, 84 in 1995, and 132 in 1996. Gaza Strip has seen a larger incidence of closures—26 days in 1993, 76 in 1994, 102 in 1995, and 138 in 1996. Figure 4.1 illustrates that the RWBGS has experienced increasingly longer periods of closure over the 1993-96 period. The business community and workers cannot anticipate the incidence, frequency and duration of any episode of border closure, which adds a substantial planning risk, over and above the shocks' actual impact.

Jerusalem and the Rest of the West Bank

Since application of the permit policy, it has not been possible for the majority of Palestinians to enter Jerusalem. During a border closure, permit-holding Palestinians from Gaza Strip and the rest of the West Bank (RWB) are not allowed to enter Jerusalem. Preventing entry into Jerusalem physically separates the RWB into two halves and inhibits the movement of people (all reasonable routes between the northern and southern parts of the West Bank pass through Jerusalem). As East Jerusalem's economic links are primarily with the West Bank, economic activity in East Jerusalem is devastated by closure. The health and education sectors are particularly impeded, since Jerusalem houses the major hospitals that serve the entire West Bank. Patients, doctors, students, and teachers cannot reach their institutions during closures (Box 4.1).

Limitations on Movement of Goods

Closures largely constrain the mobility of goods and factors of production. Vehicles owned and registered in the RWBGS generally are denied entry into Jerusalem and Israel, and permits are largely made invalid. Only Israeli-owned and operated vehicles or those owned and operated by Jerusalem Palestinians can move between the areas. Closures prevent Palestinian expediters from reaching Israeli territory, and thus, restrict the clearance of Palestinian imports and exports (factors of production or finished goods) through Israeli custom ports.

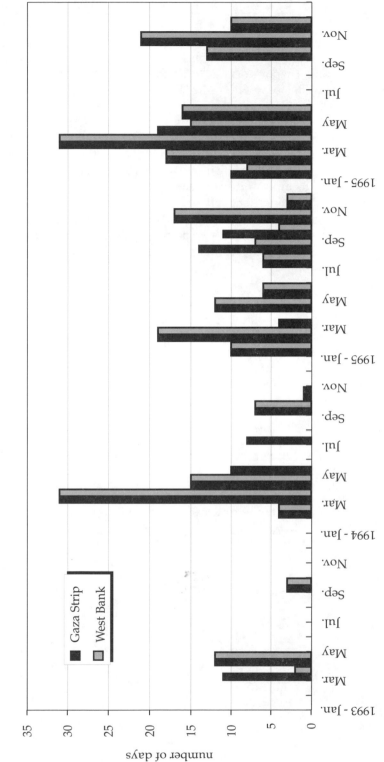

Figure 4.1 *Incident of Border Closure (days per month)*

Source: Authors' computation based on data from Palestinian Ministry of Labor.

Limitations on the movement of goods result in a decline in total trade with or through Israel. Generally, during closures Israeli exports to the Palestinian areas decline, but Palestinian exports decline much faster. This asymmetry in the effect of border closure is reflected in Figure 4.2. The magnitude of trade has traditionally been measured in relation to the number of truckloads moving across the borders. Figure 4.2 is based on the monthly number of trucks moving through the Karni/Muntar crossing point between Gaza Strip and Israel (the only crossing point where 1996 data for movement of trucks show the direction of border crossing). As the incidence of closure increases in a given month, total trade (exports plus imports) declines, and Palestinian exports decline faster than Israeli exports. The correlation coefficient between the number of monthly closure days and the total number of trucks crossing the Karni/Muntar checkpoint in 1996 is -0.38. The correlation coefficient of closure days with the share of exporting trucks in total truck movement is -0.32 during the same period.

Internal Closure

"Internal" closure emerged following implementation of the Oslo II Agreement, when authority over the majority of West Bank urban centers was transferred to the Palestinians in fall 1995. During periods of internal closure, Palestinians cannot move among urban centers within the West Bank or to and from the surrounding villages. As a result, West Bank towns and cities have become small isolated islands, surrounded by the Israeli army. Internal closure was applied

Figure 4.2 Total Trade Declines with Closure, but Exports Decline Faster than Imports

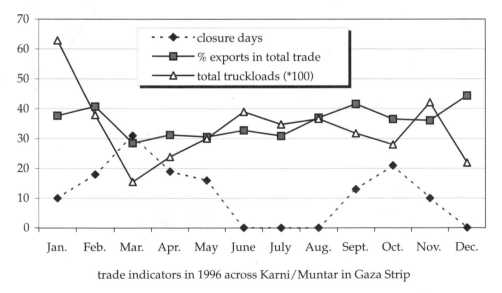

trade indicators in 1996 across Karni/Muntar in Gaza Strip

Sources: Authors' computation based on UNSCO (1997) and Palestinian Ministry of Labor.

following a sequence of suicide bombings in February-March 1996 and after violence erupted when Israel opened a tunnel in the old city of Jerusalem in September 1996. Internal closure is the most economically devastating form of border closure applied to date.

Box 4.1 The Human Cost of Closure

The restrictions on people's movement, which varies in intensity depending on the episode of closure, can be quite punishing for RWBGS residents. To enter Jerusalem or Israel, the required permit is issued from one day (such as for medical personnel) to a maximum of three months. It usually takes one week to three months to obtain. Often, applications for a permit are denied. To travel to a non-Arab country, a Palestinian needs a one-day permit to go to Jerusalem or Tel Aviv to apply for a visa, and needs a second permit to enter Israel to fly out of Tel Aviv's Ben Gurion Airport. The process of granting permits is not transparent and lacks any meaningful opportunity for appeal.

Some Palestinian professionals recruited from the Gulf countries for key technical positions within the PA could not tolerate the "prison-like" restrictions on their mobility in and out of the Gaza Strip, and some have left their positions. Restrictions deny Palestinian worshippers entry to East Jerusalem and prevent them from worshipping at Muslim and Christian holy sites.

Medical treatment is severely obstructed by the closure policy. Doctors, health workers, and patients must obtain permits to reach medical facilities in Jerusalem and Israel. Permits are often denied or not renewed. During closures, emergency passes for health workers to cross Israeli checkpoints are often not issued. Even if issued, they have not been recognized on numerous occasions. Ambulance access during emergencies is far too restrictive given the urgent needs and limited medical facilities in the RWBGS. During internal closure in the West Bank, the situation is most severe, as medical workers cannot report to work, practically freezing medical care. At least nine patients in critical condition died during the first ten days of the spring 1996 closure as a direct result of delayed or denied access at the checkpoints.

Education is also severely affected by closures. In May 1995, Israel passed regulations prohibiting the issuance of permits for study in Jerusalem to any Palestinian not previously registered in an educational institution there. Preventing the entry of any new students endangers Jerusalem's educational institutions, which have served Palestinians for decades. Closures covered 41 percent of the 1995-96 school year in the West Bank.

Source: Mostly based on Human Rights Watch/Middle East (1996).

Increased Intensity of Closure

Each time borders are sealed the conditions under which the borders would be selectively opened are harsher than in the past. For example, West Bank cars were initially allowed to enter Gaza Strip with the proper permit. Then, only cars with Israeli license plates were permitted to enter Gaza Strip. Currently, Israeli Arabs and Jerusalem residents with Israeli license plates are not permitted to enter Gaza Strip. Travelers with required permits must walk across the Gaza Strip borders. Back-to-back movement of goods is now the norm. Goods have to be unloaded from one truck to another truck at the Gaza Strip-Israel border. The inspection process of individuals and permitted vehicles (for example, vehicles with diplomatic plates or senior-level Palestinian policy makers) has become much more time-consuming and intrusive.

Macro Impact of Closure and Permit Policies in the Short-run

Losses to the WBGS economy arise from (i) the direct loss of income by Palestinian workers in Israel; (ii) the indirect impact of reduced expenditure on total production and income through the multiplier effect; and (iii) the disruption to trade that leads to permanent losses in export markets and interruptions to the flow of imports (which, in turn, disrupts domestic production and supply).

The most immediate macroeconomic impact of closure is the loss of earnings of Palestinians working in Israel, which is counted in the aggregate demand under "foreign income from abroad." The wider impact of this income loss depends on the extent to which households smooth their consumption over time, which depends on their perception of how transitory or permanent the income loss is. This analysis assumes that consumption adjusts by half as much as the income loss. The reduction in consumption expenditure depresses aggregate demand (production and income), an effect that is known as the multiplier effect of the initial reduction in expenditure. Based on previous analysis of Palestinian consumption behavior and aggregate demand, the multiplier size is here taken to be 3. Besides the direct and indirect impact of income losses of those working in Israel, the Palestinian economy suffers from trade disruptions. This leads to export market losses and disruption in the domestic supply of goods and services linked to imports. Limited information and data make it difficult to estimate trade losses. For purposes of this estimation, it is assumed that such losses equal 10 percent of the value of exports and 5 percent of the value of imports during the closure period.

The magnitude of economic losses from permit and closure policies depends on the benchmark against which the economy is compared. Here we estimate loss relative to a situation characterized by the labor and trade flows prevailing in 1992, prior to the imposition of permit and closure policies. It is reasonable to use 1992 as a benchmark since it reflects the pre-peace process employment level, and as such could be considered the "normal labor movement" that Israel committed to maintain in the 1994 Economic Protocol.

Computation of the cost of closure is shown in Table 4.1. The fraction of days that Gaza Strip was subjected to closure was 7.1 percent in 1993, 20.8 percent in 1994, 27.9 percent in 1995, and 37.8 percent in 1996. The fraction of days of closure applied to the RWB was 4.7 percent in 1993, 15.9 percent in 1994, 23.0 percent in 1995, and 36.2 percent in 1996. Two clear conclusions emerge from Table 4.1. First, closure has been significantly more costly for Gaza Strip than for the RWB. Second, the cost of closure has increased over the 1993-96 period, whether measured in absolute amounts or as a ratio of GNP. The sum of losses from closure policy only in the RWBGS was equal to 1.7 percent in 1993, 4.2 percent in 1994, 5.4 percent in 1995, and 7.3 percent of GNP in 1996. The RWBGS cost of both closure and permit policies in relation to the 1992 situation, and as a percent of the combined GNP, amounted to 6.5 percent in 1993, 16.3 percent in 1994, 20.6 percent in 1995, and 24.2 percent in 1996.

In absolute amounts, the cost of closure policy only is large (Figure 4.3). Cumulative losses over the 1993-96 period reached $775 million for closure policy only and $2,815 million for both closure and permit policies (in 1995 dollars). These cumulative losses amounted to 20 to 70 percent of one year's GNP, respectively. The higher cost estimate is about twice the amount of donor assistance that was disbursed over the same period.

Figure 4.3 Short-term Losses to Palestinian Economy from Border Closure and Permit Policies (1993-96)

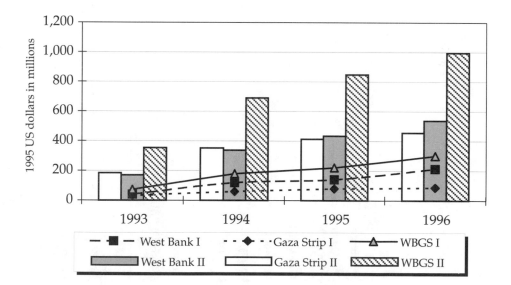

I: Cost of border closure policy only.
II: Cost of border closure and permit policies.
Source: Authors' computations.

Table 4.1 Total Cost of Border Closure and Permit Policies (1993-96)

	Rest of West Bank				Gaza Strip			
	1993	1994	1995	1996	1993	1994	1995	1996
GNP (in $ millions at 1995 prices)	3,226.6	3,124.1	2,926.9	2,951.2	1,168.3	1,120.0	1,189.7	1,152.8
Closure days/year	17	58	84	132	26	76	102	138
% days under closure	0.047	0.159	0.230	0.362	0.071	0.208	0.279	0.378
Losses ($ millions at 1995 prices)								
Closure Policy Only*	40.6	119.1	141.5	198.7	32.5	60.6	79.8	84.8
Closure & Permit Policies**	137.4	337.8	434.1	500.9	146.4	351.8	412.9	456.1
Losses (% of GNP)								
Closure Policy Only*	1.3	3.8	4.8	7.2	2.8	5.4	6.7	7.6
Closure & Permit Policies**	4.3	10.8	14.8	18.2	12.5	31.4	34.7	39.6

*   The cost of closure policy only is measured in relation to the declining flows of labor as a benchmark.
** The cost of closure and permit policies uses 1992 labor and trade flows as the benchmark.
Source: Authors' computation.

Labor Market Impact

Since 1993, Palestinians are required to have an Israeli-issued permit to work in Israel. The number of permits has declined and fluctuates in response to the political environment (Figure 4.4). The number of workers who actually obtain employment has generally deviated from the number of permits. In the early 1990s, the number of Palestinian workers in Israel exceeded the number of permits issued, often by a large margin. The situation changed after the establishment of the PA. Workers employed in Israel is much less than the number of permits issued to Palestinians. For example, the estimated average number of Palestinian workers in Israel in 1996 was lower than the average number of permits by 25 percent in the West Bank and 45 percent in Gaza Strip. This discrepancy stems directly from the increased application of closure over the 1994-96 period.

Unemployment Rate Increases During Closure

The immediate impact of closure is that Palestinian workers cannot reach their jobs in Israel, even if they have a work permit. In some cases in the West Bank, workers may get to their job site, bypassing Israeli checkpoints and walking through mountainous areas, often with help from their Israeli employers. But this has become more difficult due to greater policing of the borders and harsh punishment applied to Palestinians who are caught violating the Israeli ban on entry.

During closures, unemployment immediately increases in the WBGS, on top of an already very high unemployment rate. In September-October 1995, the rate of unemployment was 18.3 percent. It reached 28.6 percent during the harsher period of closure in April-May 1996 (Figure 4.5). Between these two periods, the number of unemployed workers increased by 38,000 in the West Bank and 19,000 in Gaza Strip. This suggests that the increase in unemployment in response to border closure equals the actual number of Palestinian workers in Israel during periods of non-closure. Clearly, some Palestinian workers working in Israel find employment opportunities in the domestic labor market during a closure period. But the impact of this adjustment is nullified by the indirect increase in unemployment in the domestic Palestinian economy as a result of border closure. Thus, unemployment increases during closure by the number of Palestinian workers unable to reach their jobs in Israel.

Labor Force Participation Rate Increases

The labor force participation rate appears to increase during closure periods. In general, the impact of increased unemployment on labor force participation is subject to two opposing trends. First, the discouraged worker effect causes people to drop out of the labor force, discouraged by the lower probability of finding a job. Second, the income loss to the household from unemployment may lead to

Figure 4.4 *Work Permits Issued to Palestinians for Work in Israel and Settlements*

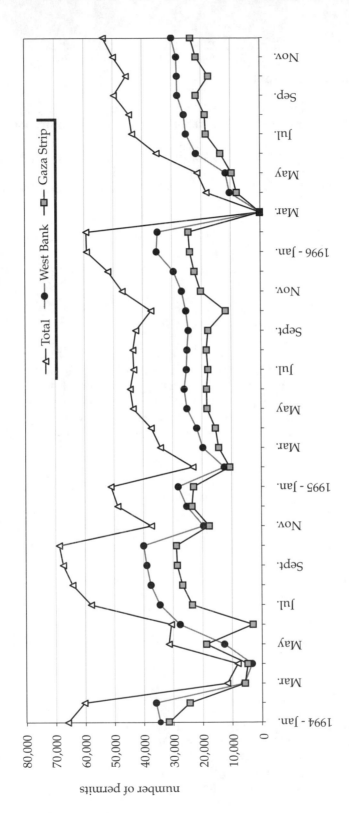

Sources: Israeli and Palestinian ministries of labor.

Figure 4.5 Unemployment Rate Increases During Closure

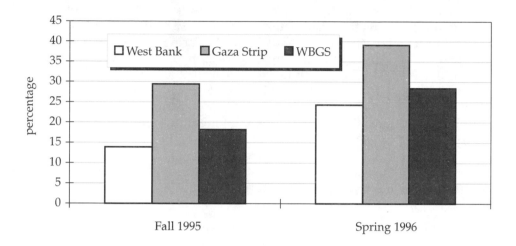

Source: PCBS (1996d and 1996e).

more members searching for and potentially obtaining jobs. The effect of income loss to the household appears to outweigh the discouraged worker effect, leading to higher labor force participation during a period of increased unemployment as a result of closure. The strength of the income loss results from the cumulative effect of negative shocks in the 1990s that have depleted household assets and limited their ability to smooth out income fluctuations (see "Household Adjustment" section). The increase in labor force participation during closure is characteristic of females as well as males.

The evidence of increased labor force participation as a result of closures comes from two separate sources. First, in comparing two PCBS surveys, the labor force participation rate for the population aged 15 years and older increased from 39 percent in September-October 1995 to 42.2 percent in April-May 1996 when closure was harsher and unemployment was higher. Second, in comparing the labor force participation rate for the West Bank across weeks of the September-October 1995 survey, it is obvious that labor force participation rates are lowest for weeks with no closure, and highest during the weeks of full closure.

Sectoral Distribution of Employment is Affected

The sectoral distribution of employment is also affected by closures (Table 4.2). In the West Bank, employment in the construction and manufacturing sectors are reduced. Agriculture operates as a shock absorber during closures as laborers work on family farms or in agricultural-related activities. In Gaza Strip, construction jobs are lost largely due to the difficulty in obtaining raw materials.

Two data sets illustrate the effect on sectoral distribution. First, the agricultural share of employment in the West Bank increased from 14.7 percent in September-October 1995 to 19.8 percent in April-May 1996. Second, micro data analysis reveals that the fraction of rural West Bank residents working in agriculture increased significantly by 0.094 during periods of partial closure and by 0.125 during full closure. The fraction of West Bank employment in manufacturing declined from 19.9 to 17.8 percent and in construction from 12.8 to 9.7 percent between September-October 1995 and April-May 1996, respectively. The micro evidence is consistent with the decline in manufacturing employment; the fraction of employment in manufacturing significantly declined by 0.011 during partial closure and by 0.014 during full closure. The micro evidence on construction employment is less clear, as it seems to be related to the nature and length of the closure and whether the import of construction materials is affected or not.

Table 4.2 Sectoral Distribution of Domestic Employment in the WBGS (Excluding Employment in Israel and Settlements)

Sector	September-October 1995			April-May 1996		
	West Bank	Gaza Strip	WBGS	West Bank	Gaza Strip	WBGS
Agriculture	14.7	10.7	13.6	19.8	10.2	17.3
Industry	19.9	15.4	18.6	17.8	15.8	17.2
Construction	12.8	14.0	13.1	9.7	7.4	9.1
Services	52.6	59.9	54.7	52.7	66.7	56.4
Total	100.0	100.0	100.0	100.0	100.0	100.0

Source: PCBS (1996d and 1996e).

Nominal and Real Wages Decline

With the sharp drop in the demand for labor during a closure period, the real and nominal wage rate drops (reflecting labor market flexibility and an absence of institutional impediments). For example, with deteriorating labor markets between September-October 1995 and April-May 1996, the average nominal daily wage fell for males from 44.6 to 41.5 shekels in Gaza Strip and from 58.5 to 49.4 shekels in the West Bank. This amounts to a 7-percent and 16-percent reduction in the nominal wages over a 7-month period in Gaza Strip and the West Bank, respectively. Given an inflation rate of 6 percent in each area, the real wage rate dropped by 13 percent in Gaza Strip and 22 percent in the West Bank from November 1995 to May 1996.

Household Adjustment

The loss of earnings during closures necessitates household adjustments in terms of income, assets, expenditure, and debt. Analysis of the results of a small sample of 300 households in Gaza Strip reveals that the average household income declined by 22 percent during the prolonged closure beginning in February 1996 in comparison to the period preceding that closure. The fraction of households (sample average household size of 9.4 persons) with a monthly income less than 600 NIS increased from 31 percent before the closure to 48 percent during closure. The most severely affected households are those with some members working in Israel. The income loss severely affects workers who depend on the transport or industrial sector, where employment is negatively affected during closures. Prolonged periods of closure also affect those working in the construction sector.

It is expected that households would attempt to smooth their consumption pattern. Consumption smoothing is carried out by drawing down household savings (such as selling jewelry, accumulating debt); adjusting eating habits to reduce expenditure while maintaining basic nutritional needs; and obtaining relief from welfare agencies, relatives, or neighbors. According to Table 4.3, 30 percent

Table 4.3 Household Adjustment During Spring 1996 Closure

Household Indicator	Before Closure	During Closure	Percentage Change
Average monthly income (NIS per household)	1,130	884	-21.8
% of households with monthly income < 600 NIS	31.0	48.0	54.8
% of households with no working adult	13.8	24.7	79.0
Fraction of households borrowing money (%)	28.0	56.3	101.0
Average debt of the indebted households (NIS)	1,028	1,225	19.2
% of households forced to use savings or sell jewelry	8.7	30.0	244.8
% of households receiving assistance		17.4	
Patterns of monthly household consumption:			
Average meat consumption (kg per household)	5.3	3.7	-30.2
Average egg consumption (number per household)	105.0	82.0	-21.9
Average flour consumption (kg per household)	106.7	106.9	0.2

Source: Authors' computation based on survey by Ard El Insan of 300 households in Gaza Strip.

of Gaza Strip households were forced to draw down their financial savings or sell their jewelry to finance current consumption during the prolonged spring 1996 closure. A sale of jewelry usually indicates serious hardship, given the difference in the sale and purchase price of jewelry.

Alternatively, households finance current consumption through indebtedness, mostly to shopkeepers and relatives who account for roughly one-half and one-third of total debt, respectively. The fraction of sample households financing their consumption through borrowing doubled from 28 percent before the spring 1996 closure to 56 percent during the spring 1996 closure. In addition to increasing the number of indebted households, closure intensified indebtedness, as the average debt of these households increased by 19 percent during closure compared to the preceding period.

Another way for households to adjust to income shortfalls is to reduce food expenditures. Evidence in Table 4.3 suggests that households did not reduce their consumption of flour, a basic need, but lowered consumption of relatively expensive goods such as meat and eggs by 30 percent and 22 percent, respectively. The average household maintains caloric intake, but protein intake probably suffers during closure.

Household consumption is also maintained through assistance provided by formal social safety nets (such as the United Nations Relief and Works Agency (UNRWA), or Ministry of Social Welfare) and the informal network of relatives, neighbors, and *Zakat* committees. Roughly 17 percent of the sample households received emergency assistance during the spring 1996 closure. More than half of those receiving assistance obtained it through the informal safety net of relatives, neighbors, and *Zakat* committees.

Impact on Firms

The impact of closure on firms in the industrial and service sectors is strongly negative. The Palestinian economy's integration with the Israeli economy ever since the 1967 occupation created very strong links between Palestinian and Israeli firms, whether in procuring inputs or supplying output. Closure has increased the cost of operations to such a level that trade between the West Bank and Gaza Strip and with Israel has become very costly and risky. The longer-run impact of recurrent and unpredictable closures would force the Palestinian areas to move toward a closed economy (autarky), with production aimed at the local market using local inputs. This outcome can be avoided only if there is a credible commitment to the free movement of goods and individuals between the WBGS and Israel. Furthermore, Palestinians should be permitted to freely access international markets directly through the Gaza airport and port (not yet open for operation) and be allowed free movement through a corridor connecting the West Bank and Gaza Strip.

Closure affects firms in several ways. It interrupts the production process, delays the procurement of raw materials and intermediate inputs, interrupts the movement of workers and personnel, and increases the cost of delivering goods and services to customers. Further, closure makes it very difficult to market goods and assure customers of reliable delivery, resulting in a loss of market share. It also increases the financing cost of doing business since collecting receivables and bad debt becomes difficult. At the same time, closure induces Israeli suppliers of inputs to demand advance payment for RWBGS firms' purchases. The net result is that sales decline, inventories build up, and operating costs skyrocket.

Declining Sales and Competitiveness

Table 4.4 documents the decline in sales for selected WBGS firms representing various industrial activities following the spring 1996 closure. The decline in sales is quite steep, ranging from 9 to 90 percent, and averaging 57 percent. Part of the decline in sales is a reflection of reduced aggregate demand from that follows closure. Despite effective demand for products, some firms suffer from a reduction in sales because they are unable to deliver the goods to the customers. They face difficulties in transporting manufactured goods or concluding sales due to restrictions on moving personnel and customers across borders with Israel. These factors are usually associated with excess inventories held by an establishment, as is the case with food processing, leather, and textiles. Other firms suffer a substantial reduction in production and sales with the interrupted delivery of key inputs that are imported either from or through Israel, such as chemical, pharmaceutical, metals, and construction firms. Clearly, establishments

Table 4.4 Impact of Spring 1996 Closure on Sales of Selected Firms

Firm	Normal Sales	During Closure	Percentage Decline
Reem Sports Shoes (1000 NIS/month)	180	40	78
Al-Shorouq Carton Industry Co. (1000 NIS/month)	150	73 in March 96	51
		136 in April 96	9
Aweida Food Products (1000 NIS/month)	500	140	72
Palestinian Tractor Co. (1000 NIS/month)	850	200	76
National Palace Hotel Restaurant (1000 $/month)	27	13.2	51
Riziq Textile Co. (1000 NIS/month)	225	157	30
Nasser Oriental Trading & Mfg. Co. (1000 NIS/month)	1,000	100	90
Sylvana Co. (1000 NIS/day)	65	20	69
Jordan Chemical Lab (1000 NIS/month)	500	300	40

Note: Figure for "during closure" refers to March and April 1996.
Source: Derived from case studies on the impact of closure on firms, assembled by Mattin and Palestinian Trade Promotion Organization (1996).

in the latter industries can build up their inventories of inputs or outputs, at a substantial cost, to reduce the impact of closure. This, however, would be fruitful only if the demand for their products and services is local and is relatively immune to closure conditions.

Difficulties in marketing Palestinian goods in Israel has led to a reduction in the Israeli market share for Palestinian firms. The increased cost of moving goods across borders and the unpredictability of deliveries adds to the cost of trade with Palestinian firms. For example, the Israeli market share in the output of the Reem Sports Shoes company declined from 50 percent in 1993 (prior to closures) to 10 percent in 1996.

Border closures are applied asymmetrically. Palestinian goods are largely prevented from entering or going through Israel, while Israeli goods continue to flow into Palestinian areas, particularly the West Bank. While it is possible for some Palestinian firms to marginally increase their market share at the expense of Israeli firms, the overwhelming impact of the asymmetry is a decline in the market share, size, and competitiveness of Palestinian firms.

Increased Costs of Production and Operation

Closures substantially increase firms' costs of production and operation. Inventory costs increase due to the undesired accumulation of inventories—inputs or outputs—or planned higher levels of inventories designed to mitigate the impact of shocks. Financing costs increase, as it becomes difficult for personnel to cross borders to collect payment and bad debt. Many Israeli suppliers have started to demand advance payment during closures instead of payment-upon-receipt to protect themselves from collection difficulties. With increased financing difficulties, liquidity problems arise as banks tighten their credit line or become unwilling to extend additional credit. The inefficient payment system that arises from closure is certain to reduce profitability and the size of production. This risky environment is well known to commercial banks, which as a result have become even more conservative in extending credit to private businesses, reducing the maturity of credit, and raising the cost of credit to WBGS firms. Commercial banks keep a higher liquidity ratio during closure periods in order to meet increased demand on withdrawing deposits.

Transportation costs increase substantially as a result of border closure. For example, the transportation cost for a truckload of goods between the West Bank and Gaza Strip was around NIS 500 in 1993 and reached NIS 1,500 in 1996. The increase arises from newly imposed rules that require goods to be unloaded at the border from one truck to another. The back-to-back system may require goods moving between the West Bank and Gaza Strip to be loaded on three separate trucks, for a journey that is less than 100 miles.

To the extent that some inputs are imported and some outputs are exported, closure increases the cost of clearance, storage, and shipping since company staff are unable to do the work. Firms have had to rely increasingly on Israeli agents for shipping and clearance at higher costs. During periods of closure, delayed delivery of goods at Israeli ports increases storage costs. There have also been numerous instances of spoilage of perishable goods due to the transportation bottleneck (Box 4.2).

Some firms react to reduced sales by laying off workers, scaling down the number of shifts in operation, or shortening the operation schedule. Firms are more likely to keep workers who have job-specific skills and to continue paying their wages, in order to save the cost of training new workers when sales begin increasing again.

Long-term Impact on Growth

Border closures have a less obvious yet detrimental impact on long-run economic development by instigating lower levels of investment and reduced efficiency of investment. These two related but separate effects of closure both imply lower rates of economic growth.

Low Levels of Investment

Closure policy can largely explain the difference between the substantial interest of local and Diaspora Palestinians to invest in the economy and the actual low levels of investment to date. First, the strong interest is based on a rosy scenario of long-term economic development; but the demand for investment has diminished under closure policy because of an overall decline in aggregate demand. Second, closure generally interrupts sales and increases operating costs, thus reducing overall profitability as well as the incentive for new investment. Third, investment is deterred by the increased risk arising from uncertainty in the timing, duration, and intensity of closures. This uncertainty is over and above the strategic uncertainty of interim status and the lack of clarity on the permanent status of the WBGS. Fourth, closure has reduced public investment as donor funds have been largely aimed at income maintenance and budgetary support in an effort to cushion the impact of closures. To the extent that investment in public infrastructure is complementary to private investment, lower levels of private investment also result from the inability to upgrade public infrastructure.

In addition to the above factors that curtail the demand for investment, closure reduces the supply of funds available for investment and increases the cost of such funds. Commercial banks have become much more conservative in their lending practice than they may otherwise be, leading to lower debt-financed investment levels.

Reduced Efficiency of Investment

In addition to low levels of investment, the wrong investment decisions are likely to be made in the context of border closures. Instead of developing into an export-oriented economy, the signals sent by the closure policy drive the economy

Box 4.2 Trade in Perishable Goods and Closure

Perishable goods that are traded, such as high-value agricultural products from the Gaza Strip, are heavily penalized by the closure policy. Perishable food and agricultural commodities can be destroyed during closures—a loss that cannot be compensated at a later stage.

The required back-to-back shipping of goods and extended delays negatively affect product quality. Sylvana, a major West Bank chocolate factory, practically lost the Gaza Strip market for its traditional products following the spring 1996 closure. Boxes of chocolate had to be loaded on three separate trucks using the back-to-back mechanism and utilizing the services of an Israeli company in the intermediate step. About 20 to 30 percent of the shipped chocolates were damaged as a result of loading and unloading and extended border delays.

Investment in producing perishable agricultural commodities for trade is proving disastrous to Palestinian farmers. The story of strawberry and carnation production in the northern areas of Gaza Strip is illuminating. Both are high-value crops and were introduced to Gaza's farmers through the ICA's Department of Agriculture. Production of these crops expanded rapidly in the early 1990s. Currently, about 1000 dunum (one dunum = 1000 square meters) in Gaza Strip is cultivated with carnations. About 75 percent of Israel's export of strawberries are produced in Gaza Strip.

The crops are marketed through the Israeli AGREXCO export company, mainly to Western Europe. The carnations and strawberries are shipped by the exporter from an Israeli airport. Extended delays at the border for security checks, limited movement of trucks, and expensive refrigerated storage facilities are making it very difficult for farmers to cover their production costs. During the 1995-96 season, an estimated 15 million stems of carnations were lost due to closure-related reduction in export (at a per farmer loss of approximately $2 million). Clearly, the farmers' investment to transform their land to high value-added export crops, purchase green houses, and acquire the requisite skills to produce these crops has placed them in financial difficulties during the 1995-96 and 1996-97 seasons. Continuation of closure policy without alternative direct export routes will ultimately force these Palestinian farmers out of production for export and into production for domestic consumption.

Closure policy also generates peculiar outcomes with wide variation in prices of perishable commodities among the markets of the West Bank, Gaza Strip, and Israel. For example, the low supply of Israeli tomatoes in summer 1995 made their price skyrocket in Israel and the West Bank from NIS 2-3 to around NIS 10 per kg. But the excess supply of tomatoes in Gaza Strip was prevented from entering Israel (and hence the West Bank), making their price in Gaza Strip drop to unusually low levels.

into localized autarky, with production aimed at the local market. This arises from the differential impact of closure on firms depending on the importance of tradable goods in their inputs and output.

As Table 4.5 illustrates, firms least affected by closure utilize local materials and sell their product in the local market. These firms may even benefit if a foreign competitor is unable to deliver goods to the local Palestinian market. Firms that sell products in markets across borders suffer a reduction in sales and market share. Firms that need imported inputs suffer higher inventory costs or sustain interruptions to production.

The more open to external trade the firm is, the more costly is closure policy. This is an ironic outcome, as the economic vision accompanying the peace process and donor assistance revolves around moving the Palestinian economy from exporting labor to exporting goods and services that utilize Palestinian labor. Investment decisions based on this vision have been heavily penalized by closure policy.

Facing these realities, firms may decide to mitigate the impact of the closure by locating the production process in the same location as inputs and product market. New investment activities could include producing goods for the domestic Palestinian market or services consumed in the region, such as tourism. Industries that produce export goods will attract very little investment without open borders and political stability. The Palestinian economy could move toward autarky, with limited trade with the rest of the world.

The non-contiguity of the West Bank and Gaza Strip generates additional peculiarities for an economy mainly serving domestic markets. To the extent that both the West Bank and the Gaza Strip are important for a firm's product, the firm may have to invest in two separate plants to cater to the markets separately. The result would be a closed economy with both little trade to the outside world and limited trade between the West Bank and Gaza Strip.

The closed-economy outcome would prevent the WBGS from reaping substantial benefits from the international division of labor that accompanies world trade. Skilled and educated workers are likely to be punished more severely from limited international trade, since their skills would be underutilized by the market. This would be particularly damaging to the Palestinian economy, given its abundant endowment of educated workers. Low and stagnant levels of income, coupled with reduced benefits, would push educated workers to seek better employment opportunities by migration. The resulting situation could generate dissent and strengthen opposition to the political process.

Impact on the Government

Border closure has affected government operations by reducing revenues, increasing expenditure on income maintenance and job expansion, and shifting the priorities of donor assistance away from public investment to short-term budgetary and income support. With the negative impact on income and production levels, closure has resulted in revenue losses for the PA. The losses are hard to

*Table 4.5 Difficulties Encountered by Firms During Closure
by Location of Inputs and Markets*

A Firm Located in the West Bank

Market

Inputs	West Bank	Gaza Strip	Israel	Abroad
West Bank	minimal	delivery	delivery	delivery
Gaza Strip	access	access + delivery	access + delivery	access + delivery
Israel	access	access + delivery	access + delivery	access + delivery
Abroad	clearance + access	clearance + access + delivery	clearance + access + delivery	clearance + access + delivery + clearance

A Firm Located in Gaza Strip

Market

Inputs	West Bank	Gaza Strip	Israel	Abroad
West Bank	access + delivery	access	access + delivery	access + delivery
Gaza Strip	delivery	minimal	delivery	delivery
Israel	access + delivery	access	access + delivery	access + delivery + clearance
Abroad	clearance + access + delivery	clearance + access	clearance + access + delivery	clearance + access + delivery + access

Categories of difficulties:

access = delivery of inputs to firms is interrupted or becomes very costly

delivery = delivery of output to customers is interrupted or becomes extrememly expensive

clearance = difficulties are encountered in customs clearance either for imports or exports trace given the incremental transfer of revenues from the Israeli to Palestinian authorities, and given the difficulty in assigning government revenues to specific time periods of accrual.

More obvious is the impact of border closure on increasing PA expenditures, such as welfare programs to mitigate increasing levels of poverty. A significant part of increased public expenditure is due to the substantial increase in public sector employment, some of which may be an effort to alleviate the impact of high unemployment.

Closure presents challenges to the operation of the PA, whose offices are located in the geographically non-contiguous areas of the West Bank and Gaza Strip. Coordination between the offices is substantially more difficult and costly as officials are restricted from moving freely between the two areas. Staff training, workshops, and any type of government operation has to be done twice— once in the West Bank and once in Gaza Strip. The difficulty in mobility for government officials poses a danger of having two government bodies develop and implement different policies in the two areas.

Border closure has negatively influenced the official assistance programs of donor countries. Reduced revenues and greater expenditures have increased PA budget deficits, which has increased the demand for donor budgetary support at the expense of investment in public infrastructure. Donor aid has been re-oriented away from long-term development projects toward employment-generation projects (see Chapter 10). The latter can be implemented quickly with an immediately visible impact of alleviating unemployment and poverty. Further, the delivery of donor assistance has often been interrupted by closures as imported goods face difficulty in clearance or as aid workers' mobility is hampered.

* * *

The recent negative performance of the Palestinian economy can largely be attributed to the sudden disengagement of the Palestinian and Israeli economies as a result of permit and closure policies. Continuation of the closure policy in the next few years will only perpetuate negative economic outcomes. Private investment will be deterred, and firms will increasingly adjust their investment to the local market. The optimal policy would be to open up the border, allow for open employment of Palestinians in Israel, and assure the free and uninterrupted movement of goods within WBGS, between the West Bank and Gaza Strip, and between the WBGS and Israel. If this is deemed impossible, fundamental changes will have to be made that allow the Palestinian economy to function with minimal links to Israel.

Bibliographic Note: This chapter draws on the background papers of Arnon (1996), Pissarides (1996), and Abu Dagga (1996). Additional sources include PCBS labor force surveys, Iyyada, Hannon, and Ard El Insan (July 1996), Human Rights Watch/Middle East (July 1996), UNSCO (1997), and Mattin and Palestinian Trade Promotion Organization (1996).

Part II

Policies for Growth and Job Creation under Adverse Conditions

In the long term, the Palestinian economy cannot grow on a sustainable basis without a favorable resolution of the peace process. In the next few years, the economy is likely to remain vulnerable to external shocks and political uncertainty, and stabilization policies will not be sufficient to meet the job creation challenge. To build a solid basis for growth in spite of the ups and downs of politics, Palestinian society can take advantage of its unused assets—the skills and capital of its population and Diaspora, a broad array of profitable investment opportunities, and the goodwill of the international donor community.

To nurture these assets toward their potential, a good policy framework should be designed to

- diversify away from economic reliance on Israel;
- remove artificial constraints to allow the economy to jump closer to its potential;
- foster more risk-sharing among the WBGS, international donors, and financial markets; and
- resist the temptations of myopic policies with large social costs down the road.

The PA has sufficient authority to implement many of the policies identified throughout Part II of this book. However, some policies—such as changes in trade regime, taxation, or land zoning—hinge on further negotiations with Israel or resolution of the final status issues.

Chapter 5

Private Investment

Osama Hamed

Introduction

Traditionally, domestic savings and investment in the WBGS have been relatively high, but most of this investment has been concentrated in housing. This was due to a combination of forces: a high level of risk requiring high precautionary savings; financial and regulatory repression, with taxes on local businesses that discouraged productive investments; and low public investments, a consequence of fiscal compression and significant tax leakage to the Israeli treasury (Figure 5.1).

Figure 5.1 Composition of Total Investment as Share of GDP

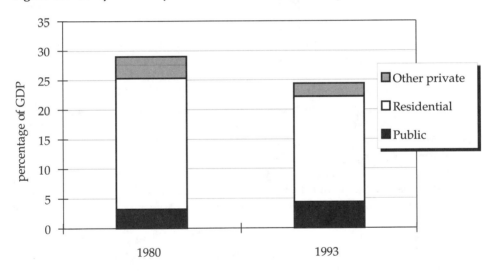

Source: Annex, Table A.1.

The signing the Oslo Agreement generated much optimism regarding the capacity of the private sector to absorb accumulated savings of WBGS residents and to attract Diaspora investments. To date, however, this investment has not materialized. Private investment has been falling over the last three years. The housing sector, which absorbed most of private investment in recent years, is showing signs of slowing down. The main difference between the present and the pre-1993 situation is that investment is currently weighted down by uncertainties about the future rather than by regulatory repression. However, good policies can unlock investments in some sectors.

This chapter focuses on the short- and medium-term impact that private investment has on the construction, infrastructure, and tourism sectors. A potentially large private growth area is in utilities and collective infrastructure, such as electricity, telephone, water, trash collection, and the construction of large projects, such as ports and an airport. Donor assistance has not managed to make a large difference in these sectors. The challenge is to find the arrangements that will allow the blending of donor support (preferably linked to capital with high resistance to political risks) with private sector investment (where the key advantages include flexibility and more efficient management).

Another possible growth area is tourism. The tourism sector currently captures extraordinarily low revenues compared with its immense potential in a land filled with historical sites and unusual geological formations. Events such as Bethlehem 2000 could attract millions of tourists. Lower regulatory restrictions now provide the opportunity to try and win back some of the tourism infrastructure, such as hotels and buses, that was dominated by Israel in the past.

Legal and Regulatory Framework

A transparent and independent legal system promotes investment by providing efficient mechanisms for settling disputes among private sector agents and by protecting these agents from undue government intervention in economic affairs. The present legal environment needs significant improvement to attract investors, which should include avoiding political intervention in legal affairs and resolving conflicts between different layers of legal codes (Israeli military orders as well as Ottoman, British, Jordanian, and Egyptian codes). Immediate attention is needed to secure legal protection against expropriation and confiscation of foreign investment property, and to provide legal guarantees that insure the repatriation of capital and profits.

While most of the elements of the investment framework require urgent attention by the PA, several initiatives are already in progress.

- The court system is being reconstructed, including adoption of a civil procedure law. Courts will need to clarify areas of jurisdiction in accordance with the judicial hierarchy.
- In the property rights sphere, a new apartment ownership law is being implemented and a registration system for movables is underway.
- New banking laws and regulations as well as a new intellectual property law are being drafted.
- A number of ministries are assessing existing laws in the economy through field surveys and databases.

Special tax incentives may or may not be effective in encouraging investment. If tax incentives are deemed necessary, these incentives should be well targeted, and it would be advisable to modify the present draft of the PA investment law to make it more effective in stimulating investment. First, emphasis should be shifted from tax holidays (which recent experience in developing countries has shown to be ineffective in attracting investors) to tax credits and investment allowances. Second, incentives should be performance-based rather than registration-based. Third, all decisions for granting and canceling incentives should be based on clear criteria and guidelines. In contrast, the present investment law draft gives substantial discretionary power to bureaucrats in charge of implementing the law.

The above is a tall order that can only be implemented over a considerable time period. In the meantime, it would be desirable to enact some short-term measures that stimulate investment and help overcome the critical employment problem. One widely used measure is the creation of special economic zones (Box 5.1). Other actions can encourage the development of sectors that are more robust to political turmoil, such as housing and other types of infrastructure with a large pent-up demand.

Box 5.1 Industrial Estates

A series of industrial zones has been planned to help jump-start industrial development. These are zones with closure-free movement of goods and labor established in a legal and regulatory environment attractive to potential investors. The estates would, in effect, sidestep the many obstacles that presently impede employment, investment, exports, and business transactions through the WBGS.

The Gaza Industrial Estate (GIE) is the first phase of a broader program of industrial estate development. The GIE is targeted primarily but not exclusively at export markets. A German-funded project in Jenin is the second export-oriented border estate. Municipal industrial estates (with a proposed project for Nablus initially) constitute the third dimension of the program; these focus primarily on the domestic market, are designed to provide facilities for small workshops in local areas, and incorporate a policy dimension to address newly enforced municipal zoning requirements.

The total cost of the GIE pioneer project is estimated at $64 million, of which $34 million is expected to come from private sector investors, including the developer, Palestinian Development International Company (PADICO), local private sector investors, the International Finance Corporation (IFC), and the European Investment Bank. The remaining $30 million for technical assistance and off-site infrastructure components will be covered by the donor community. When used at its full capacity, the GIE could have 17,000 permanent jobs, with an additional 20-30,000 jobs created indirectly for services and other manufacturing operations.

(box continues on next page)

Barriers to Growth in Agriculture

The industrial sector has experienced some expansion in the transition period. For example, industries catering to domestic consumption, such as food processing, expanded after years of retarded growth under Israeli administrative restrictions. However, restricted access to international markets and uncertainty about the future are major barriers to investment in the industrial sector. Lack of market access inhibits the development of export-oriented industries, which represent a major potential source of growth in the WBGS (see Chapter 6).

This has led some to recommend a larger role for agriculture. However, prospects for the agricultural sector are even less promising. Export barriers in the short term and limited access to land and water resources in the long term inhibit agricultural growth. Land use in 40 percent of the Gaza Strip and 74 percent of the West Bank is still controlled by Israel. Israeli-controlled areas are vulnerable to expropriation for settlement and bypass road construction. Farming in some areas, such as regions of the Jordan Valley, is restricted for security reasons. Most WBGS agricultural products are still not allowed to enter Israel despite the provisions in Economic Protocol to gradually phase out all barriers to trade in agricultural products between the WBGS and Israel. Regional and international exports are inhibited by cumbersome customs procedures and closures.

In the long term, a permanent political settlement that results in Palestinian control of WBGS water and land resources will no doubt enhance the prospects for agriculture. Such a settlement can also improve WBGS access to regional and international markets. Nevertheless, the long-term growth potential of the WBGS agricultural sector is very limited because of intrinsic water scarcity.

Economic development means growing water demand from agricultural and industrial production, population increase, rising living standards, and preservation of environmental sustainability. Any economic growth will substantially

---

(Box 5.1 continues)

Viability of industrial estates will hinge on critical success factors.

- *Security and Access Agreement.* Success is dependent on political and legal agreements of a binding nature that will insulate these zones from border closures. Negotiations are presently underway to formulate security procedures and access agreements to insure closure-free operation.
- *The Policy Environment.* Significant progress has been made recently in advancing the legal framework and the institutional arrangements to assure transparency, efficiency, and investor confidence. Further progress is still required in gaining legislative approval for the investment law and the industrial and free zones law.

increase water demand. However, current available renewable water resources in the WBGS (based on the Oslo II Agreement) are only 115 cubic meters per capita per year—among the lowest in the world (Table 5.1). Regardless of the final status settlement, water resources will be extremely limited in both the West Bank and the Gaza Strip and will pose a serious constraint for the economy, even with minimal growth scenarios. This requires re-thinking economic growth patterns and a change in attitudes to water use. One dramatic implication is that agriculture is unlikely to remain the mainstay of the Palestinian economy in the future.

Presently, WBGS agriculture uses, on average, 70 percent of all extracted water (strikingly, Gaza Strip uses 150 percent of annually renewable water resources) and the sector contributes about 15 percent to GDP. By comparison, industry and construction use about 13 percent of available water resources and contribute about 25 percent to GDP. The value added per unit of water is much higher in industry. Typical value added by irrigated agriculture in the region varies between $0.15 and $0.30 per cubic meter of water, while value added by most industries can be as high as $30 to $50 per cubic meter of water used. For future economic growth, less water should go to agriculture, and more should go to industry. But less water use in agriculture does not necessarily mean lower agricultural outputs. Conversion of current irrigation practices to more efficient methods could protect and use less of the available freshwater resources. Nevertheless, given the large share of the labor force in agriculture (20 to 25 percent), the required future adjustment is considerable.

Table 5.1 Regional Water Resources (1995)

Country	Resources BCM* per year	Consumption BCM per year	Resources cubic meters per capita per year
Israel	2.1	1.9	375
Jordan	0.8	1.0	213
Lebanon	4.8	0.8	1,200
Syria	5.5	3.3	385
WBGS	0.2	0.2**	115

* billion cubic meters
** Actual Oslo II allocations (interim) are 264.5 million cubic meters (MCM) (248 MCM renewable and 16.5 MCM from Israel).
Source: World Bank (1995a).

Translating Potential Housing Demand into Actual Units

Investment in housing exploded with the start of the peace process, causing land prices to skyrocket. By 1996, it started to falter, as indicated in Figure 5.2 by the sharp drop in building permits. Most new construction has been in residential housing at the upper end of the market, with new apartments bought by relatively well-to-do returnees or the small new professional class of public servants, university professors, and bank employees. While there is still a demand for expensive residential housing, mainly in the Palestinian Diaspora, its potential is largely dependent upon political improvements. Demand is potentially stronger and much more robust to political uncertainties at the middle and lower end of the market. However, before this potential can be realized, improvements are needed in the legal framework and financial markets. Also, efficiency gains must be realized in the construction industry.

Measured by floor area per person, the WBGS does not seem to have a serious housing crisis. The median usable space is around 15.1 square meters, which is about average for countries at a comparable level of development (Table 5.2). This figure, however, masks crowding problems among lower-income households, particularly in refugee camps. Based on a 1995 PCBS demographic survey, 34.7 percent of all households in the Gaza Strip and 26 percent in the West Bank have more than three persons per room. Comparable figures for refugee camps are 41.1 percent for the Gaza Strip and 31.1 percent for the West Bank.

Figure 5.2 Building Permits Issued by the City of Ramallah (1991-96)

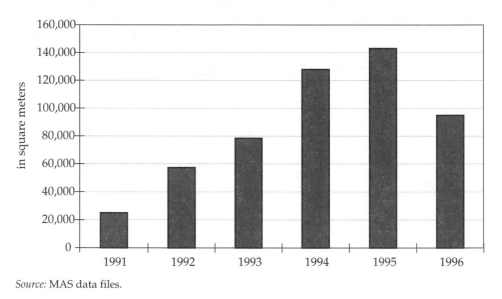

Source: MAS data files.

High Demand and Limited Supply

Housing prices are relatively high. The most common measurement for the relative cost of housing is the house price-to-income ratio, defined as the ratio of the median free-market price of a dwelling unit and the median annual household income. There is hardly any market for existing housing units because of cultural factors, limited mobility, and lack of well-defined property rights for a significant share of the housing stock, particularly in the West Bank. Hence, it is justifiable to use the selling price of newly built units in calculating the house price-to-income ratio. The WBGS house price-to-income ratio is around 10, which is significantly higher than other countries at a comparable level of development (Table 5.2).

The share of rental units in the housing stock is very low—only 4.9 percent in the Gaza Strip and 11.4 percent in the West Bank. Housing finance, which plays an important role in facilitating the purchase of dwelling units in most countries, hardly exists. Limited rental units and the effective absence of housing finance makes it difficult for households to smooth housing consumption, which, in turn, decreases the probability of translating potential housing demand into actual demand.

Table 5.2 Housing Indicators for Selected Countries in the Region

	GNP per capita US$ (1990)	Floor area per person (square meters)	House price/income
Egypt	600	12.00	6.67
Morocco	950	6.00	7.15
Jordan	1,240	10.00	3.39
Tunisia	1,440	6.47	6.11
Turkey	1,630	17.00	5.03
WBGS	1,700	15.10	10.00
Algeria	2,060	8.54	11.70
Israel	16,680	24.80	5.03

Source: All figures in this table are based on Mayo (1995), except the house price/income for the WBGS which was estimated by the authors.

Enormous Potential Demand for Housing

In the short term, a high natural population and a decreasing family size could generate a strong housing demand. The number of housing units needed to accommodate this demand for the period 1997-2000 is estimated at around 217,000. Housing demand will be much larger when considering the need to replace units removed from the housing stock due to deterioration or lack of suitability, and the need to reduce overcrowding. In the long term, a permanent political settlement may result in the return of a substantial number of Diaspora Palestinians and the resettlement of Palestinian refugees, creating even more demand for housing: If potential demand is translated into the production of new housing units, the housing sector could be a major source of economic growth in the long and short term.

In the long term, the absorption of Diaspora Palestinians and the resettlement of refugees could require the construction of new cities and major investments in infrastructure. This would require enormous financial resources and a quantum leap in construction management and know-how. Possible sources of finance are mortgage loans from the domestic financial sector, commercial investments by Diaspora Palestinians, financial compensation obtained by resettled refugees, and international aid. The technical expertise in construction can be provided by Diaspora Palestinians, some of whom are major players in the regional construction market, particularly in the Gulf (see Box 1.1 in Chapter 1). However, major expansion of mortgage lending by commercial banks and other financial institutions will be contingent upon the success of the permanent settlement to increase political stability. A substantial contribution of financial resources and technical expertise by Diaspora Palestinians will also depend on the effectiveness of the permanent settlement to integrate these Palestinians in the WBGS body politic. Finally, the feasibility of building new cities will be determined by the size of the landmass controlled by the PA under the permanent settlement.

Enhancing the Housing Market

In the short term, the high population growth rate and decrease in the average family size may not necessarily translate into the production of new housing units, unless measures are taken to relax some supply and demand constraints that currently inhibit development of the housing sector. On the demand side, potential demand for housing by many households cannot be translated into actual demand because of insufficient income or the lack of long-term financing. On the supply side, the construction of new housing units is inhibited by rent control laws and Israeli zoning restrictions.

Increased housing costs and poverty in the last few years have made housing unaffordable for a significant segment of the population without some assistance. One approach is to provide cash-based housing assistance. Lower-income households that do not earn sufficient income to cover basic needs could receive rent vouchers. Housing assistance to moderate-income households could be in the form of a loan subsidy.

The present economic and political environment in the WBGS makes commercial banks and other financial institutions reluctant to commit significant financial resources to mortgage lending because of high credit and liquidity risks. This limits demand for housing even among households that can afford a house. A significant increase in mortgage lending cannot be expected in the present environment without finding ways to reduce liquidity and credit risks. Some reduction in credit risk could be achieved by providing banks with partial credit insurance. Liquidity risk could be reduced by creating a secondary mortgage facility that provides banks with long-term funds (see Chapter 7).

Rent control laws limit the supply of rental housing. Generally, these laws entitle the tenant to remain in the rented property after the lease period expires, and the rental terms (including rent payment) legally continue to bind the parties indefinitely. This is supposed to make housing affordable to the poor. Recent evidence, however, indicates that the main beneficiaries of rent control are not the poor. The poverty rate is much lower among renters than the population as a whole. Based on a poverty line of $650, only 5 percent of WBGS renters are poor, compared with the overall poverty rate of 19 percent. Meanwhile, rent control laws depress investment in the construction of new rental units and make it unprofitable for current owners to maintain or renovate them. A complete repeal of the rent control law, however, is not politically feasible at present. A more realistic approach would be to allow owners of new rental units to increase rent by the rate of inflation.

Israeli restrictions make it extremely difficult for Palestinians to obtain building permits in more than 70 percent of the West Bank and almost 40 percent of the Gaza Strip, where zoning is still under Israeli control. Limited PA control over zoning has increased demand for land in the rest of the WBGS, resulting in higher land prices and construction costs. The relaxation of zoning rules in the Israeli-controlled areas of the WBGS, therefore, is essential to the development of the housing sector in the transition period.

Attracting Private Investment in Infrastructure

For a small economy such as the WBGS, infrastructure acquires a special importance. Trade links as well as communications with the rest of the world are particularly important. Studies show that export growth is associated with rapid growth in telecommunications services. Foreign investment is similarly attracted by a good infrastructure.

The infrastructure is deficient and unreliable due to years of neglect under Israeli occupation. In the 1980s and 1990s, investment levels in infrastructure were minimal, ranging from $20 to $30 million per year. To some extent, these low expenditures reflect the fact that much of the responsibility for infrastructure supply lay with Israeli providers, thereby eliminating the need for some direct expenditures in the WBGS, such as power generation and international telecommunications switching equipment. However, lack of maintenance and general neglect has resulted in huge equipment losses, which in turn, has increased prices to consumers (see Chapter 13).

In the last two years, a number of infrastructure rehabilitation projects were financed by donors. Total investment in these projects in 1995 was around $60 million, which represents under 2 percent of GDP. Much of the investment went to water and sanitation, where health needs are urgent and environmental benefits are significant. Investment in infrastructure is still inadequate if the WBGS is to attract foreign investment and expand the role of exports in its economy. If the average for developing countries is accepted as the target for ongoing infrastructure investment in the WBGS, (with an additional 1 percent of GDP allocated to continue rehabilitation to make up for past neglect), then annual investment in infrastructure should be between 4 to 5 percent of GDP. This presently amounts to $140 to $175 million.

Private Infrastructure

The private sector could contribute some of the investment required for infrastructure. The extent of private sector financing will depend on the form in which the private sector participates in infrastructure delivery and, hence, in risk-taking. For example, in electricity and telecommunications, the private sector could be induced to bear most of the costs. In water, the private sector might be limited to a management contract.

The first step toward private sector involvement has already taken place with the newly established regional water and sanitation authority in the Gaza Strip, which awarded a four-year management contract to an international operator through competitive bidding. In telecommunications, a private company, the Palestinian Telecommunications Co. (Paltel), was awarded an exclusive franchise for rebuilding and operating fixed and mobile phone systems for a 15-year period, with a non-exclusive franchise for another 15 years. In electricity, the Palestinian Electricity Authority (PEA) is presently negotiating the development of a power-generating plant in the Gaza Strip under a 20-year build-operate-transfer contract with a private company that will ultimately provide 215 megawatts (Mw) of power.

Private provision of infrastructure requires building sufficient regulatory capacity to ensure that societal interests are met. Where competition is effective, service providers have the right incentives to price in a socially desirable manner. Hence, regulation should be limited to non-price issues, such as safety and environmental protection. Where market power rests with providers, a price regulatory mechanism needs to be put in place. An increasingly popular form of price regulation calls for capping prices at a pre-specified level. In contrast with the rate of return method (traditionally used to regulate infrastructure providers with market power), price caps tie the provider's return to performance.

The principle of creating incentives for performance is already being adopted for infrastructure projects in the WBGS. Compensation has been tied closely to performance in the Gaza Strip water supply management contract. In the Gaza Strip power plant, the price paid for electricity will evolve according to a pre-specified formula, in the spirit of price cap regulation. Operation and maintenance (O&M) costs will be tied to a cost of living index, and energy costs will be tied to a world energy price index.

Financing Infrastructure

Infrastructure provision is accompanied by substantial risks, including expropriation, the ability (or lack of) to convert and transfer currency, and regulatory reversals that render the enterprise financially impracticable. In the WBGS, the risks associated with setbacks to the peace process are an additional, perhaps critical, concern. These risks limit entry of private providers even where large profits could be made. Thus, risk mitigation and management is a crucial element of government and donor strategies.

A co-financing facility can serve as a transitional mechanism for attracting finance to infrastructure and leveraging donor and government sources. Such a facility, utilizing concessional resources to share risks with the private sector, was used in Pakistan for financing private power investments and in Sri Lanka for all infrastructure investments. Leveraging is achieved by supplying a limited portion of project financing, for example 25 percent, on average. Private sponsors provide the equity, the facility is the source of subordinated debt, and private lenders provide the senior debt. Thus, a dollar of money from the facility can leverage another three dollars of private money for effectively structured projects. The subordinated debt is provided at market interest rates (although for Pakistan and Sri Lanka, the grace period and overall loan maturity is much higher than would be available from the market).

Another possible mechanism to mitigate risk is to supply private investors with guarantees from multinational institutions, such as the World Bank and the Multilateral Investment Guarantee Agency (MIGA), and bilateral agencies, including export credit agencies and specialized insurance entities, such as the Overseas Private Investment Corporation (OPIC). The additional security offered by these international agencies is required when private sponsors and lenders are reluctant to take country risk.

Leveraging Human Capital through Information Technology

Given the high skill level of the Palestinian work force, there exist large profit opportunities in the knowledge-based sectors. Conversely, since Palestinians lack significant natural resources, the economy's future will be largely determined by the capacity to construct a knowledge-based economy. The pillar of such an economy is a modern telecommunications infrastructure.

Looking ahead, the development of information technology capabilities would open up a series of possibilities for the economy.

- As a Middle East financial center, it could tap into the resource of specialized Palestinian bankers, provide a safe haven for investors, integrate regional stock markets, and serve as a center for currency trading and clearing credit card obligations.
- By encouraging information processing industries, it could exploit decreasing long-distance telecommunications costs to enter new markets in off-shore information processing and software engineering (as in Barbados and India).
- As a hub for high-skill professional services, the WBGS could provide legal services, insurance, investment banking, consulting, education, specialized medical treatment, advertising, and software development.
- Information technology capabilities would give a boost to the tourism sector that requires high-tech infrastructure, including modern communications for hotels, resorts, and restaurants in historic sites.

Increasing the Competitiveness of the Tourism Sector

Tourism has played an increasingly important role in less developed countries (LDCs). In 1991, tourism accounted for 2.4 percent of LDCs GNP, 8.5 percent of their exports, and 39.8 percent of their services exports. Tourism is also becoming a major source of employment in many LDCs. In some island economies, the share of tourism in total employment is as high as 50 percent.

Constraints amidst Potential

The WBGS has great potential as a tourist destination because of its religious, historical, archeological, natural, and cultural attractions. The number of tourists to the WBGS has increased substantially in the last few years. By 1995, the annual number of visitors to the Church of Nativity in Bethlehem and archeological sites of Jericho reached one million and 300,000, respectively. Yet, the role of tourism in the WBGS economy is presently very limited. In 1995, total revenues of the tourism sector, excluding East Jerusalem, was around $26 million, compared to $155 million in East Jerusalem and $2,930 million in Israel.

The tourism sector's limited contribution is not surprising, given its stagnation in the last three decades as a consequence of political uncertainty and Israeli restrictions. Since 1967, the number of hotels has remained approximately the same in East Jerusalem and the number of licensed guides in the WBGS has dropped sharply (from 154 in 1967 to 47 in 1996). Israeli restrictions have inhibited the establishment of tourist bus companies in the WBGS, where no such companies were licensed over the three decades of occupation.

The WBGS and Israel represent a single tourism market. While this market has expanded substantially in recent years, its size is highly sensitive to political tensions. Such sensitivity was apparent with the sharp decline in tourists following the series of suicide bombings in Israel in March 1996 (Figure 5.3). The WBGS' share in total revenues of the combined market is a function of the competitiveness of its tourism sector with Israel's. All tourist sites in the WBGS are within a one-hour drive from Israel. Without border formalities, tourists can visit WBGS sites on one-day excursions and spend their nights and most of their expenditures in Israel, and many of them do just that. This is apparent in the disparity between the number of visitors to major WBGS tourist sites and the WBGS' share in total revenues of the combined market. In 1995, the Church of Nativity in Bethlehem and the historic sites of Jericho were visited by 40 percent and 10 percent of total tourists to the combined market, respectively. In the same year, the WBGS' share in total revenues of the combined market was only 1 percent.

Policies and Prospects

The tourism sector's long-term prospects will be highly influenced by the permanent political settlement. First, if final status negotiations result in a significant reduction in political tensions in the region, the flow of tourists to the combined

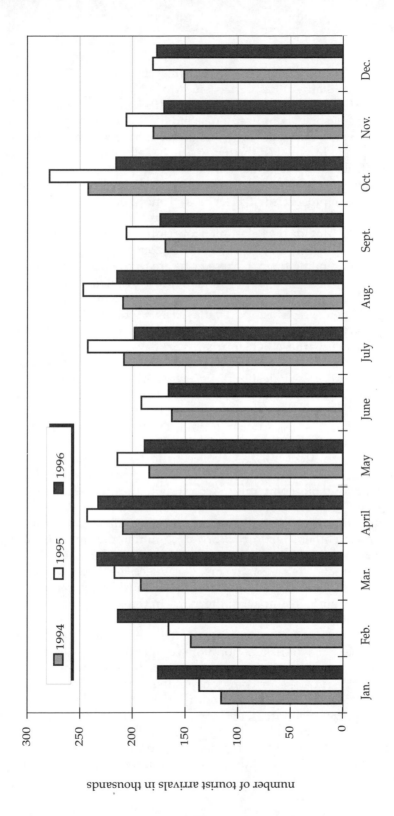

Figure 5.3 Tourist Arrivals to the Combined Market

number of tourist arrivals in thousands

81

Sources: ICBS, Tourism and Hotel Services Quarterly, several issues.

market may increase substantially. Second, final status negotiations are supposed to determine the status of East Jerusalem, which historically has been the nerve center for the Palestinian tourism sector. Since 1967, the development of Palestinian tourist establishments in East Jerusalem has been severely restricted by Israeli licensing procedures and other institutional barriers. These measures have been compounded in the last three years by Israeli restrictions on the travel of WBGS residents to East Jerusalem. If the final status negotiations end these restrictions and allow East Jerusalem to resume its leading role in Palestinian tourism, its long-term prospects will be enhanced enormously. Third, final status negotiations are supposed to determine the status of the Dead Sea areas. These areas, which can provide the Palestinian tourism sector with an important source of growth, are presently classified as part of zone C, giving Israeli authorities control over developing them. If these areas are to come under PA control, they could serve as an asset of great potential in health tourism. Fourth, a permanent political settlement could lead to a significant increase in Muslim tourism. This segment of market, which historically played an important role in the Palestinian tourist industry, has disappeared almost completely since 1967.

In the short term, the WBGS tourism market will continue to be integrated with the Israeli market. With Israeli control over WBGS borders and ongoing political uncertainties, Palestinian policy makers will have little influence over the combined market. Hence, efforts to increase the contribution of tourism to the Palestinian economy in the transition period should focus on increasing competitiveness to enable the tourism sector to capture a higher share of the combined WBGS-Israel market.

One policy area that will greatly affect short-term competitiveness is the implementation of the Palestinian-Israeli agreement regarding the mobility of tour guides and bus companies. According to these agreements, tour buses are supposed to move freely between PA-controlled areas and Israel, and tour guides who meet mutually agreed-upon standards are supposed to be honored in each other's territories. So far, common standards for tour guides have not been established, which effectively prevents PA-licensed guides from working in Israel. The free movement of buses has been enjoyed only by Israeli-licensed buses. This has given Israeli tourism operators a clear advantage over their Palestinian counterparts in the competition for tourists in the shared market.

Improvements in infrastructure are another important area in which policy actions can make the tourism sector more competitive. The current state of the infrastructure presents serious constraints to the tourism sector's development. Water supply disruptions are common, particularly in the summer, and power outages are frequent. This causes additional expenses in water truck containers and power generators, and lowers the standard of services provided by tourist establishments. Telephone lines are difficult to get. The two newest hotels in Bethlehem, for example, managed to obtain only four lines each to cover office, fax, and guest use, which is highly inadequate for the size of the hotels.

* * *

Unlike most developing countries, capital does not represent a serious constraint to economic development in the WBGS. However, large-scale investments cannot be expected before there is a significant improvement in political stability. Under a proper investment climate, accumulated savings of WBGS residents (most of which are presently invested abroad either directly or through the domestic banking system) could provide a major source of funds. Substantial investment funds can be mobilized from Diaspora Palestinians, and the WBGS could attract significant foreign investment because of its relatively well-educated labor force and ability to establish strong market links with other countries in the Middle East. However, it is difficult to imagine a sustained boom in investment supporting a long period of growth in the current circumstances of political turmoil and acute uncertainties for future conditions. Yet, unfavorable factors that depress private investment in the short term can be removed by well-crafted policies. Removing those constraints would allow for a burst of growth, stimulate jobs, and prepare the ground for a period of sustained growth—which can start once, and if, the peace process advances.

Favorable conditions depend heavily on regulatory and institutional changes, such as defining and monitoring norms in the construction business and improving zoning practices to lower construction costs; establishing better land titling and a functioning legal system to allow for mortgage lending and financial sector development; and setting up a housing insurance fund to cushion against unmanageable political risk.

Bibliographical Note: The section on housing draws from Abdulhadi (1992), Mayo (1995), World Bank (1996c), and Foreign Investment Advisory Service (1995). The section on infrastructure draws from Mody (1996). The section on tourism draws from Khano and Sayre (1997).

Chapter 6

International Economic Relations: Access, Trade Regime, and Development Strategy

Ishac Diwan

Introduction

In recent years, trade fell dramatically as a result of repeated closures and high transaction costs at the border. Merchandise exports were nearly cut in half, from 11 to 6 percent of GDP between 1992 and 1995. Imports also fell, from 46 to 38 percent of GDP over the same period (Figure 6.1).

Figure 6.1 Merchadise Exports and Imports in the WBGS (1990-95)

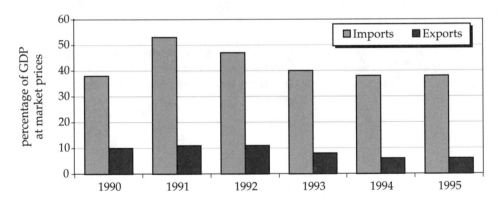

Sources: ICBS and World Bank.

The recent cut-off with Israel due to repeated border closures leaves the Palestinian economy in a difficult predicament. Starting with the occupation in 1967, a one-sided customs union (CU) has resulted in a preponderance of trade with Israel at the expense of other partners. The resulting imbalance in trade is proving to be extremely costly in the face of the repeated border closures. It also creates a difficult policy dilemma since any sudden redirection of trade away from Israel will be extremely costly in the short term.

This chapter discusses the choices facing Palestinian society as it tries to establish the required infrastructure and the preferred policy regime to facilitate and regulate its international trade. Admittedly, both the infrastructure for trade (ports, airports, bridges, roads) and the trade regime (customs union, free-trade area, non-discriminatory regime) can be only partially improved within the bounds of the existing agreements with Israel. An important inquiry of this chapter is whether a change in the economic agreement itself should be pursued when final status negotiations start.

From 1967 to the 1994 Economic Agreement

In 1967 the WBGS had no relations with Israel. After occupation, the Palestinian economy was cutoff from its traditional trading partners and a completely different set of economic relations was created with access to the much larger economy of Israel. This brought huge increases in the movement of both labor and goods. Over time, up to one-third of the WBGS labor force came to be employed in Israel, and another large share found employment in the Gulf and elsewhere during the oil boom. In the same period, trade with Israel expanded significantly.

There are four particularly striking aspects of the pattern of trade: (i) the large size of the trade deficit (35 percent of GDP in 1993); (ii) its concentration in industrial products (70 percent of exports in 1987—the last date at which good trade statistics were collected) (Figure 6.2); (iii) the orientation of trade toward Israel, amounting to 90 percent of imports and more than 70 percent of exports in 1987; and (iv) the sharp decline in labor and exports beginning in 1987 with the *Intifada*.

Figure 6.2 Exports by Category of Goods

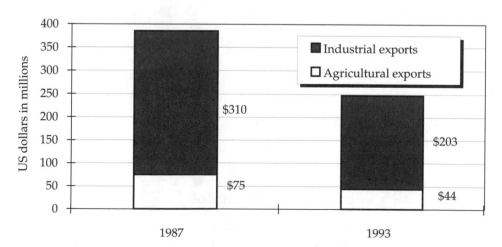

Source: El-Jafari (1995).

These trade patterns—export of labor rather than goods, export of industrial rather than agricultural goods, and trade relations dominated by the relation with Israel—were due to the economic incentives that prevailed under occupation. Palestinians have been free to sell skilled labor to the Gulf and unskilled labor and manufactured goods to Israel (but expansion of manufactures was restricted). Palestinians have faced difficulties in other trade sectors, due to the repression of domestic production, restrictions on agricultural exports to Israel, and weak trading networks to the rest of the world. In addition, the Arab boycott, by preventing the export of Palestinian goods with Israeli content, effectively eliminated all Palestinian manufactured exports to neighboring countries. There were no restrictions on imports of Israeli goods to the WBGS, but for imports from the rest of the world, the economy operated under the highly protectionist Israeli trade regime. In the absence of these restrictions, the patterns of trade would have looked very different. Various modeling exercises have shown regional trade and trade with Asia would have been much larger, and trade with Israel much smaller, in the absence of the CU. By some estimates, imports from Israel may have been lower by as much as half.

By the mid-1980s, when the growth in labor movement started to taper off, manufactured exports started to rise, reaching a high point in the late 1980s (at about $400 million per year or 20 percent of GDP). Initially, these exports represented mainly subcontracting-type business with low value added in labor-intensive industries such as shoes, garments, or plastics. After a dip related to the beginning of the *Intifada*, the early 1990s saw an expansion in exports, particularly to Israel, which was facilitated by Israel's attempt to revitalize the Palestinian economy and offer inducements to new investors. For example, shoe production based in Hebron supplied as much as half the Israeli shoe market by the early 1990s.

The Economic Protocol signed in 1994 both regularized the existing trade relation and improved some of its aspects.

- There is no customs border between the WBGS and Israel and, subject to Israeli quality standards, trade between the WBGS and Israel is mostly free. The only theoretical exceptions are five agricultural goods with quotas until 1998 (but effectively hard to enforce given the non-existence of a customs border).
- Trade relations with third countries—tariffs, standards, and quotas—are largely determined by Israeli policies, albeit with some limited exemptions (see below).
- Custom revenues and VAT—but not other levies—raised on goods coming from third countries are partially returned to the Palestinians. The VAT operates on a destination basis; the VAT on imports from Israel is remitted by the Israeli treasury to the PA.

Characteristics of the Economic Protocol

Instead of the expansion expected under the Economic Protocol, trade flows have collapsed in recent years. This was mainly due to repeated closures, but also to flaws in the agreement, some of which—but not all—can be corrected within the existing framework. There are four main weaknesses: disposition of tariff revenues, the need for more policy independence toward WBGS trade with third parties, problems of access to the Israeli market, and difficulties in access to third countries.

Tax Leakage

In the current system, VAT is treated on a destination basis. The Palestinian treasury receives VAT on goods consumed in the WBGS (and produced in Israel or in another country). A clearance system that operates on a transaction basis has been set up to collect these revenues and transfer them to the PA. In 1996, VAT and other tax clearances were the largest single source of PA revenue, amounting to 65 percent of total tax revenues, or 14 percent of GDP.

However, the Economic Protocol does not foresee the return of purchase taxes paid to Israel. The treatment of customs and purchase taxes paid at the border on goods imported from third countries that end up in the WBGS is also problematic (see Chapter 8). Those revenues are remitted to the PA only when the shipment identifies a firm in the WBGS as the final destination. This means that revenues on imports that are resold to WBGS firms via Israeli wholesalers, or directly to Palestinian consumers, or that are imbedded as inputs in Israeli products, are not remitted to the PA and leak instead to Israel. The extent of these leakages is unknown, but could be as large as 5 percent of GDP.

To collect some of the lost revenue, the PA has begun to oblige Palestinian distributors to buy directly from abroad (through a system of control of distributors) some of the goods with high tariffs or with high purchase tax. This is good for revenue collection; perhaps as much as $100 million, or 15 percent of 1996 revenues, could be raised on cigarettes, alcohol, and electrical products alone. However, this system runs a risk of being captured by distribution monopolies if import permits are not distributed in a competitive fashion.

More drastic solutions might require a customs border between Israel and the WBGS, but a solution that still falls within the general framework of the existing agreement is exemplified by the revenue-sharing agreement under the Southern African Customs Union (SACU), which comprises South Africa, Lesotho, Swaziland, and Namibia. In the SACU, trade policy is determined by South Africa, all border taxes are collected in a common revenue pool, members other than South Africa receive 1.4 times their share in total consumption within the union, and South Africa receives the residual. The agreement is easy to apply because it is based on a macro formula, and it compensates the smaller members for accepting a trade policy designed for the benefit of South Africa.

Policy Independence

On the positive side, the trade agreement mandates a relatively open trade regime. In the past few years, Israel has liberalized much of its manufactured trade regime. There is free trade in manufactured products with both the US and Europe (the destination of 85 percent of Israeli exports). Tariffs on imports from other countries average 8 percent for intermediate goods, and 12 percent for final products. All quotas have been removed, including for agriculture (in accordance with the Uruguay Round). Protection remains highest in agriculture, textiles, garments, furniture, and shoes. There is also high tariff escalation resulting in high rates of effective protection on consumer goods. The use of high excise or purchase tax on imports (revenues from taxes are about five times more than from custom duties) and quality standards (especially on food items) remain important instruments of non-tariff barriers. Services have not yet been liberalized as much.

To a large extent, the Palestinian trade regime has already been anchored by the FTAs signed with the EU and US in 1996. However, in the short to medium term, the rules for trading with Israel and the rest of the world remain crucial. From the Palestinian point of view, the Israeli trade regime has several disadvantages compared to an ideal regime chosen independently by the WBGS. Imports are not allowed from countries that do not have trading relations with Israel, including Arab countries. Quality standards in the current regime are perceived to be above what would be desirable given Palestinian income levels. For example, in the midst of border closures, which led to meat shortages in the Gaza Strip, meat could not be imported from Egypt because of quality standards restrictions.

The current situation allows, at best, for limited trade policy independence with respect to trade with third parties. While there are common tariffs in trade with third countries, the Economic Protocol allows for some exceptions. For a few goods whose market can be easily monitored (such as registering cars or dyeing gasoline with a different color), the PA can set tariff rates independently and import quantities that are not restricted (provided these goods are not marketed in Israel). For a longer list of goods (such as food, gasoline, cement, construction materials, cars, and some investment goods), tariffs can be set independently only on some pre-specified quantities ("Palestinian estimated needs").

The Palestinians have already begun to exercise this latter option. Ten bilateral trade agreements have been signed to date. In a recent agreement with Jordan, the tariff rate was set to zero on most of the allowed list. There have also been other attempts at reducing the constraints imposed by the agreement. Some goods were added to the list, and some quantities were increased. New regulations for Arabic packaging are used to prevent tax leakages to Israel and create a more transparent border.

Trade with Israel and Border Closures

Closures hinder Palestinian exports to Israel, not imports from Israel. Thus, closure policy effectively eliminates the potential gains that the Palestinian economy could derive from the existing free trade agreement with Israel. Even if the Palestinians had free access to the rest of the world and could redirect trade to other markets during closures, a preferential trade agreement under these conditions would end up one-sided and not be in their favor. This is because an FTA or CU is a discriminatory trade relation between two economies with each side giving the other preferences over other competitors. Whether such an exchange is in the interest of the WBGS depends on how the value of the preferences given by the WBGS to Israel compare to the preferences Israel gives to the WBGS.

Under ideal border conditions, free trade with Israel offers important advantages for the Palestinian economy. An attractive feature of the agreement is that the Israeli tariff structure is particularly protectionist in the sectors where the Palestinians have a strong export potential—namely, agriculture and labor-intensive manufacturing (such as shoes, garments, furniture). The large potential value of these preferences explains why the Economic Protocol was expected to generate rapid job creation (agriculture in the short term, and labor-intensive industry in the longer term).

But while these trade preferences are important on paper, their value has turned out to be almost negligible under repeated closures since agricultural exports are highly perishable, and industrial subcontracting requires a high degree of predictability. Under the current arrangement, expectations of future closures affect production negatively. For example, agriculture is shifting back from high value crops to less valuable, less perishable, and less risky ones (see Box 4.2 in Chapter 4). Gazan firms specializing in subcontracting have cut business in half over 1995.

Simultaneously, the preferences accorded by the Palestinians to Israel involve real costs. The alternative to the CU, such as a system with non-discriminatory tariffs for all imports, would allow Palestinian importers to purchase goods from third parties at prices cheaper than Israel's and raise extra custom revenues. The value of these preferences is not negligible given the size of the trade deficit with Israel (a larger deficit means larger preferences) and the relatively high level of tariffs applied to the goods (mainly consumption goods) that Israel exports to the WBGS. The WBGS represents the third largest market for Israeli exports after the EU and US, amounting to 10-15 percent of Israel's exports.

Closures and the Necessity of Open Access to Third Countries

While trade with Israel has suffered under closures, there has been little substitution from other sources. Even though imports from Jordan and Egypt jumped significantly (from $20 to $80 million between 1993 and 1996), this was insufficient to compensate for the lost trade with Israel. The lack of trade infrastructure inhibits large quantities of goods from entering either directly (no ports or airport), or through Egypt and Jordan (where crossing points have old infrastructure and limited capacity). Also, exporting to and through these countries remains restrictive, partly because the Palestinians are not in a position to reciprocate.

The possibility that closures will remain a fact of life and the need to enhance competition among service providers make it necessary to consider diversifying trading routes. This means that besides direct routes (Gaza port and airport), increased capacity for going through Egypt and Jordan is needed, and investments in border administration and infrastructure must also be secured. Investment in security infrastructure is also needed. Such policies do not run against the interest of Israel. If the WBGS has free and good access to the rest of the world, Israel cannot afford to use closures as a security measure.

Free Access: Moving People and Goods

The movement of goods and people is central to the well being of the Palestinian economy. Whatever trade regime ultimately emerges in the future, new transportation linkages are required to the rest of the world, as well as within the Gaza Strip, within the West Bank, and between the Gaza Strip and West Bank (see Chapter 13).

At present, all movement in and out of the WBGS to the rest of the world must take place through ports of entry and exit located in Israel, Jordan, and Egypt (Table 6.1). The most developed of these ports—and the passage for over 90 percent of Palestinian trade—are in Israel. As part of the Oslo II Agreement, "equal treatment" was to be accorded to Palestinian exporters and importers at these points of entry and exit. In practice, besides the port fees, goods from or to the WBGS are typically subject to stringent security checks, and thus long delays.

Table 6.1 International Ports of Entry and Exit

Border Country	Name of Port or Border Crossing	Conveyance	Port Fee
Israel	Ben Gurion	Air	2.5 percent of CIF value
	Ashdod	Sea	2.5 percent of CIF value
	Haifa	Sea	2.5 percent of CIF value
Jordan	Karameh (Allenby) Bridge	Land	None
	Damiah Bridge	Land	None
	Sweimah Bridge	Land	None
Egypt	Rafah Crossing	Land	None

Sources: The Small Business Support Project (1996) and the PA (1995).

Of the crossover points to Jordan, only two of the bridges, the Karameh (King Hussein or Allenby) Bridge and the Damiah (Prince Mohammed) Bridge, are presently functioning, but in a limited fashion. The bridges are in disrepair and security checks restrict the number of trucks (presently 35 per day) that can be handled at these ports. The land crossing to Egypt at Rafah is limited also by the lack of access roads and supporting infrastructure.

Expanded options for trade and the movement of people are clearly required. Rehabilitation and enhancement of the crossover points to Jordan and Egypt are immediate lower-cost options. Physical rehabilitation of the Jordan-West Bank bridges can be accomplished for about $60 million. However, further development of access and infrastructure that permit speedy customs checks—freeways to the bridges, warehousing facilities, customs check points—will require at least an equal expenditure. Two additional bridges may be needed if trade grows.

Direct access from Palestinian areas of control will provide increased options, and hence greater comfort to traders, tourists, and internationally mobile workers. Two projects under active consideration are a port and an airport in the Gaza Strip. There has been some concern that the port and airport require large initial investments and may not be economically justified for a small economy such as the WBGS. Most small economies typically do have their own port and airport because they have no other choice. It has been argued that it would be better for

---

Box 6.1 The Gaza Port and Airport

The Gaza port is to be located five kilometers (km) south of the Gaza City border. According to the PA, the plan is to provide international access to traders all over the WBGS and industrial estates in the immediate vicinity and, possibly, establish a free trade zone for the assembly of light manufactured goods.

In the first phase, a 600-meter berth in deep water plus a petroleum products berth are planned. At the end of the first phase, the port would be able to receive small container vessels with a maximum size of 15,000 deadweight tonnage (DWT). Port equipment is expected to be elementary, including mobile cranes. A multipurpose container terminal with the ability to handle much larger vessels would be constructed in the second phase. Upon completion of the third phase, with an expanded breakwater and a new multipurpose terminal, the port would be able to handle larger vessels (50,000 to 70,000 DWT) and function as a major transshipment facility.

Costs for the first phase are expected to be about $60 million for the port and $40 million for supporting land development, equipment, and rail facilities for cargo movement. Various European donors have indicated an interest in financing this phase. Operations are likely to be undertaken through a management contract.

In contrast to the Gaza port, construction of the physical infrastructure for a new airport at the southeastern edge of the Gaza Strip is largely completed. The airport includes terminal buildings and a runway capable of accommodating Boeing 747-400 long-haul jets. Funding for this work, which cost about $20 million, was made available mainly by Egyptian commercial banks. However, operation of the airport continues to be delayed pending approval by the Israeli authorities, who have cited security concerns. Such concerns have also been cited in delaying the clearance to import essential equipment for airport operations and three aircraft provided by donor countries as part of their assistance programs.

Source: Mody (1996).

the WBGS to use the highly developed facilities in Israel. That argument loses force in view of the serious uncertainties associated with using Israeli facilities even under normal conditions and especially during closure periods. Direct international access from the Gaza Strip, consequently, has an important "option value." In addition, if a free economic zone is to be created, direct access to a port is essential. To Israel, the benefits accrue in the form of reduced expenditures on security checks of goods and people moving through Ben Gurion, Ashdod, and Haifa.

To be useful, the Gaza port and airport must provide effective facilities, especially for traders. This implies the ability to handle large ships and bulk cargo speedily and without damaging the goods. According to present plans, port capacity is to be built in phases and airport construction is largely completed (Box 6.1). Though initially donor-financed, private financing can be expected for the second and third phases of Gaza port.

Trade Regime and Development Strategy

To assess the existing trade agreements and propose improvements, it is necessary to form views about the broader development and strategic options facing the Palestinian economy. At the outset, the major goal of WBGS trade policy is to attract investment into the economy. This requires, first and foremost, trading rules that are credible and stable. If this is not possible, establishing a clear policy path is needed so that investors can form expectations with high chances of being realized. Beyond this, trade policy will have to open up new growth opportunities based on comparative advantage. With limited natural resources, the focus will have to be on manufactured products. Advantages include a relatively sophisticated and hard-working labor force; a strategic geographical position; a relatively open economy with an industrial base that has shown resilience and can sustain foreign competition (foreign competition is mainly in agriculture); and a revenue base that does not rely on customs duties.

Given these advantages and starting conditions, there are three main (non-exclusive) types of industries that are likely to grow. These also correspond to successively more sophisticated and skill-intensive stages of development.

- *Strategy A: Labor-intensive growth.* Low- and medium-skilled exports to the West, starting with Israel and expanding to the rest of the world, especially the EU and US.
- *Strategy B: Gateway to the West.* Transforming raw and semi-finished, unskilled labor-intensive, regional products into more valuable exports.
- *Strategy C: Gateway to the East.* Transforming Western technologies and adapting technologically intensive goods to better fit the specific needs of neighboring Arab countries.

Strategy A would build on the existing base of $400 million in potential exports to Israel in recent years, in the absence of closures. This requires continued openness to Israel, and increased openness to richer markets in the OECD). Strategy A would militate for continuing a free trade relation with Israel (at least until Israel becomes more open multilaterally), and will be helped by the recent signing of FTAs with the EU and US. Under the current regime, it is possible to envision a quick expansion of manufactured exports to the EU and US, if the trade infrastructure was to improve.

Strategy B is more difficult in terms of prerequisites. It requires large improvements in trade infrastructure, but it also has higher payoffs. Its premise is that neighboring countries need time before they can afford to open up. If the WBGS could trade freely with these countries, its economy would be able to exploit its free access to the OECD, adding value to labor-intensive regional manufactured goods for the benefit of the region as a whole. The West Bank could ally itself with Jordan, and the Gaza Strip with Egypt. Free trade with these regional partners would be necessary, and therefore, this strategy cannot be followed within the existing agreement with Israel. Gains would also be possible if the four neighboring countries integrated more closely in trade, as long as the WBGS remains less regulated and, therefore, more attractive as a location that can access all these markets.

Strategy C provides a challenging vision for the medium term and is the most demanding in terms of human resource development and modern infrastructure. Similar to strategy B, it requires open trade relations with both the West and the region, but integration with these markets needs to be deeper, extend to services, and provide protection of intellectual property rights. Such a strategy would take advantage of raising skills and cultural advantages, and could encompass sectors ranging from telecommunications to the information industry and finance.

One important question is whether there is a trade-off between links with Israel and the OECD, and links with the region. From an economic perspective, the two approaches are complementary as the ability to develop links with the rest of the region is made more valuable through deeper links with Israel and the OECD.

Which Trade Regime with Israel?

The choice of an optimal trade relation with Israel is complicated by the uncertain political outlook. On the one hand, in a peaceful environment, there are likely to be large gains to a CU with Israel; but such an agreement becomes one-sided and ineffectual with repeated closures. On the other hand, moving to an independent and non-discriminatory trade regime would improve the situation if the border was nonporous; however, it would have negative effects compared to free trade under workable border arrangements. In the context of this dilemma, is an FTA with Israel that falls short of an agreement on third-country relations (such as a CU) a good intermediate solution?

There are several positive aspects to an FTA. Trading relations with Israel would remain open, but would potentially avoid protectionist aspects of Israel's trade regime (especially in trade with the region) that are ill-suited to the high value-added strategies discussed above Establishing a customs border would help avoid tax leakage and allow for more realistic quality standards. Taxes that now leak to Israel could be collected at the (new) custom border Revenue would rise even if the tariff rates to third countries are set at zero because an FTA would allow for recapturing much larger purchase and excise taxes. Simulations suggest that under an FTA with Israel and zero tariffs to third countries, Palestinian revenues could rise significantly. Finally, a strategy of free trade with third parties would improve the bargaining position of Palestinian trade negotiators, perhaps resulting in more efficient operations at the border.

Several problems must be dealt with for the FTA solution to become attractive.

- A potential costly problem concerns the low value added in the Palestinian economy. Under an FTA, free trade only applies to goods that have a minimum share of domestic content (such as 40 percent). Trade preferences given to Israel, in which the share of domestic value added in goods is large, could be much more valuable than those accorded to the WBGS if only a few such goods exist. This may not seem problematic for several traditional exports (such as stones, agriculture, and shoes) where the share of domestic value added is large. In textiles, however, some form of derogation would be needed.
- An FTA has the same weakness as the current system with respect to border closures. To reduce this problem entails reducing the preferences accorded to Israel. This can be done without losing preferential access to the Israeli market by reducing the tariffs that apply to third parties. If tariffs are set to zero, free trade with Israel would not entail any costly preferences. Indeed, there would be no preferential relation anymore.
- An FTA would remove tariffs on third parties, which would then come under the influence of lobby groups, with potentially very high costs to consumers. One solution is to use some commitment mechanism to bind these rates. The World Trade Organization (WTO) provides such mechanisms through potential trade agreements with other parties (in particular, the US, EU, and other Arab countries) or by establishing free trade zones.
- Finally, moving to an FTA would involve renegotiating the economic agreement. The issues of Jerusalem, settlements, and the geographical separation of the West Bank from the Gaza Strip complicate such an agreement. However, these issues do not make it impossible to achieve an independent trade regime with low tax leakages, especially for the Gaza Strip.

There are further difficulties in moving to the third alternative—a non-discriminatory trade regime that would treat all trade partners similarly, including Israel. Certainly, giving up a preferential trade agreement with Israel and preferential treatment for Palestinian exports would be extremely costly in the short to medium term. It would expose Palestinian exports to Israel (80 percent of total WBGS exports) and to the relatively large tariffs that Israel imposes on third countries. Yet, while the current system is likely to be advantageous when borders are open, it is very costly with frequent closures. In 1996, total exports to Israel were estimated at $200 million. By some estimates, the figure could have been $600 million in the absence of closures.

Such a choice will be partially dictated by expectations about the frequency of future closures. Repeated closures render the current trading relation with Israel inadequate. Unless new ways are found to isolate security issues from the passage of goods and people between the WBGS and Israel, a more independent trade regime could be preferable from a Palestinian economic point of view. Choosing improvement within the current agreement (the only short-term choice) would be boosted by increased Israeli cooperation on issues such as improved revenue-sharing systems, more fluid borders, increased trade independence with neighboring countries (in terms of longer lists of allowable goods and larger quantities), and larger labor flows. The alternative of renegotiating the agreement would be more attractive if the current situation does not improve.

One daring possibility worth investigating seriously is a free trade zone in the Gaza Strip (and in the West Bank as soon as the border situation allows it). This would involve renegotiations with Israel, but for positive and forward-looking economic reasons, rather than defensive purposes. Turning the Gaza Strip into a free trade zone would send a strong signal that Gaza is open for business. It would send the message loud and clear that there is no room for rent-seeking activity, monopoly behavior, or special treatment, because the government is out of the business of trade. Together with its large and relatively skilled labor force, such an initiative would make the Gaza Strip very attractive as an export platform to the US and EU (and because nearly no custom revenue is presently collected on manufactured imports, there would be little effect on fiscal revenues).

* * *

In the past three decades, the Palestinian economy exported mainly people to the expanding labor markets of Israel, GCC countries, and other parts of the world. This regional labor demand has tapered off, probably permanently. In the future, the WBGS economy will not be able to grow in a sustainable fashion unless it manages to increase substantially its export of goods and services.

In this context, the choice of a trade regime becomes more important. The outcome of recently signed FTAs with the EU and US will be determined in the years to come. For these agreements to be useful, however, rapid improvement in the physical trade infrastructure is necessary. The existing trade relations with Israel also require improvements that allow for a mix of greater tax collection, lower consumer prices, and greater policy independence.

One important choice is whether the optimal mix is better achieved by marginal changes within the existing agreement, or by renegotiating the economic agreement and setting up a customs border. As a matter of principle, the WBGS probably stands to gain most, and to acquire greater security, not through seeking economic "independence" in an autarkic sense, but through playing a role in interdependent networks in the region—linking both to Israel and the Arab world.

Bibliographical Note: The analysis in this chapter is based on the background papers of Panagariya and Diwan (1997), Kanafani (1996), Arnon (1996), and El-Jafari (1995). Fiscal leakage estimates are from Jawhary (1995). The chapter also draws on Halevi and Kleinman (1994) and Mody (1996).

Chapter 7

Financial Intermediation

Osama Hamed

Introduction

The Palestinian financial system has expanded substantially in the last three years. The expansion was particularly large in the banking sector, where deposits increased sevenfold. Some expansion has also taken place in the equity market. In contrast, loans rose at a much slower pace, and lending NGOs, which accounted for most lending in the WBGS before 1994, saw a decline in their relative weight in the financial system.

The banking system expansion was remarkable. By end-1996, the number of bank branches in the WBGS reached 71, compared to 13 at end-1993. This translates into 35,699 persons per branch, which is average by Middle East standards, but still a small share of the full potential in the WBGS (Figure 7.1). The jump has affected nearly all households. At end-June 1996, 14.7 percent of people over 18-years old had deposit bank accounts (20.3 percent in the West Bank and 6.4 percent in Gaza Strip). Urban residents held the most, followed by those in rural areas, and lastly, those in refugee camps.

The banking system has been much more effective in the last three years in attracting deposits than in channeling these deposits to local borrowers. At end-1996, the loan-deposit ratio was only 0.24. The ratio has remained low because the demand for loans is constrained by political and economic uncertainties and institutional limitations. Under any circumstances, lending could not have been expected to keep up with the rapid growth in deposits. It is unrealistic to expect the loan-deposit ratio to reach the 0.6 to 0.8 levels observed in other countries in the region before successful conclusion of final status negotiations and decreased political uncertainty. But a significant increase in lending can be achieved even in the present political environment if certain policy actions are taken to improve the institutional framework.

This chapter covers the main issues confronting the Palestinian financial sector. These issues include appropriate policy to take advantage of expanding bank deposits to increase bank lending; increasing the maturity of lending in order to foster long-term investment; and the role of the nascent stock market in encouraging a broader sharing of risks.

Figure 7.1 Persons per Branch in the Middle East

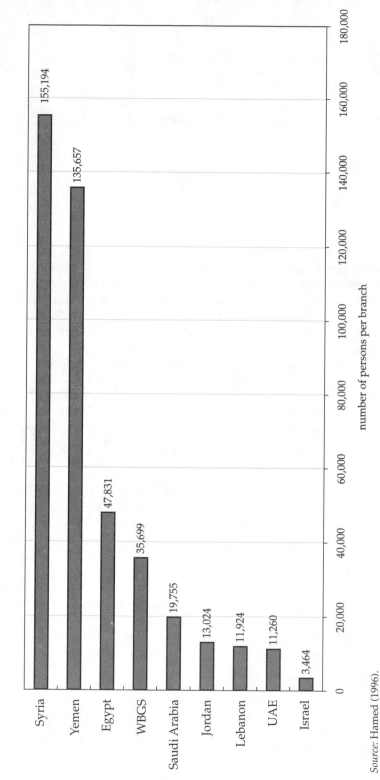

Syria — 155,194
Yemen — 135,657
Egypt — 47,831
WBGS — 35,699
Saudi Arabia — 19,755
Jordan — 13,024
Lebanon — 11,924
UAE — 11,260
Israel — 3,464

number of persons per branch

Source: Hamed (1996).

Issues In Banking

Regulation and Supervision

Considering the number of branches per capita and the number of adults with bank accounts, the banking system still has room to expand. Bank expansion, however, should be gradual so as to give the PMA, presently in charge of bank regulation in the WBGS, the chance to develop its regulatory regime and build sufficient supervisory capacity.

Adequate regulation and supervision are instrumental for achieving stability and confidence in the banking system. Bank regulators usually institute failure-prevention measures, such as asset restrictions, capital adequacy, and reserve requirements. Knowing that preventive measures cannot eliminate bank failures completely, regulators also set up failure-containment mechanisms, such as deposit insurance and discount lending to prevent limited failures from destabilizing the banking system. To ensure compliance with bank regulations, regulators conduct frequent site examinations and require commercial banks to provide them with regular financial reports.

Without deposit insurance in the WBGS and with limited discount loans, it is difficult for regulators to contain individual bank failures. Hence, bank regulation should focus on failure prevention. This requires imposing strict capital adequacy rules, relatively high liquidity ratios, and restrictions on foreign-currency

---

Box 7.1 Islamic Banking

The operations of Islamic financial institutions can be divided into two major categories: *Murabaha* and *Mudaraba*. *Murabaha* is basically a cost-plus-resale contract in which the Islamic financial institution buys the goods that the borrower wishes to acquire and sells them to the same person at an agreed-upon higher price. This can be easily accommodated under the regulatory approach advocated in this book. The most common *Murabaha*-based operations are in consumer and international trade finance. In *Mudaraba* operations, the provider of capital agrees to finance a project to be carried out by an entrepreneur on a profit-sharing basis at predetermined ratios. This involves a high degree of risk and should not be conducted by Islamic banks, if they are to be allowed to accept deposits from the public. This type of operation should be conducted instead by Islamic investment companies that cater to customers who are willing to accept a high degree of risk. Islamic banks operating in the WBGS should limit their operations to *Murabaha*, and Islamic institutions involved in *Mudaraba* should not be allowed to collect deposits from the public.

Source: Hamed (1996).

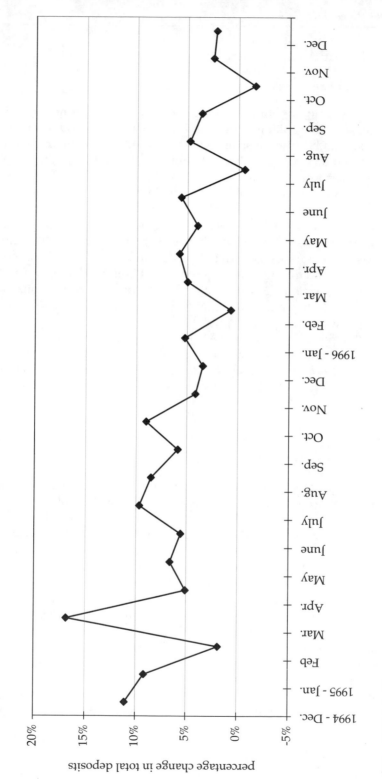

Figure 7.2 Percentage Change in Total Deposits from Previous Month

Source: MAS data files.

100

exposures, as well as restrictions on acquiring risky assets such as real estate and stocks. To be effective, these regulations should apply equally to all financial institutions that accept deposits from the public, including Islamic banks (Box 7.1).

The lack of deposit insurance and the high level of political risk constrain the growth of the local deposit base (Figure 7.2). Growth in bank deposits has been very high since 1993. By end-1996, total deposits in the WBGS banking system were $1,711 million, compared to $219 million at end-1993 (see Chapter 2, Figure 2.4). The deposit to GDP ratio at end-1996 was 0.535, much lower than other countries in the region, such as Jordan (0.825), Kuwait (0.771), Israel (0.734), and Egypt (0.728). If this ratio is to become equal to Jordan's, total WBGS bank deposits can potentially reach $2,640 million. However, this is not expected to happen before successful conclusion of final status negotiations since political uncertainties encourage many WBGS residents to maintain bank accounts abroad.

The Role of Foreign Branches

The banking system's phenomenal growth was made possible by the importation of banks and regulation from abroad. As a result, foreign branches dominate the system. At end-1996, only 4 of the 17 banks and only 20 of the 71 branches were locally chartered. The dominance of foreign banks is particularly strong in the West Bank, accounting for 42 of the 49 branches in operation at end-1996.

Establishing foreign branches was key in the development of WBGS banking. In expanding their operations, foreign banks were able to rely on their head offices for technical and managerial support and to train new employees. Without foreign branches, it would not have been possible for banking services to expand as fast as they did in the last three years. The expansion took place at a time when bank supervisory capacity in the WBGS was extremely limited. In such an environment, home offices abroad closely supervised their branches. This provided the banking system with badly needed help in maintaining safety and stability.

However, the dominance of foreign banks places a number of restrictions on the development of the WBGS banking system.

- Decision makers for the foreign branch are usually located at the bank's head office, which makes it less likely for them to receive direct and timely information about political and economic changes affecting the local market. The foreign branch usually keeps a significant share of its assets as deposits with the head office and tends to depend on the head office as a source of liquidity, thus inhibiting the development of a domestic interbank market.
- Because foreign branches have access to borrowers outside the WBGS, they may delay their investment in the risk assessment system necessary to extend credit in the WBGS, making it less likely for them to lend there. The primacy of access to foreign borrowers has a negative impact on lending in the WBGS that may continue even after the foreign branch sets up a risk assessment system, because of what is referred to in economic literature as credit rationing. Under credit rationing, when credit conditions are tight, lenders tend to give

preference to their established long-term customers at the expense of new customers who lack track records with the lender.

• Foreign banks present serious challenges to bank regulators. Regulating foreign branches is not an easy task even under the best circumstances due to transfer pricing problems and the ability of a foreign branch to avoid regulations by swapping assets with operations abroad. Such regulation in the WBGS is particularly difficult because of the absence of a national currency.

While foreign branches will undoubtedly continue to serve an important function, their dominant role cannot be maintained indefinitely. Eventually, the PMA should require foreign banks to convert their WBGS operations into subsidiaries. To avoid disruption, the conversion should be done gradually. Meanwhile, the PMA should reduce dependence on foreign branches by encouraging locally chartered banks. Such encouragement, however, should not in any way compromise the safety and stability of the banking system. The PMA should work closely with the home regulatory authorities of foreign branches, particularly the Central Bank of Jordan, to develop a common strategy for supervising foreign branches.

Size and Maturity of Loans

Domestic lending by banks operating in WBGS is very limited and the majority of credit extended is in the form of overdraft facilities. At end-1996, total credit (outstanding loans and overdrafts) accounted for merely 19 percent of total assets and 23.9 percent of total deposits. At the same time, the share of overdraft facilities of total credit was 64.4 percent (Figure 7.3).

Figure 7.3 Asset Composition of WBGS Banking System (December 1996)

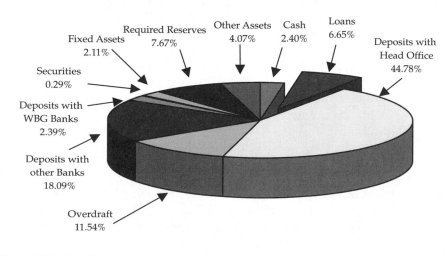

Source: MAS data files.

Low lending ratios are caused by both demand and supply factors. On the demand side, political and economic uncertainties inhibit investment and, hence, demand for credit. On the supply side, domestic lending is hampered by the limited availability of collateral. Lending ratios cannot be expected to reach the levels of neighboring countries before conclusion of final status negotiations. In any case, lending cannot possibly be expected to keep up with the rapid growth in deposits.

There is substantial pressure on the PMA to implement policies that increase bank lending. In the present environment, increased lending should be carefully implemented to avoid endangering deposits. The PMA should be more conservative in its approach than is usually the case, given its inability to act as a lender of last resort in case of a banking crisis. In particular, quantitative restrictions in the form of minimum lending ratios should be avoided as they force banks to provide bad loans, endangering bank deposits. Collateral enhancement is the most effective policy to increase lending in the current environment. It is worth carefully exploring a market-oriented policy that uses changes in the reserve requirement on deposits lent in the WBGS to change the share of deposits lent internally.

A substantial increase in average loan maturity is possible only if a parallel increase in deposit maturity takes place (which is not expected without a significant decrease in political uncertainty). Otherwise, average loan maturity can only be increased if a mechanism for hedging against unexpected change in interest rates is created, given the need to guard against possible sudden withdrawals caused by political instability. Normally, hedging is done by using futures and options market instruments or interest rate swaps. None of these hedging instruments is presently available on WBGS markets and the situation is unlikely to change soon. Meanwhile, commercial banks can be encouraged to provide some long-term credit by setting up a mortgage insurance program and a secondary mortgage facility.

Collateral Enhancement

Present economic uncertainties limit the appeal of cash-flow lending to firms. In this environment, increasing the availability of collateral and enhancing its value to lenders is essential for expanding credit. The most effective way to increase the availability of collateral is to establish clear property rights to land—the main asset for many Palestinians. Presently, only 30 percent of the land in the West Bank and 90 percent in the Gaza Strip is properly registered. The registration process for the remaining land has been frozen by the Israeli authorities since 1967. The signing of the Oslo II Agreement put the PA in a position to resume land registration in the Gaza Strip and in zone A of the West Bank. Therefore, the PA should resume land registration in these areas without delay. In zones B and C of the West Bank, the resumption of land registration is contingent on the Israelis, and all efforts should be made to obtain their cooperation.

The PA can increase the availability of collateral by registering tractors, agricultural tools, industrial machinery, and other movables. Registered tractors are attractive to banks as collateral because of their marketability. Tractor registration can use the existing automobile registration system. Registering industrial machinery is more problematic because of its limited marketability and the need for a special registration system.

Apart from increasing the availability of collateral, the PA needs to introduce legal reforms that make it easier for lenders to engage in leasing or foreclose in the case of non-payment. The PA should negotiate with neighboring countries, especially Israel, about the priority of claims on properties sought by debtors in more than one country. This is particularly relevant to automobiles, which move easily across borders, and thus are subject to confiscation. The PA needs to control the export of industrial machinery to protect against moving registered collateral outside the country. Finally, a law for securities and leasing would be useful.

Dual Reserve Requirement

Normally, the ability of banks to acquire foreign assets is constrained by the need to avoid foreign-exchange risk, since the bulk of their liabilities are usually denominated in local currency. This constraint does not apply to banks operating in the WBGS due to the absence of a national currency. In addition, foreign banks have access to the borrower base of their head offices abroad. This reduces the pressure to set up the risk assessment system needed to enlarge their WBGS borrower base. Given this lack of incentive, is there a way to encourage banks to increase domestic lending?

One policy suggestion is for the PMA to reward domestic lending, or impose a cost on placing funds outside the WBGS, by reducing the reserve requirement on deposits lent locally or used in acquiring other local assets. This could be done either through a straightforward reduction in the required reserve ratio on deposits lent locally, or an equivalent subsidy financed by PMA income from investing required reserves. (A straightforward reduction in the reserve ratio below the ratio in Israel is not possible for the NIS under the Economic Protocol.) Another view is that a modest subsidy to domestic lending would not encourage reduction of reserve requirements. Subsidies may actually result in higher bank profits rather than lower borrowing costs; may create incentives for banks to classify operations in such a way as to benefit from the subsidy without increasing their domestic lending; and may increase risks to the deposit base, thereby encouraging depositors to deplete or close their accounts (disintermediation). The validity of these arguments requires serious empirical analysis. But careful consideration of the potential outcomes should be exercised before dual reserve requirement policies are implemented.

Mortgage Lending Instruments

Mortgage lending by commercial banks is presently negligible. If such lending is to be seriously considered by banks in the present economic environment, mechanisms for reducing credit and liquidity risks must be instituted. Credit risk could be reduced by the newly created mortgage insurance program (MIP). Liquidity risk could be alleviated by setting up a secondary mortgage facility (SMF).

The MIP should provide insurance covering default loss on residential mortgage loans extended by commercial banks. To maintain an incentive for proper underwriting and risk management by the lenders, the coverage provided by the MIP should be partial. To be viable, the MIP will require an ongoing subsidy to cover catastrophic risks, such as prolonged closures, in addition to start-up costs. These premiums cannot be expected to cover more than the program's operating expenses and "normal" risk.

Initially, the SMF should allow banks to purchase long-term loans by using mortgage loan portfolios as collateral. To minimize the SMF's credit risk and ensure a net injection of funds into the housing sector, these loans should be over-collateralized. Over time, the SMF may be able to stimulate mortgage lending by serving as a source of liquidity through loan purchasing. An initial source of funds for the SMF could come from donors, probably as loans to the PA. The SMF, however, should eventually be able to raise its own funds by issuing bonds and obtaining bank loans.

Financing Micro-entrepreneurs

Despite their recent decline, lending NGOs still have an important role to play in the WBGS financial system. Unlike other NGOs, such as those involved in health and education, lending NGOs serve a function that has not been assumed by the PA. Lending NGOs extend loans to small enterprises that lack collateral and credit history, and therefore are not of interest to commercial banks.

If small enterprises are to become sustainable, they need to become less dependent on subsidies. To do so, lending NGOs may have to eliminate most of their interest subsidies (as some have done already) and find ways to minimize default risk without relying solely on collateral. One option is use of the group risk-sharing method, which was pioneered by the Grameen Bank in Bangladesh and recently implemented by UNRWA and Save the Children. The Grameen Bank, which targets rural women farmers lacking access to credit, demonstrated extremely high rates of punctual repayment. The bank organizes borrowers into small groups and requires each group member to bear collective responsibility for default by any of its members. By doing so, most of the default risk is shifted from the lender to the borrower. This motivates borrowers to use local information (unavailable to the lender) to exclude bad risk and peer pressure among members to ensure payment. The UNRWA's Solidarity Group Lending program, offering working-capital loans to women micro-enterprise owners, consistently has achieved 100 percent repayment rates since its inception in 1994.

The Emerging Financial Market

While there is still no bond market in the WBGS, a stock market opened in 1997. The role of equity in the Palestinian financial system had been limited in the past to over-the-counter trade in a handful of public companies, most of which are family-controlled. Equity could play a substantially larger role in the WBGS' high-risk environment. One of the most promising areas of growth for the equity market is infrastructure. However, a substantial investment by private companies in infrastructure in the present political environment requires guarantees by donors or international organizations (see Chapter 5).

There are presently around 50 joint stock companies in the WBGS (accounting for less than 1 percent of establishments). The stocks of these companies are not listed on any stock exchange, which reduces their liquidity and hence their appeal to investors. Consequently, these stocks do not change hands frequently and, when they do, the sale is often arranged by the company itself.

More than half of existing stock companies were established in the last three years. Demand for equity from 1994 through mid-1996 was strong and many of the stock issues that floated in those two years were oversubscribed. In contrast, companies that attempted to raise funds on the equity market in the second half of 1996 faced a weaker market (Table 7.1). Even a company like Paltel, whose stock was heavily oversubscribed when it was first issued in 1995, experienced some difficulty in collecting the second installment on the stock price.

The newly established stock exchange can play an important role in stimulating demand for equity. Centralized trading provided by the exchange for listed companies will increase the liquidity of their stocks and hence their appeal to investors. The required publication of standardized annual and semiannual balance sheets for list companies will increase the ability of potential stockholders to evaluate the risk of investing in these companies. The shares of a listed company will be traded in the first six months at the previous year's average sale price. Thereafter, the stock price will be determined by supply and demand, subject to a daily limit on variability (which provides accurate value of stock at any point in time). This increases the value of stocks as collateral as well as their appeal to investors. Stock prices will be available electronically, which makes the information easily available to Diaspora Palestinians, who represent a major potential source of funds for the equity market.

The WBGS stock market will increase the access of small investors to stock ownership in a region where less than 0.5 percent of people over 18-years old own stocks. Increased access, however, will carry some risk. The lack of experience in financial portfolio management (due to the effective absence of financial institutions in the last three decades) may result in excessive risk-taking by some small investors. This could result in massive selling during price declines. Selling, in turn, it could affect public confidence in the stock market and financial system, and finally result in depositors depleting or closing their accounts (disintermediation). Therefore, some temporary restrictions on the access of small investors to the stock market might be necessary.

Other Financial Institutions

Pension funds and insurance companies do not play important roles in the financial system and are not expected to increase significantly in the near future. The

Table 7.1 Demand and Supply for Stocks in the WBGS (1993-96)

Company Name	Issue Date	Total Supply (JD)	Total Demand (JD)	Total Subscription Ratio (4/3) (%)
Palestinian Investment & Development Co.	Sept. 93 - Oct. 93	6,000,000	7,500,000	125
Arab Investors	June 94 - July 94	12,000,000	9,452,328	79
Palestinian Cement Co.	June 94 - Sept. 94	6,000,000	3,300,000	55
Beit el-Mal el-Falastini	Sept. 94 - Nov. 94	10,000,000	11,400,000	114
Eastern Co. for Chemicals	Nov. 94 - Dec. 94	750,000	900,000	120
Palestine Industrial Investment Co.	Dec. 94 - Jan. 95	3,750,000	3,750,000	100
Palestinian Telecommunications Co.	Oct. 95 - Oct. 95	18,750,000	36,943,354	197
Palestine Islamic Bank	Apr. 96 - May 96	1,965,100	1,961,000	100
Jerusalem Building & Investment Co.	May 96 - June 96	3,600,000	3,253,320	90
Palestine International Bank	June 96 - Sept. 96	14,000,000	9,743,127	70
Arab Hotel Establishment Co.	July 96 - Jan. 97	10,000,000	2,500,000	25

Source: MAS data files.

insurance business is dominated by auto insurance, which is a cash-flow business that does not generate long-term investable funds. In comparison, life insurance, which provides a major source of long-term funds in many countries, hardly exists. Pension funds do not presently represent a major source of investment funds. While central government employees are entitled to pensions when they retire, these pensions are financed by the annual budget on a pay-as-you-go basis. In comparison, UNRWA employees are covered by a provident fund that pays them a lump sum at the end of service. However, the fund's portfolio does not include any investment in the WBGS. In the private sector, very few firms have employee pension funds, and existing pension funds are invested mostly in bank accounts.

In the absence of sufficient retirement benefits from the workplace, children and other family members represent the main source of financial support for the present generation of WBGS retirees. Family support, however, may not be as viable for the next generation of retirees because of changing family structures and decreased job opportunities in the Gulf (where a significant share of family financial support had originated in past decades). In this environment, serious consideration should be given to setting up a national social security system. Apart from providing a stable source of retirement benefits, a social security system can provide a major source of long-term investable funds for the economy, provided that it is kept financially independent from the central government. This should probably be the case given fiscal conditions of the PA.

Large holding companies have emerged recently as an attempt by major investors to deal with the difficult conditions. Several large funds were established in 1993, mainly by Palestinian businessman from the Diaspora, such as the Akkad Group and PADICO (Box 7.2). These funds share various characteristics. They have managed to provide a broad base of risk-sharing capital for the investments undertaken. The funds typically reserve 25 percent of the fund for commission; another 25 percent is sold over-the-counter to the public (and traded in the recently opened stock market), and the remaining 50 percent of the fund is received from banks in the form of medium-term loans. This structure provides enough risk capital to ride a rocky investment climate, manages to attract many investors to cooperate on large and long-term investment plans, and at the same time provides large shareholders with incentives to monitor the project carefully. The funds reduce risk by diversifying across various sectors of the economy. This provides an important avenue of investment to shareholders that are still unable to use the emerging stock market to diversify their holdings (especially in infrastructure, construction, tourism, and on a much smaller scale, manufacturing).

* * *

The development of the WBGS financial system is limited by economic and political uncertainties. A decrease in these uncertainties cannot be accomplished before a permanent political settlement is reached. However, some growth and deepening of the financial system can be achieved before then, especially in the rapidly expanding banking system and equity market. To facilitate this progress,

---

Box 7.2 PADICO

The Palestinian Development International Company (PADICO) has emerged since 1993 as the largest private sector investment company in the WBGS, with over $1 billion in planned investments by the end of the decade. PADICO was founded by some of the most prominent Diaspora Palestinian business-men and two of the main Palestinian banks, the Arab Bank and the Cairo Amman Bank (holding 10 percent and 5 percent of shares, respectively). PADICO's mission is "the furtherance and development of the Palestinian citizen on the Palestinian soil as a national objective and sacred task." The company has 200,000 shares with an aggregate value of $200 million, offered in a public subscription in June 1994. PADICO was set up as a holding com-pany, in which its investors own 49 percent of the various subsidiary operat-ing companies while local investors hold the remaining 51 percent. This struc-ture was chosen in order to allow local entrepreneurs and businessmen in the WBGS to participate to the fullest extent possible.

The primary aim of PADICO is to invest—directly, or through subsidiary companies, joint ventures, mergers or affiliations with other companies—in diverse projects that will help rebuild the economic infrastructure of the WBGS, while providing reasonable financial returns to company sharehold-ers. PADICO currently invests in tourism, real estate and housing, industry and manufacturing, finance, power generation, and telecommunications.

Source: Zuaiter and Abdou (1996).

---

policies are needed to boost financial markets and encourage more financial in-termediation, despite high levels of political risk permeating the system.

Possible actions that can increase lending include building an efficient regula-tory system, taking measures to increase the availability of collateral, and insti-tuting disincentives to discourage banks from acquiring foreign assets. There is also a need for a tighter regulation of banking, a stronger court system, the devel-opment of land registration, greater availability of financial vehicles for risk-shar-ing, and the emergence of larger financial market players. The equity market can potentially have a more important financial role than the debt market under the existing risk level in the WBGS. However, despite its recent expansion, the equity market is still very small and presently shows signs of weakness. The opening of the Palestinian stock exchange in 1997 provided the equity market with an im-portant mechanism for realizing its potential.

Bibliographical Note: The section on commercial banks draws heavily from the background papers of Hamed (1996), Hamed and Khano (1995) and Hamed and Shaban (1995). For housing finance, see World Bank (1996c); for PADICO, see Zuaiter and Abdou (1996).

Chapter 8

Fiscal Management

Ali Khadr

Introduction

In 1992, a year before the Declaration of Principles, central administration of the WBGS was in the hands of the ICA. It reported collecting $328 million in revenues, spent $252 million on salaries and other recurrent items, invested $59 million on public projects (much more than in preceding years when the annual average fluctuated around $30 million), and employed 18,000 civil servants. The budget was in surplus by $17 million. In contrast, in 1996 the PA was a much larger organization. It received $684 million in revenues (more than twice the collection of the ICA), spent $779 million on salaries and other recurrent expenditures (over three times more), and invested $160 million (almost three times more). Its public employees numbered more than 75,000 by end-1996 (over four times more). A little under half were in the newly created police force, implying that the number of PA civilian employees was more than twice that of the ICA (Figure 8.1).

Two major sources of revenue not previously featured in the central budget enabled this significant expansion to occur so rapidly. First, the erstwhile tax leakage (historically an average of nearly 10 percent of GDP) now accrues to the PA in the form of tax clearances remitted by the Israeli treasury. These amounted to $420 million in 1996 (61 percent of total revenues). Second, much larger levels of donor financing have been made available; in 1996 this amounted to $293 million (the full amount of the 1996 fiscal deficit) of which $160 went to finance capital expenditure with the remainder shared between financing current expenditure ($84 million) and direct employment generation ($49 million).

This chapter reviews the circumstances under which this huge expansion took place. It examines the fiscal revenue and expenditure structures, considers how revenues can be increased, and explores how the quality of expenditures can be improved. Attention is then focused on the civil service and the sustainability of expenditures at current levels. The chapter closes with a discussion of local government finances.

From Takeover to Maturity

A key feature of fiscal outcomes has been their disproportionate subjection to external factors, though outcomes have also been shaped by PA policies. The PA's fiscal operations since inception can only be interpreted when set against

Figure 8.1 Evolution of Fiscal Revenue and Expenditure

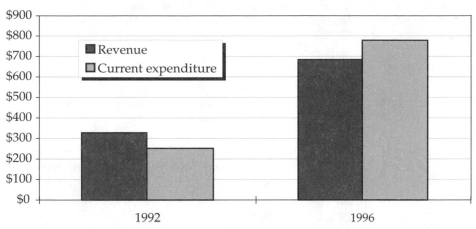

Source: Annex, Table A.5.

the evolving and often turbulent Palestinian-Israeli relations, with its phased transfer of powers and responsibilities and increasingly frequent border closures. Fiscal outcomes and prospects for medium-term public finances have been substantially influenced by the PA's discretionary actions—particularly, the massive recruitment of public service personnel and capacity-building in revenue administration and expenditure management.

Transfer of Public Sector Functions under the Agreements

The process of gradual Palestinian empowerment was set in motion by the Declaration of Principles. The stepwise increases in the PA's recurrent expenditure and revenue between mid-1994 and late 1995 are largely due to the discrete transfer of responsibility for public service provision and revenue-raising from the ICA to the PA.

The PA's initial level of monthly recurrent expenditures was around $10 million, comprising among other things the payroll of the approximately 7,000 Palestinian employees inherited from the ICA and a 9,000-strong (largely returnee) police force. Under the Economic Protocol, PA revenue collection was largely confined to the same tax and non-tax instruments previously employed by the ICA, with little leeway to vary indirect tax rates. Revenue collection proved insufficient to cover expenditures, in part owing to a sharp dip resulting from the disorderly transfer of revenue administration. Even by late 1994, domestic revenue collection in the Gaza Strip and Jericho was averaging only about $3.6 million per month.

A second milestone in the Oslo process was the PA's December 1994 assumption of jurisdiction, under the Early Empowerment Agreement, over six public service sectors in the West Bank. These include health, education, social affairs, tourism, and the administration of direct taxation and VAT (currently confined to domestically produced goods and services). The immediate budgetary impact was a jump in PA recurrent expenditures by $6 million per month, mainly to cover salaries of 17,000 employees inherited from the ICA payroll.

At the same time, monthly revenues increased by some $5.4 million. This reflects a smooth transfer of tax administration functions, though falling slightly short of Israeli negotiators' stated intent for balancing expenditure transfers with added revenue collection instruments. Additional revenue came mainly from the income tax and VAT. Property tax revenues were also transferred, although these continued to be collected by the ICA for remittance to the Palestinian treasury. With a growing monthly recurrent expenditure level and recovering revenue collection in the Gaza Strip and Jericho, total expenditures and revenues were $110 million and $63 million, respectively, for the PA in the first quarter of 1995. Under the Protocol on Further Transfer of Powers and Responsibilities, in August 1995 eight additional public sector functions (commerce and industry, insurance, gas and petroleum, postal services, labor, local government, census and statistics, and agriculture) further increased recurrent expenditures and, to a lesser extent, revenues.

The most recent component of the Oslo Accords—the September 1995 Interim Agreement, to which was annexed a slightly revised Economic Protocol—provided for the transfer to the PA of all remaining public sector functions in the West Bank (along the lines of the Gaza-Jericho blueprint), with the exception of those relating to water and sewerage. This transfer was to apply to zone A (major urban areas populated by Palestinians) and zone B (adjoining areas) by end-1995, and to zone C (rural and other areas) during the 18 months following the election of the Legislative Council in January 1996. (Israel retained functions relating to public order and security in zone B, while these were transferred to the PA in zone A.)

The Interim Agreement was implemented roughly on schedule in late 1995 and early 1996 (with the exception of Hebron, for which separate arrangements came into effect in January 1997). The jump in recurrent expenditures associated with the transfer of functions in zones A and B under the Interim Agreement was relatively modest. In part, this was because the only major function remaining to be transferred was public order and security in zone A. The PA had geared up for this by recruiting additional police force personnel in the preceding months. The administration of remaining revenue instruments and entitlement to the revenue collected was also transferred. Provisions for revenue clearances from customs duties, excise taxes, and VAT on West Bank imports went into effect. Initially, these transfers yielded an average of $3 million in additional "domestic" revenue and $4 million in revenue from clearances per month.

Outside influences notwithstanding, revenue and expenditure trends have been significantly shaped by the PA's fiscal policy stances as well as by institution-building efforts to strengthen revenue administration and expenditure management. (For an itemized breakdown of the PA's fiscal operations, see Tables A.5 and A.6 in the Annex.)

Fiscal Revenues

Capacity-building efforts (and in a few cases, slow progress therein) have helped to shape revenue administration and expenditure management trends. Despite grave problems in revenue collection during the first few months of self-government in the Gaza Strip and Jericho, it is generally acknowledged that by late 1995 revenue administration was on sound footing. Progress is reflected in consistently higher-than-projected revenue collection. Good revenue performance can be ascribed to both the domestic tax collection effort and the revenue clearance mechanism provided for under the Economic Protocol. Tax collection ratios (at a respectable 21 percent of GDP on an annualized basis in late 1996) can probably still be improved upon through more comprehensive audit and enforcement activities. In 1996, tax revenues collected in the WBGS by the PA were as high as those collected by the ICA in 1993, at about $170 million (Figure 8.2). This implies that the revenue collection effort is satisfactory. It also suggests potential for further increases through strengthened administration, since the PA has political legitimacy that its predecessor lacked. However, major revenue increases should not be expected. An exception arises in connection with trade-related taxes, as discussed below, but this is due more to the design of the system than its administration.

Figure 8.2 Composition of the Fiscal Revenue

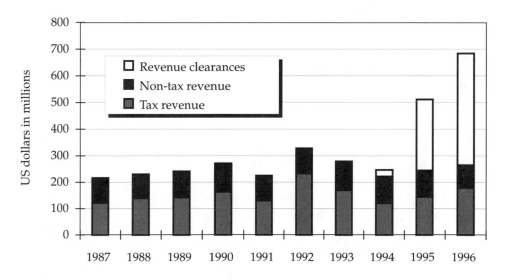

Sources: IMF/IBRD Joint Mission (1995) and World Bank (1996b).

There has been significant progress in the organization, staffing, and equipping of revenue administration departments; coordination and negotiation with the Israeli authorities on transferring taxpayer information and revenue clearances, and resolving outstanding arrears, credits, and enforcement issues; and strengthening customs administration and enforcement. Several issues remain unresolved or under implementation, such as developing formal work rules and instructions for revenue administration staff, reconnecting Gaza Strip's revenue administration facilities to the ICA's computerized former taxpayer records, and strengthening customs administration management.

Budgetary Transparency

Certain revenue sources accruing to the PA are not subject to regular Ministry of Finance (MOF) budgetary controls, prompting questions about the disposition of the funds. For example, transfers of petroleum excise revenue from Israel under the clearance mechanism and some domestically collected excise revenue have gone through channels not directly controlled by the MOF. Similarly, profits from quasi-private monopolies that distribute several key commodities in the Gaza Strip (such as petroleum products and cement) accrue at least in part to the PA. However, no such receipts are recorded in the budgetary accounts, and their disposition is not publicly disclosed. In response to concerns expressed by several donors at the December 1996 Ad Hoc Liaison Committee meeting, the PA undertook to consolidate all revenue accounts under MOF control by March 1997, to audit dividend income accruing to the PA from "commercial" operations, and to discontinue the PA's participation in such operations by end-1998.

Impact of Border Closures

While it is clear that closures adversely affect fiscal revenue, it is difficult to precisely estimate the impact (see Chapter 4). Direct revenue losses include (i) income tax on lost earnings in Israel (roughly $30 per worker per day multiplied by the marginal effective income tax rate of about 7 percent); and (ii) losses of customs, excise, and/or VAT on closure-restricted flows of goods and services imported into the WBGS. Indirect (or second-round) losses include tax and possibly non-tax revenue losses stemming from the general decline in economic activity. The decline is triggered by the loss of factor income earned in Israel, the loss of export revenue, and disruptions in domestic production (resulting from interruptions in intermediate import supplies). Revenue losses, particularly indirect, are almost certainly characterized by a complex lag structure, and also depend on seasonal and other factors.

The long and severe closure beginning in late February 1996 exemplified the significant effect that prolonged closures have on fiscal revenue. Revenue in the second quarter of 1996 was about 7 percent below first-quarter revenue. The bulk of the reduction was in clearance transfers generated on factor services and merchandise trade with Israel. The largest fall occurred in health fees, income taxes, and VAT. While significant, the decline in second-quarter revenue is relatively modest compared with the fall in output and income during the closure period. This may at first appear to be due to the consumption-based nature of the bulk of taxes collected (coupled with a tendency for consumption-smoothing to occur in the face of output and income fluctuations). But on closer inspection, the mitigation of tax revenue decline can be attributed partly to the revenue administration capacity-building efforts that were implemented in early 1996. Such efforts include the introduction of tax enforcement measures, establishment of large taxpayer units, and implementation of issue-oriented auditing.

Revenue Collection and Financing Potential

Against this backdrop, total revenue stood at about one-fifth of GDP on an annualized basis as of late 1996. Projections for 1997 are at roughly the same ratio. As shown in a regional comparison in Figure 8.3, this ratio is a respectable one by developing country standards. However, it can probably be improved upon at the margin through further improvements in revenue collection efficiency. For example, while comparable in absolute size to the revenues collected under Israeli control, "domestic" revenue collection in 1996 was below the ICA's early 1990s collection ratios. Given the PA's political legitimacy, there should be scope to spread the tax net through more comprehensive tax collection enforcement. A public awareness campaign to educate taxpayers on the link between the provision of public services and revenue collection could prove beneficial. However, aside from possible improvements in revenue collection at the margin, major increases in revenue over the next few years are unlikely, barring significant changes in the design of the tax system and other revenue collection instruments, or in current application of revenue-sharing formulae.

Figure 8.3 Fiscal Revenue by Category and as Percentage of GDP

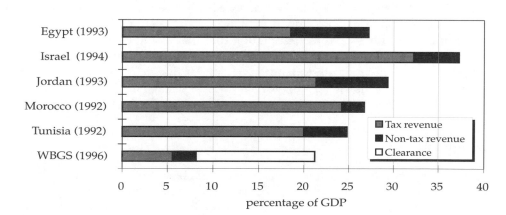

Source: Government Finance Statistics Yearbook (1995).

Any such changes would be predicated on re-negotiating parts of the Economic Protocol with Israel. If that proves politically feasible, at least two areas would merit attention. First, the present revenue-sharing formula for customs duties on imports in the prevailing quasi-customs union with Israel is based on the destination principle. It allocates to the Palestinian treasury a share of revenue calculated on the basis of recorded import flows that are explicitly designated for final use in the WBGS. Palestinian officials frequently bemoan the significant leakage which occurs in practice when administering this formula, such as the shortfall in revenue accruing to the PA compared to what ought to accrue under the destination principle. The leakage is reportedly due to the high proportion of indirect imports. These imports into Israel are sold to final users in the WBGS but are not explicitly designated as such at the initial point of entry.

The PA recently attempted to capture a larger share of customs revenue by requiring that certain goods offered for sale in the Palestinian market be imported through licensed agents to ensure that the imports are recorded as direct. Although these efforts have had some success, it is argued that the customs revenue yield could be increased by several percentage points of GDP if the present revenue-sharing formula were abandoned in favor of a presumptive formula. The latter is based on an estimated share of imports into Israel intended for final use in the WBGS. Based on a presumptive macroeconomic-level formula used in the Southern Africa Customs Union, one study estimates potential customs revenue for the Palestinian treasury. It argues that, in the 1994-96 period, annual leakage amounted conservatively to 4 to 6 percent of GDP. Advantageously, a formula that addresses the problem of underreporting imports would avoid the transaction costs arising from additional red tape associated with broadening the import licensing system.

The second area concerns seignorage revenue—the real resources appropriated by a governing authority as it increases the money (currency) base in the economy. The Interim Agreement rules out near-term issuance of a Palestinian currency. So, no independent seignorage can be generated for the Palestinian treasury. For the present, continued abstinence from issuing an independent currency may be the best policy option for Palestinian policy makers, in light of prevailing fiscal duress and the temptation that this would create to monetize deficits. However, there is no provision for allotting a share of the seignorage collected by Israel to the Palestinian treasury under the present currency union arrangement. A defensible formula for sharing seignorage on the shekel might yield between 0.2 and 5 percent of GDP annually in additional revenue to the PA.

Expenditure

Several administrative decisions have raised budgetary expenditures in recent months, but none as much as public sector employee recruitment. The creation of the Ministry of Supply and the Ministry of Higher Education in mid-1996 and the start of Legislative Council operations in early 1996 entailed start-up and additional operating costs. What long-term impact these administrative changes will have for the budget remains uncertain. For example, it is unclear whether the Ministry of Higher Education will eventually incorporate university budgets into the central budget.

Wage Expenditures

Within the rubric of recurrent expenditures, wage expenditures have grown particularly rapidly. At year end-1996, the number of public sector employees at the central level (excluding employment by municipalities and village councils, and those hired directly under donor-funded job creation programs) stood at 75,047, a 28-percent increase since the beginning of January 1996 (Figure 8.4). Of the end-1996 figure, 41,020 individuals were employed in the civil service (mainly education and health), and 34,027 were in the various branches of the Palestinian security services. At about 13.5 percent of the labor force (11 percent for the West Bank and 19 percent for Gaza Strip), the relative size of public sector employment at the central level is significant even by regional standards (Box 8.1). As of late 1996, the wage bill (on an annualized basis) was over $400 million (12 percent of GDP). The projected 1997 recurrent expenditure level at $866 million (57 percent consists of wage payments, at $495 million) assumes added recruitment of 6,700 employees (3,700 in the civil service and 3,000 in the security services) and suggests further increases in public sector employment ratios ahead.

Clearly, part of the public sector increase stems from the phased transfer of public sector functions and associated personnel previously employed by the ICA. A strong case can also be made for some new recruitment (on top of employees

Figure 8.4 Public Sector Employment (end of year)

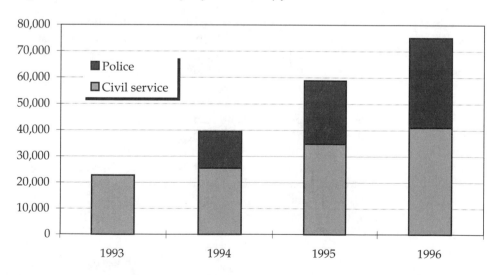

Source: World Bank (1996b).

inherited from the ICA) to (i) provide for enhanced delivery of public services that were widely perceived as sub-standard under occupation; (ii) staff senior ranks of the civil service, which under the ICA had been confined to Israelis; and (iii) fulfill functions (mainly relating to public order and security) for which no ready-made apparatus was bequeathed by the ICA. In addition, the *de facto* restrictions on mobility between the West Bank and the Gaza Strip for all but the most senior officials makes some duplication of employee functions (thus increasing staffing ratios) inevitable.

Nevertheless, there is growing concern that extra recruitment has already met the level needed to fulfill public sector functions under a market economy blueprint. Also, the incentive structure for the civil service is not geared toward ensuring optimum staff performance. Continued recruitment at the same pace as in recent past could threaten medium-term fiscal stability. It could compromise the PA's ability to provide adequate O&M allocations and thus, service provision.

Box 8.1 Rapid Expansion in Public Sector Employment

The public sector has grown rapidly in the wake of the progressive transfer of authority to the PA. Public sector growth since mid-1994 has occurred in several stages. Parts of the structure and staff were inherited from the ICA, notably in the areas of education, health, and social welfare. But former under-provision of public services necessitated a substantial increase in the civil service. In acquiring security responsibilities, the PA introduced and subsequently expanded the police force.

Public sector employment grew from 35,000 employees (including 12,000 police staff) in October 1994 to over 49,000 (including 19,000 police staff) in October 1995. Extension of the PA's authority in fall 1995 resulted in additional increases in subsequent months. By January 1996, government employment stood at 59,000, and increased to about 75,000 by end-1996. While a substantial fraction of the increased public employment is accounted for by returning cadres of the PLO, the increase has also helped provide employment opportunities.

PCBS labor force surveys provide an independent assessment of the relative size and recent evolution of public sector employment, as depicted below. Public sector employment was 13.5 percent of the total labor force in April-May 1996, a 1.9 percent increase of the labor force from seven months earlier. Public sector employment is more significant in the Gaza Strip, at 19 percent of total labor force and 30 percent of the employment. In the West Bank, it amounted to 11 percent of the total labor force and 15 percent of employment in April-May 1996.

(Box continues on next page)

Public Sector Organization

There is much potential for streamlining within the PA's organizational structures and personnel management policies. For several functions the mandate has been spread across more than one ministry or agency. These include economy-wide development strategy formulation and public investment planning; coordination and monitoring of donor assistance; environmental monitoring and regulation; overall coordination and regulation of NGO activities; and overseeing the implementation of public works projects. Although overlapping functions are currently being addressed, substantial efficiency gains and greater cost-effectiveness could be achieved through clearer distinction among the mandates of various ministries and agencies.

(Box 8.1 continues)

A substantial fraction of the increase is clearly defensible given the numerous responsibilities acquired by the PA, the undersized public sector inherited from the Israeli authorities, and restrictions on PA staff mobility between the West Bank and the Gaza Strip. However, substantial increases are difficult to sustain, given budgetary pressures. Further public sector expansion to address labor market pressures would be ineffectual in reducing unemployment and counter-productive to private sector job creation. Such expansion would be insufficient to absorb the estimated 30,000 new entrants into the labor force each year.

Size of Public Sector Increase

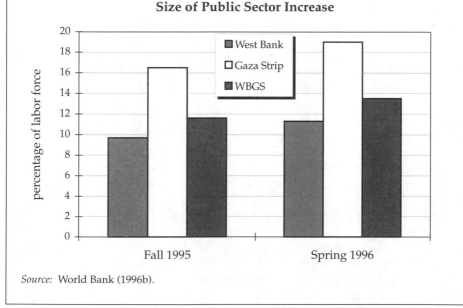

Source: World Bank (1996b).

Expenditures and Border Closures

Closures have affected public expenditure. During and after the prolonged closure that began in February 1996, the PA spent almost $25 million on employment-generation initiatives through end-1996. These were entirely financed by donor grant funds through the World Bank-administered Johan Jorgen Holst Peace Fund (Holst Fund) and were not strictly on budget. The bulk of job creation expenditures were undertaken by PECDAR. Though later consolidated with general budget expenditures in MOF reports, PECDAR expenditure is not subject to budgetary procedures under MOF oversight, as line ministries are. Nevertheless, job creation programs clearly entailed public expenditure of a relief nature. Expenditure on job creation projects by UNRWA, United Nations Development Programme (UNDP), and bilateral donors was also significant (about $24 million in 1996). However, these expenditures were not strictly on-budget and subject to regular budgetary procedures under MOF oversight. At the height of the March 1996 closure, the PA spent more than $5 million to secure supplies of staple foods and to alleviate hardship among needy households.

Public Investment

Over the period 1993-96, public investment hovered at about 5 percent of GDP, a relatively modest sum by regional standards (Figure 8.5). Of total public investment, substantially less than half, or no more than $50-60 million (1.5-2 percent of GDP) was invested in new major infrastructure projects. The remainder went toward rehabilitation, upgrading, or extension of existing infrastructure (see Chapter 13).

Expenditure Management

The capacity for monitoring budget execution, early detection and correction of slippages, auditing, and cash management remains limited. Although several measures to enhance expenditure management capacity are either planned or under implementation, in many cases they occur with outside technical assistance. The installation of a computerized Government Financial Management Information System is now underway, which will prepare monthly instead of quarterly expenditure reports of PA ministries and agencies. It brings financial comptrollers in the spending ministries and agencies under the authority of the MOF and consolidates a multiplicity of cash management channels into a single account.

The tools needed to translate policy decisions into practice include an effective budgeting process (with appropriate incentives for spending ministries and agencies to remain within budgetary ceilings); devices for monitoring budget execution and detecting overruns; an efficient cash management system for processing payments; and effective control and auditing mechanisms to foster compliance with procurement and payment processing procedures. Despite the sub-

Figure 8.5 Capital Expenditure (as share of GDP)

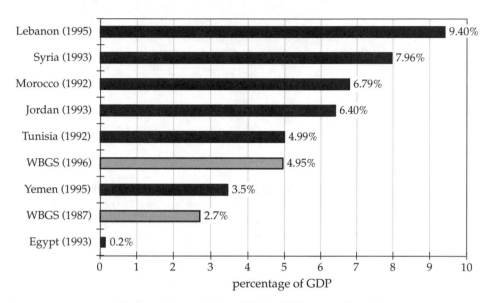

Sources: Government Finance Statistics Yearbook (1995), ICBS data, and World Bank estimates.

stantial progress in building up revenue administration, MOF expenditure management capacity has been slower to develop. Annual budgeting has until recently been viewed as a formality by spending ministries and agencies. Not until June 1996 was a formal circular issued to signal the start of the 1997 budget cycle. A 1997 public investment program was prepared in fall 1996 for presentation to the donor community (on which virtually all public investment continues to rely). But preparation of the program was not mirrored by a formal capital budgeting process by prospective implementing agencies under MOF direction. Progressive integration of public investment plans with a formal capital budgeting process is targeted for 1998 and subsequent years.

Auditing and control mechanisms are likewise being strengthened. The Auditor-General's Department, established by presidential decree in 1994, has the mandate to monitor the use of public funds to ensure adherence to proper standards of accountability. Its first formal report, dated May 23, 1997, provided an overview of the limited auditing and control work since the department's establishment. Its scope was confined mainly to Gaza Strip branches of most PA ministries and a fraction of the large number of other public institutions, municipalities, village councils, and public associations within the department's audit responsibility, also mainly in the Gaza Strip. While the report has not been publicly released, there has been substantial media reporting to the effect that more than $300 million has been subject to mismanagement or misuse. The report's limited scope of coverage was criticized and its methodology of estimating this sum has been disputed by some PA officials (who argued that much of this money represents lost opportunities for generating revenues or reducing expenditures). However, the report's findings have been taken seriously by the PA. A national independent committee was appointed to investigate the content of the Auditor-General's report. The committee submitted its internal findings to the President of the PA in July 1997. The Legislative Council carried out its own oversight of PA operations and released its critical report in August 1997. This financial control and investigative work reveals the widespread recognition within the PA of the importance of accountability in managing and disposing public funds, and strengthening mechanisms of financial control.

Deficit

The considerable recurrent budget deficits that have characterized fiscal outcomes since the PA's inception—about $65 million (2 percent of GDP) in 1994, $67 million (2 percent of GDP) in 1995, and an estimated $95 million (3 percent of GDP) in 1996—have been financed largely by grant assistance from donor countries. Domestic commercial bank overdrafts (chiefly from the Gaza-based Bank of Palestine) have also been tapped as a source of financing and liquidity. Donors funded over one-half of the 1994 recurrent deficit and approximately twice the 1995 recurrent deficit. Likewise, almost the entire $95-million recurrent budget deficit estimated for 1996 was covered by donor grant funding. Over half of the total 1994-96 recurrent cost funding was made available through the World Bank-administered Holst Fund. The balance came through a mechanism administered by UNRWA (for payments in support of the Palestinian police force), or through bilateral bank transfers (such as EU support for education sector salaries). Investment expenditure and spending on employment-generation initiatives have been funded entirely by donor assistance, largely on grant terms.

The availability of bountiful grant assistance to date has avoided—or at least deferred—any threat of a medium-term debt burden. In the face of mounting donor fatigue regarding recurrent cost funding, it is unclear how much, if any, further grant assistance will be made available for this purpose. At the same time, donor willingness to support the PA's budget appears responsive to adverse political developments. Despite growing concern with the opacity of certain off-budget operations, many donors proved willing to put their reservations aside and mobilize $35-$40 million in additional recurrent budget and employment creation support in the month following the outbreak of Palestinian-Israeli clashes in late September 1996.

Notwithstanding the difficulties associated with forming reliable point-estimates of steady-state revenue and expenditure levels, a central question concerns whether expenditures may be close to—or, indeed, may already exceed—their maximum sustainable level. As of end-1996, monthly recurrent expenditures alone stood at about $67 million (on an annualized basis, close to one-quarter of GDP) (Figure 8.6), an above-average ratio in relation to many comparable countries. For 1997, the MOF (with IMF assistance) projects a recurrent (wage and non-wage) expenditure level of $866 million, again roughly one-quarter of projected GDP. The projected revenue ($814 million) and deficit ($52 million) figures hinge on the assumptions of average Palestinian employment in Israel of 35,000 individuals and of real GDP growth of 5.5 percent during 1997. These assumptions are reasonable as a baseline and the actual outturn on employment flows in Israel has compared favorably with them (though past experience suggests that employment is subject to considerable downside risk). As of the end of May 1997, budgetary outcomes were still pointing to a small surplus, mainly because expenditures had been held in check during the first quarter of the year pending approval of the 1997 budget by the Legislative Council. However, the trend was one of emerging deficit.

Against a backdrop of modest near-term prospects for increasing revenue, demands on expenditure are likely to continue to grow. Unchecked expenditure growth would risk generating large public sector deficits and crowding out potential private investment. Once the present grant and concessional funding from donors dwindles, it may not be possible to finance sizable public sector deficits without threatening macroeconomic stability. In the absence of demonstrated capacity for macroeconomic management and in the present climate of political uncertainty, prospects for foreign commercial borrowing and domestic non-bank borrowing are likely to be limited. This forces a reliance on substantial additional borrowing from the domestic banking system and a further build-up of payments arrears.

The risk of closure-induced shocks to revenue and, to a lesser extent, expenditure appears more significant. Following the January 1997 deployment of Pales-

Figure 8.6 Evolution of the WBGS Fiscal Balance

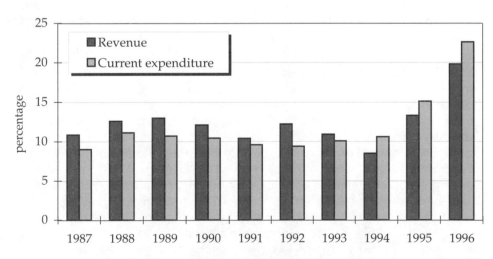

Note: Certain revenues accruing to the PA following the 1994 Economic Protocol were not counted as revenue prior to 1994.
Sources: Annex, Table A.5, and World Bank 1994-96 GDP estimates.

tinian security forces in Hebron, the only remaining transfers of public sector functions to the PA are in zones B and C of the West Bank. The recurrent expenditure increases associated with these remaining transfers will be minor. Zone C is sparsely populated, and the PA's structures—particularly its security forces—have been gearing up for some time to expand their areas of jurisdiction.

Fiscal Fragility

Expenditure and revenue directly attributable to further transfers of public sector functions are likely to be minor over the remainder of the Interim Agreement period. Concerns about the sustainability of fiscal operations arise from the fact that not all potential public expenditure needs are fully provided for in the PA's ongoing or planned spending patterns. As a result, it would be unrealistic to expect that future growth in expenditure can be kept in line with real income growth. At least three factors can be cited where costly public sector intervention may be required in the future.

- UNRWA runs parallel systems of education and health care for the refugee population both inside the Palestinian self-government areas and in neighboring countries. Integrating the operating costs of these systems into the PA's budget—which already bears the cost of public education and health care—will arise as a serious option over the medium term.
- The paucity of quality and funding sources for municipal services provided by local authorities may call for inter-governmental fiscal transfers over the medium term to support service improvement and extension.
- Not only will public investment expenditure need to be funded, at least in part, from central budgetary resources once exclusive reliance on donor funding is no longer feasible, but new public sector assets will also require additional outlays to cover their O&M costs.

The last point is worth stressing given the recent and current scale of donor support for public investment. In particular, the absence of a structured investment budgeting exercise (which is fully integrated with the recurrent budget cycle) poses a serious risk of inadequate planning and provision for the future O&M requirements. Global experience indicates that in cases where public investment expenditure is improperly integrated into the recurrent budgeting exercise (often the case when public investment programs are donor-driven), the result is a build-up of the public sector's capital stock to levels beyond what can be sustainably operated and maintained in the medium term. In the WBGS, the disconnect between recurrent and capital budgeting has probably fostered only modest capital stock bias to date, given that much public investment has been concentrated on rehabilitating and upgrading existing infrastructure. However, the need for integrated recurrent and capital budgeting is acquiring greater cogency as the focus of public investment activity shifts increasingly from rehabilitation to construction of new infrastructure.

Local Government

Traditionally, local government entities in the WBGS (which comprise 28 municipalities, 82 village councils, and 347 villages headed by a *Mukhtar*) have varied considerably in terms of service provision and revenue-raising capability. As a rule, their consolidated deficits have not been significant. Municipalities serve the urban population, which comprises roughly two-thirds of the WBGS population. Municipalities provide services such as local roads, street lighting, pest control, public libraries, fire protection, solid waste collection, and in many cases water, sewerage and electricity services. Revenue sources include property tax (collected at the central level and remitted to municipalities); fees on construction and other activities, and in many cases rental income on municipal properties; sewerage connection charges; and water and electricity tariffs. Any capital (or "development") expenditures undertaken by municipalities traditionally had to be covered by a recurrent budget surplus or by donor assistance, either directly or (since 1994 only) through a central-level intermediary such as PECDAR. Prior to the PA's assumption of central-level governing powers, but not since, capital transfers from the central level (the ICA) were funded by a surplus in recurrent budget operations at that level.

For illustrative purposes, a 1993 sample of six municipalities (Ramallah, Hebron, Jericho, Nablus, Gaza, and Khan Younis—accounting for roughly half of the urban population in WBGS) posted revenues totaling some 2.5 percent of GDP. Their recurrent expenditures amounted to some 2.1 percent of GDP, but almost three-quarters of this amount represented payments to Israeli bulk suppliers of electricity and water. Thus, what is in effect a retailing function inflates the true expenditure (and service provision) picture. Development expenditures amounted to less than one-third of one percent of GDP.

Inter-governmental Fiscal Relations

An essential building block of sound medium-term fiscal management is a framework that ensures fiscal discipline among local government entities, including clear rules for fiscal relations between the central and local government. In choosing which level of government delivers a given public good or service, key considerations include lowering enforcement costs, improving service provision, and encouraging institutional learning and demand management. The classic argument in favor of decentralized provision is that local government provision offers better accountability and responsiveness to beneficiaries. Typically, decentralized municipal government functions include local road construction and maintenance, local police, fire protection, primary and secondary education, street lighting and cleaning, water supply and sanitation, trash collection and disposal (landfills), and land use and zoning. Municipal governments commonly set broad standards to determine land use patterns in urban areas, such as green space, watercourses, public transport networks, commercial areas, and industrial and residential areas. The common trait of such services is that their benefits are largely captured by the immediate community, in contrast to such services as national defense.

Successful delivery of high-quality services by local government entities hinges on the capacity to raise resources to fund them, as well as local institutional capacity and discretion. Funding mechanisms for local government services include user fees and charges, taxes on local residents, and transfer payments from the central level of government. Unlike the tradition in the WBGS, revenue-generating utilities are typically managed by an autonomous authority to separate commercial service provision from political influences. Providers of utility services (not WBGS municipal governments) typically collect the utility charges.

The conceptualization, design, and implementation of a framework for sound inter-governmental fiscal relations and municipal finance, which was initiated shortly after the start of self-government in the WBGS, now needs to be accelerated. The first key component of the framework is to articulate local government service provision responsibilities as part of an overall blueprint of the public sector's role in the private and NGO sectors. Another component is to empower local governments to provide quality services by reviewing and codifying their revenue entitlements (possibly including transfers from the central level of government); developing local-level capacity for economic and financial management; and enhancing central supervisory capacity (Ministry of Local Government). Many elements of this framework are already well underway, including the drafting of a new Local Government Law and a pilot capacity-building initiative for certain municipalities.

* * *

The desirability of limiting public sector deficits militates strongly in favor of curbing any further growth in recurrent expenditures and identifying cost savings through expenditure rationalization where possible. First, policy makers need to articulate the range of services to be provided and paid by government. This requires defining the split of responsibilities between central and local levels, based on a detailed blueprint of the role of the state under prevailing financial constraints. Once the government's service provision responsibilities have been clearly spelled out, optimal organizational designs, staffing levels, and profiles for government structures become easier to specify. Second, civil service personnel management policy warrants careful examination. Third, a framework that ensures fiscal discipline among local government entities and between the central and local government is needed to achieve sound medium-term fiscal management. Finally and most importantly, the tools to translate policy decisions into practice are required for effective expenditure management. Such tools include an effective budgeting process, devices for monitoring budget execution and detecting over-runs, and an effective cash management system for processing payments. Despite the substantial progress in building up revenue administration, much still remains to be done in this area.

Bibliographical Note: This chapter's data is based on Palestinian MOF publications and IMF and World Bank reports (see bibliography). Information and recommendations on the revenue system are mainly drawn from Abed and Tazi (1994, 1995, 1996). On revenue, the chapter is partly based on Naqib (1996). On the prevailing revenue-sharing formula for customs, see Jawhary (1995). On potential seignorage revenue from shekel circulation, see Hamed and Shaban (1993) and Arnon (1996). On public sector employment, see World Bank (1996b).

Chapter 9

Shocks and Stabilization

Osama Hamed

Introduction

The volatility of macroeconomic indicators of the WBGS economy has been substantial, even in comparison to other small open economies. To what extent can Palestinian policy makers stabilize the economy from the impact of shocks? Given the economy's enormous exposure to external shocks, it will be difficult to counter their impact, especially if integration in regional and international labor and trade markets continues as a key characteristic of the economy. Even with full state powers over economic matters and borders, it would still be difficult for Palestinian policy makers to compensate for the fluctuations of remittances from expatriate Palestinians.

However, closure-related shocks could become less severe if the permanent political settlement provides Palestinians with control over their borders, allowing direct access of people and goods to international markets. Coping with monetary policy shocks could also substantially improve in the post-transition period if the PA could issue its own currency. With limited power over stabilization tools, the PA's potential for reducing fluctuations in the interim period is currently quite limited, but some improvement can be made in the short term.

This chapter first documents the economy's vulnerability to external shocks. It then explores built-in stabilizers to adjust for closures, such as export insurance, unemployment insurance for workers in Israel, and employment-generation schemes. The next section examines mechanisms of monetary stabilization-in the short-run without currency and in the long-run when the PA can issue its own currency. While it is unrealistic to expect policy makers to end shocks of such magnitude, the policies recommended here could mitigate the wide fluctuations that currently characterize the economic aggregates in the WBGS.

Vulnerability to Shocks

Aggregate indicators of overall economic activity exhibit substantial annual fluctuations (Figure 9.1). This trend is primarily a result of three factors: (i) the economy's exposure to substantial risk, more than most small open economies; (ii) shocks over the past three decades that have significantly influenced the shape of economic development; and (iii) the economy's lack of effective built-in stabilization instruments. While the scope of discretionary policy-making has improved with the

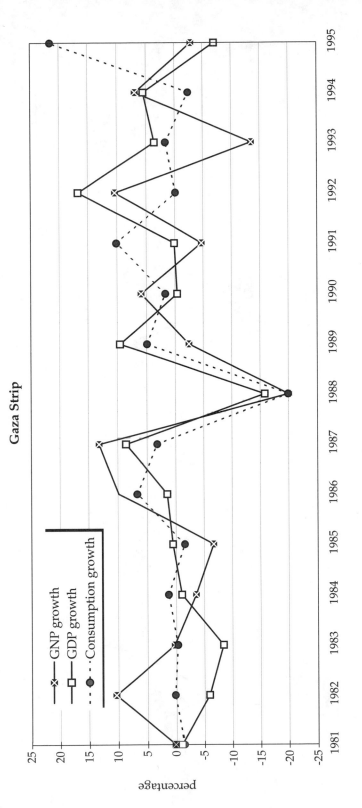

Figure 9.1 Per Capita GNP, GDP, and Consumption Growth

Gaza Strip

(figure continues on next page)

(Figure 9.1 continued)

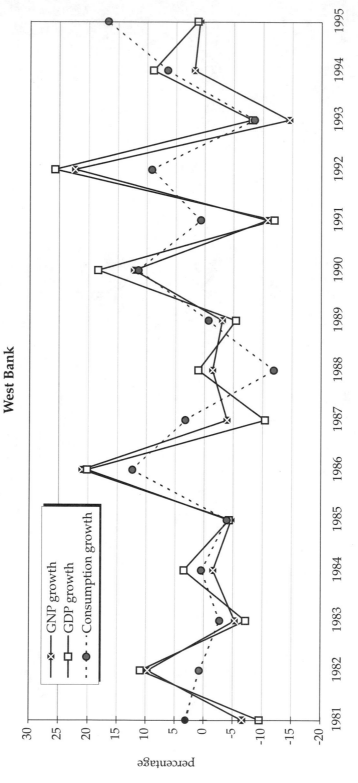

West Bank

Note: 1995 data is a World Bank estimate.
Sources: Data from ICBS and PCBS.

130

transfer of authority, the challenge of stabilization is substantial in comparison to the actual and potential instruments available to the PA.

Enormous Exposure to External Risk

Exposure to external shocks is very large relative to the Palestinian economy's size. This arises from skewed development and its asymmetric relations with Israel, which have made the WBGS economy primarily an exporter of labor and importer of consumer goods from or through Israel. The economy's excessive exposure to shocks stems from the following factors.

- The export of labor is large relative to the size of labor force. By the early 1990s about half of the potential labor force was employed either in Israel, Jordan or Gulf oil-exporting countries.
- As a result of labor export, remittances were quite large relative to total income, making the gap between GDP and GNP very large even by standards of major labor-exporting economies. The ratio of GDP to GNP ranged between 74 to 84 percent during the 1980-93 period (see Table A.1 in Annex). The GDP to GNP ratio rarely falls below 90 percent for other labor-exporting economies.
- The size of external trade is large. The ratio of imports to GDP in the WBGS ranged between 56 and 72 percent from 1980-87. Gaza Strip's reliance on imports is much higher, with its imports to GDP ratio ranging between 82 and 96 percent from 1980-87.
- The Palestinian economy does not have its own currency, and the exchange rates of the Jordanian and Israeli currencies—both used by the Palestinians— have been subject to wide fluctuations due to macroeconomic instability in the respective countries.
- The two-year cycle of the olive crop, representing a significant fraction of the West Bank's GDP, leads to substantial fluctuations in production and income.
- Palestinian policy makers do not have control over the movement of people and goods into, out of, and between the areas under PA control.
- The unresolved permanent status of the WBGS has increased the uncertainty as well as sources for potential shocks in the interim period.
- Policy-making can be a potential source of shocks until some credibility is established over the government's philosophy toward the role of markets. Will the PA support the operation of free competitive markets, as its declarations assert, or will the PA instead nurture state-owned enterprises and monopolies that deliver private goods and services?

These factors have to be taken into account above other standard shocks facing small open economies, such as terms of trade fluctuations, internal changes in tastes or behavior, or weather. The impact of numerous shocks that have affected the WBGS economy is reflected in the large fluctuations in overall economic activity, as illustrated in Figure 9.1.

Harsh Impact of Shocks

Beyond their sheer number, the nature of these shocks have had a large impact on the course of economic development. Box 9.1 catalogues the major shocks that have influenced Palestinian economic development since the mid-1970s. The most disruptive shocks were the border closures of the mid-1990s, which affected practically all aspects of economic activity (see Chapter 4). In general, various shocks can be classified by their sectoral impact as monetary, labor, or trade shocks.

Monetary shocks result from fluctuations in real money supply caused by changes in fiscal policy and conditions in Israel and Jordan. Israel's high inflation in the early 1980s and Jordan's currency depreciation during 1988-89 affected the Palestinian economy and led to substantial seigniorage losses. Though agreements signed by the PA make both Israeli and Jordanian currencies legal tender in the WBGS, the PA has absolutely no influence on the course of monetary policy in either Israel or Jordan.

Labor market shocks have resulted from fluctuations in the external demand for Palestinian labor in Israel and GCC countries. Until the early 1980s, labor demand shocks were negatively correlated, providing the Palestinian economy stability at the aggregate level. Oil price increases negatively affected the Israeli economy and positively affected the Gulf economies. However, demand for Palestinian workers has not grown in the Israeli or Gulf economies since the second half of the 1980s. The 1990s witnessed the collapse of the labor export market. Kuwait sent back many workers to Jordan and the WBGS, and Israeli demand dropped sharply and suddenly. These labor demand losses seem permanent, generating high unemployment and poverty.

The trade regime was reoriented in 1967 when the Palestinian and Israeli economies were cut off from their usual markets in the Arab world. As a result, the WBGS began to conduct an overwhelming majority of its trade with Israel. The trade regime can be somewhat reoriented under the Economic Protocol, but the major shock of the collapse of international trade remains. In addition, both external and internal trade have been disrupted substantially by border closures, causing extreme difficulty of access to goods.

Closure-related Shocks

Since 1993, closures have been imposed often, unexpectedly, and for unknown duration. This has prevented the free movement of people and goods between the WBGS and the rest of the world, as well as within the WBGS. The major macroeconomic impacts of border closure are summarized below.

- Closure damages the reputation of Palestinian firms in foreign markets, which reduces the likelihood of investment in WBGS export-oriented industries.
- Closure reduces the income and consumption of Palestinian workers in Israel and those working in export-oriented industries, which results, through the multiplier effect, in a significant decline in GDP. This, in turn, increases

---

Box 9.1 *Vulnerability and Shocks*

The WBGS economy is characterized by an unusual dependence on external sources of growth, making it very vulnerable to external shocks. The shocks of the 1970s and early 1980s often cancelled each other out, and therefore did not generate large fluctuation in the overall level of activities. Changes in recent years add up to a large and probably permanent adverse change in external sources of income. The main economic shocks are listed below.

- The mid-1970s slowdown in Israeli growth after the first oil shock led to weaker demand in the dominant market for labor and goods.
- The boom in the Gulf countries, following the oil price increases in 1974 and 1979, led to increased demand for skilled Palestinian labor and contributed to substantial revenues from Palestinian and other Arab sources overseas. This helped pick up the slack from the slowdown of Israel's economy.
- The collapse of oil prices in the early to mid-1980s contributed to stagnation in Gulf demand for Palestinian workers and started a period of stagnation in the WBGS.
- Israel's high inflation was imported into the WBGS in the early 1980s.
- The *Intifada*, starting at the end of 1987, reduced labor demand in Israel (except in construction) and labor supply from the WBGS. Economic activity slowed due to strikes, periodic border closures, and increased enforcement of claims for taxes.
- The Jordanian withdrawal of public sector salary payments after 1988 and the devaluation of the JD during 1988-90 hit many West Bank Palestinians hard, since they traditionally had used JDs for savings.
- Immigration of Jews from former Soviet countries to Israel in the 1990s increased the demand for Palestinian labor for new home construction, offsetting the reduced demand in industry and services.
- The Gulf War led to drastic short-run effects following the 40-day border closure in early 1991. Effects included permanent losses from the expulsion of Palestinians from several Gulf states, and the loss of Arab grants and reduced transfers to the cash-starved PLO.
- Expectations of a peace settlement in 1992 fueled a small boom, especially in property, generally financed by drawdowns in savings of Palestinian families with relatives returning from the Gulf. Savings repatriation may have been facilitated by relaxed ICA restrictions.
- Since 1993, increasing isolation from Israeli jobs and reduced border porosity has caused a sharp reduction in both labor incomes and domestic product. Because unskilled workers were mostly employed in Israel, the reduction in employment hit poorer households relatively hard. Since 1993, per capita incomes have dropped, in spite of a booming public sector and generous donor assistance.

investment risk in industries that cater to the domestic market and reduces PA tax revenues.

- Closure increases the variability of WBGS money supply, which is determined mostly by the balance of payments.
- Closure inhibits bank lending, forcing banks to hold excess liquidity and decrease the value of past performance of firms as a source of information for risk assessment purposes.

Lack of Effective Built-in Stabilizers

Presently, there are no effective built-in stabilizers to mitigate the impact of shocks on the local economy. While income taxes are progressive with a potential for automatic stabilization, these taxes account for a very small share of PA revenues. The non-progressive VAT functions in the tax system as an effective built-in stabilizer and accounts for much of the rest of public sector revenues. However, the significant progressive growth of the tax system is not expected in the foreseeable future due to constraints imposed by economic agreements with Israel. Unemployment insurance, which serves as a built-in stabilizer in many countries, is presently not available in the WBGS. A comprehensive unemployment insurance program should not be expected soon due to financial and institutional limitations. The current PA welfare program does not serve as a built-in stabilizer because it is targeted at the permanently poor (households lacking the capacity to work). Thus, its budget does not change with economic conditions (Figure 9.2).

Built-in Stabilizers for Border Closure Related Shocks

Some decrease in closure-related variability of output, employment, and money supply can be achieved if appropriate built-in stabilizers are put in place. These could include an export insurance program, an unemployment insurance program for WBGS workers in Israel, and employment-generation schemes. While these programs are in the right direction, their impact is expected to be minor in comparison to the overwhelming impact of closures.

An unemployment insurance program (UIP) stabilizes aggregate demand by reducing fluctuations in the purchasing power of WBGS workers in Israel. To make it self-financing, the benefits of an UIP should be limited in duration. An export insurance program (EIP) decreases investment risk and hence overall economic activity. Unlike the UIP, the EIP may have to be subsidized, especially during long closures. Targeted employment-generation schemes (EGS) channel transfers to people directly affected by long closures, such as Palestinian workers in Israel who exhaust their UIP benefits, as well as those affected by closures indirectly. To pay for the EGSs and to subsidize the EIP, a stabilization fund should be set up as part of the PA's annual budget, funded in an initial amount of about 3 to 5 percent of the total budget. Starting the stabilization fund is consistent with the policy recommendation of keeping overall expenditure under control.

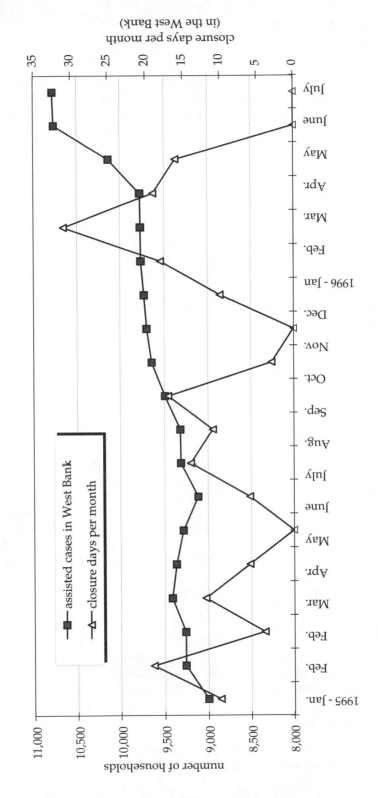

Figure 9.2 PA Social Welfare Payments are Insensitive to Closure Shock

Source: MAS data files.

Export Insurance Program for Mitigating the Impact of Trade Shocks

Export-oriented development is essential for the WBGS economy. Insuring export-ers against some losses resulting from closure would help the export-oriented sec-tor and remove one potential barrier to greater private investment. Various coun-tries establish export-import banks providing credit to ensure timely payment by foreign buyers. The MIGA insures against political risk, such as unexpected re-strictions on currency transfers, expropriation, war, and civil disturbance. WBGS exporters undoubtedly face potential loss from non-payment and civil disturbance, but the main deterrents to exports and foreign investment are constant delays and interruptions to international market access.

Shipping delays due to closure may cause exporters liquidity problems, a loss of reputation, and financial losses resulting from damages to exported goods. While a loss of reputation for exporters is hard to repair, liquidity problems and other financial troubles caused by closure can be alleviated by an EIP. The EIP would collect premiums from covered exporters, and primarily recoup financial losses caused by the failure to ship on a timely basis. Covered exporters prevented from shipping by Israeli restrictions would be paid by the EIP on the date the shipment was supposed to take place, subject to proper documentation. The payment would be treated as an interest-free loan for the duration of the delay. Should the delay result in damaging goods or loss of contract, the exporter would be compensated for the losses incurred. Setting up an EIP also can help to expand credit by enhancing the value of an exporter's balance sheet as an information source on financial performance.

Unemployment Insurance for Workers in Israel

It is not prudent to set up an UIP for all Palestinian workers at present. The PA does not have the resources to finance it, the organizational capacity to manage it, nor the infrastructure needed to compile the extensive and timely data the UIP requires. Limiting the program to unemployment resulting from closure would keep it man-ageable and avoid potential moral hazard problems. The UIP would cover all Palestinian workers who have permits to work in Israel. Eligibility should be deter-mined at the beginning of each year regardless of Israeli policy changes toward permits during the year.

Premiums collected would be the major source of funds. The program, however, should be able to draw upon funds from Israel and donors, particularly during long closures. Given the frequency of closures, the UIP is expected to have a rela-tively high premium. With the wide gap between wages earned by Palestinians working in Israel and wages in the WBGS, this may not present a problem in the labor market. Because closure risk cannot be hedged domestically, premiums col-lected from members should be invested abroad until needed during closures.

EGSs Activated During Closure Periods

The main policy instrument to mitigate the economic impact of closures has been the implementation of numerous EGSs. Most of these schemes, however, have been used primarily as anti-poverty programs. None were designed specifically as built-in stabilizers. Some EGSs perform simple tasks, which directs a relatively high share of their budgets to the poor but does not create permanent assets. Others attempt to create assets as well as help the poor, which dilutes the effectiveness of EGSs as an anti-poverty program.

Over $90 million was spent on implementing EGSs from 1993 to 1996. Table 9.1 presents a summary of some key projects, indicating their budgets, amount of money in the form of wages for unskilled workers that reached the poor, and the relative cost of delivering one dollar to the poor. The higher the cost of materials and admin-

Table 9.1 Relative Effectiveness of Employment Generation Schemes in WBGS

Area	Program	Budget ($)	Net benefit to the poor ($)	Relative Cost* ($)
West Bank	UNRWA Shelter Rehabilitation Program	$11,000,000	$3,751,582	$2.90
	World Bank Direct Hire Program	2,704,630	1,628,725	1.70
Gaza Strip	UNRWA Shelter Rehabilitation Program	7,000,000	1,070,873	6.50
	Sectoral Working Group Program	15,200,000	2,387,908	6.30
	World Bank Direct Hire Program	1,603,333	1,154,400	1.40
	UNRWA Emergency Employment Program	5,000,000	3,247,296	1.60
General	Maharashtra Employment-generation Program	–	–	1.80
	Ministry of Social Affairs Assistance Program	–	–	1.60
	Uniform Transfer	–	–	5.00

* Relative cost is the cost of getting one dollar into the hands of the poor.
Source: Al-Botmeh and Sayre (1996).

istering the project, the higher is the relative cost of delivery. The variation in cost reflects the inherent trade-off in EGSs. At one extreme, the World Bank's Direct Hire Program emphasized quick disbursement of money to unemployed poor in the wake of the spring 1996 closure without attention to the creation of assets. At the other extreme, the UNRWA's Shelter Rehabilitation Program emphasized creating better housing and, thus, ended up transferring a smaller fraction of the total budget directly to the poor in the short-run.

The record of EGSs in developing countries as permanent job creation and anti-poverty programs is not encouraging, and they should not be used for these purposes. To be effective, EGSs should serve exclusively as a built-in stabilizer instrument, having the following characteristics.

- EGSs should involve simple tasks that can be implemented directly by local municipalities or farmed out using standard contracts covering more than one period, thus shortening their time lags.
- Inputs used in EGSs should be domestically produced or easily and inexpensively stockpiled, thus making the program less vulnerable to closure.
- It should be possible to change the coverage of the EGS without causing serious disruptions in its operation.

Possible tasks that can be performed by an EGS include forestation programs, soil preservation, street sign installation, access road construction, and street cleaning. This may make it unpopular with policy makers and the public, who tend to prefer permanent asset-creating EGSs, such as road construction programs.

Monetary Stabilization in the Short-run and Long-run

This section reviews the role of monetary shocks in economic fluctuations and explores the potential for monetary stabilization with and without a Palestinian currency. The PA's right to issue its own currency was left unresolved by the Economic Protocol. Until this issue is resolved, the PA should initiate discussions with the Israeli government aimed at reclaiming the NIS seigniorage generated in the WBGS.

In the absence of a national currency, three main currencies circulate in the WBGS: the NIS, the JD and the US dollar. Of these three currencies, the NIS has established itself as the primary medium of exchange in both the West Bank and Gaza Strip. The dominant store of value in the Gaza Strip is the US dollar; the JD is the favorite store of value in the West Bank. However, the role of the JD as a store of value in the West Bank has been diminishing lately in favor of the dollar. This is apparent in the steady increase in the share of dollar-denominated deposits in West Bank total bank deposits at the expense of the JD (Figure 9.3).

In the absence of a national currency, the WBGS money supply is determined mostly by the balance of payments. Because of frequent closures, the balance of payment, and hence the money supply, cannot be expected to be very stable. Instability in money supply can result in serious disruptions to the real economy, at

Figure 9.3 Distribution of Total Bank Deposits by Currency

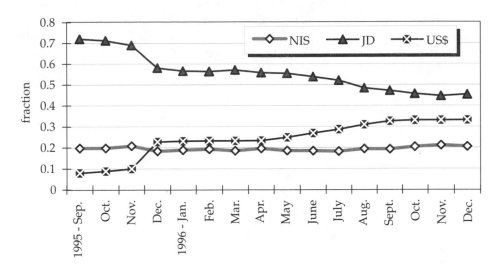

Sources: MAS data files and PMA.

least in the short term. The absence of a national currency deprives the economy of its seigniorage revenues, limits the ability of the PMA to act as a lender of last resort, and eliminates the foreign exchange rate as a policy tool in making adjustments to changes in the terms of trade. Such absence also makes the WBGS vulnerable to monetary shocks caused by unexpected change in money supply in Israel and Jordan.

Empirical estimation of changes in the WBGS money supply caused by changes in the different currency channels is not possible at this time due to lack of data, but the timelines of money supply variations are well established by economic litera-ture. This enables us to determine the impact of monetary shocks on the money supply at different stages of the adjustment process. A monetary expansion in Israel, for example, results first in an increase of WBGS money supply because of increased demand for Palestinian goods and labor services. Later on, higher prices and currency depreciation resulting from monetary expansion reduce the WBGS money supply. Because this reduction may end up canceling the earlier increase, money supply fluctuations caused by monetary policy shocks can cause serious disruptions to the real economy.

Monetary Stabilization with National Currency

If the long-run political settlement empowers the PA to issue its own currency, then it may choose to issue it or enter into a formal monetary union with a neighboring country (most likely Jordan) or countries. If it opts for its own currency, the PA can work either through a currency board that issues coins and notes (if backed by foreign exchange) or through a central bank that has some discretionary money creation power. A currency board enables the PA to reclaim parts of the seigniorage revenues that are currently lost to the countries whose currencies circulate in the WBGS. It will also reduce the vulnerability of the WBGS real money supply to unexpected changes in the money supply of these countries. A central bank with the power to create money will have the resources to serve as a lender of last resort and can use exchange rate policy to make adjustments for external shocks. These added benefits, however, come at the expense of losing the monetary and fiscal discipline built in the currency board arrangement (Box 9.2). Hence, the economy is best served if a solid record of fiscal prudence and sustainable public finances is established before any discretionary money-creation power is given to a central bank. Such practice helps to improve the acceptability of the currency and to avoid deficit-driven inflation.

Monetary Stabilization without National Currency

In the interim period, the PMA cannot effectively utilize traditional stabilization instruments. Open market operations are not presently feasible because of the absence of government securities. Changing the required reserve ratio is available as a policy instrument, but its effectiveness is extremely limited. The PMA cannot impose reserve ratios that are significantly higher than those in effect in the home countries of circulating currencies as a means to prevent deposit flight. In addition, the Economic Protocol does not allow the PMA to impose reserve ratios on NIS deposits that are lower than those imposed by the Bank of Israel on comparable deposits.

The PMA should not place any restrictions on currencies in circulation in the WBGS, either in terms of their number or exchangeability. Maintaining the multiplicity of currencies in circulation will reduce the impact of external monetary shocks on the WBGS money supply through market-driven currency substitution, as well as facilitate the future introduction of a Palestinian currency. For such introduction to take place without causing political and economic conflicts with neighboring countries, the WBGS needs to minimize its dependence on a single currency. Moreover, circulation of hard currencies, such as the US dollar, facilitates the accumulation of the foreign reserves needed to back a future Palestinian currency.

One proactive way for the PMA to offset shocks to the economy is to vary the amount of liquidity in the banking system, by moving PMA reserves in and out of the local banking system. For example, during an economic slowdown, the PMA would move some of its foreign investment reserves to the local banking system, increasing the banks' ability to lend to their customers. The domestic placement ratio, which is the fraction of PMA reserves loaned to the local banking system, would conversely be reduced if the PMA's objective is to reduce liquidity in the banking system. The full implications of this policy and its exact mechanics should be explored in greater depth. Moreover, this policy can only be implemented if the supervisory and regulatory capacity of the PMA is substantially enhanced to reduce the likelihood of a bank rescue. Thus, implementation of this policy requires careful consideration and substantial strengthening of PMA institutional capacity.

Box 9.2 Currency Boards

A currency board is a foreign exchange system under which notes and coins are issued only if backed by foreign reserves denominated in a stable currency. The currency board establishes a fixed-exchange rate between its currency and the reserve currency, and maintains unlimited convertibility between them. The reserves of the currency board usually consist mostly of high-quality interest-bearing assets. Since the currency board does not pay interest on its notes and coins, it earns a profit (seigniorage) that is equal to the difference between the interest earned on its reserves and the board's operating costs.

By design, a currency board has no money creation power. Hence, it cannot be used as a tool of inflationary government finance, making the finance of government expenditure more transparent since it has to come either from taxes or borrowing. The lack of money creation prevents the currency board from serving as a lender of last resort to the domestic banking system, or from counteracting temporary shocks to the terms of trade. The inflation and interest rates in a currency board country are determined mostly by those in the reserve currency country.

However, a government with weak fiscal conditions may be tempted to break away from the best implementation of a currency board by printing money without the full backing of foreign reserves. Given the resulting loss of credibility, governments may not carry out this measure unless other methods of financing their deficits are extremely costly. A currency board does not provide complete protection from inflationary finance. Thus, a minimal level of fiscal discipline and a good track record in budgetary management is needed for the success of a currency board.

A related concern is that foreign reserves back up high-powered money— that is, notes and currency in circulation. But bank deposits, created through the money multiplier, have no such backing. A massive withdrawal of short-term bank deposits can trigger the collapse of a currency board. The establishment of a currency board, therefore, should be preceded by building sufficient bank regulatory and supervisory capacity to ensure stability of the banking system.

Source: Wijnbergen (1996)

---

* * *

The WBGS economy is highly vulnerable to external shocks. Some of the external shocks, such as fluctuations in worker remittances, will no doubt continue into the post-transition period. The economy's vulnerability to closure can be decreased significantly if and when the Palestinians improve control over their borders, allowing them direct access to international markets. Vulnerability to monetary policy shocks can be reduced if a Palestinian currency is introduced, or by creating a balanced monetary union between the WBGS and another country or countries.

In the meantime, the PA can help minimize the economic impact of monetary policy shocks by placing no restrictions on currencies in circulation. The PMA can explore the full implications of varying the fraction of its reserves placed domestically, once its regulatory and supervisory capacity is enhanced. It can also set up a number of built-in stabilizers that minimize the impact of closures on the economy, such as EIPs, UIPs for Palestinian workers in Israel, and closure-triggered EGSs. These insurance programs will need a large compensation element for potentially long and intense periods of closure, and therefore should be heavily subsidized by external sources. Contributions by Israel would create virtuous incentives to minimizing the border closures.

Bibliographical Note: The section on EGSs draws from Al-Botmeh and Sayre (1996). The monetary stabilization section is based on Hamed (1997). The box on currency boards draws on a background paper by Wijnbergen (1996).

Chapter 10

Donor Assistance

Ali Khadr

Introduction

At the October 1993 Conference to Support Middle East Peace, the international community committed itself to jump-start the Palestinian economy and pledged $2.4 billion over the ensuing five years. Additional pledges, contributed by 38 countries and several international organizations, have raised total pledges to $3.4 billion. About three-quarters of the assistance pledged is on grant terms; the remainder consists of loans, mostly on concessional terms. With 2.5 million Palestinians, these pledges translate to $270 per person per year for 1994-98. Actual disbursements for the period 1994-96 have been lower, at $195 per person per year.

This chapter examines the impact of donor assistance on economic development in the WBGS by examining aid flows in the post-Oslo period. The analysis compares expectations and realities, reviews the reasons behind the shortfall, and offers suggestions for improving the effectiveness of donor assistance. In particular, the chapter evaluates the balance between trends in support of consumption-oriented activities versus investment underpinning longer-term development.

The Flow of Post-Oslo Donor Assistance

Numerous obstacles notwithstanding, the donors have managed to achieve satisfactory disbursement levels and successfully established institutions for channeling assistance. Unlike the experience in many developing countries, donors and the PA have made an unusual effort in coordination, giving rise to a variety of complex but functional structures and institutions, as detailed in Box 10.1. In addition, UNSCO has a mandate to coordinate UN agencies and facilitate processes on the ground. To enhance the speed and responsiveness of its operations, the World Bank devolved decision-making authority to its resident representative in the WBGS.

The donor assistance coordination mechanisms took about one year to set up. The delay can be attributed to initial weaknesses in coordinating the receipt of aid on the Palestinian side, given no ready-made apparatus was bequeathed by the ICA. Furthermore, at the time of the Declaration of Principles, donors were caught by surprise and had little time to prepare projects and their approach to aid. Therefore, urgency was balanced by donors' demand for accountability, transparency, and efficiency. Despite initial delay, by mid-1995, appropriate mechanisms to share information and, to a lesser extent, formulate development policy and prioritize investments, were in place to permit a smoother flow of assistance.

Donor assistance had an unexpected impact on institution-building in the PA. The large inflow of aid coincided with the establishment of PA ministries and public agencies. Perhaps unavoidably in a transitional phase, it led to competition between PA agencies and ministries to address donors directly. This resulted in an institutional setup with some overlap in coordination and project implementation functions. Only recently have there been visible efforts to ensure the consolidation of economy-wide policy functions, such as public investment priorities and donor assistance coordination.

The flow and composition of donor assistance has evolved somewhat differently than was originally envisaged. In 1994, donor assistance responded to po-

---

Box 10.1 Institutional Structures for Donor Coordination

Ad Hoc Liaison Committee (AHLC). The AHLC, chaired by Norway, meets two or three times a year, bringing together key donors (EU, Japan, Saudi Arabia, and US), the PA, and the Israeli government, with the World Bank as secretariat. The AHLC was established by the Multilateral Steering Group of the Multilateral Talks on Middle East Peace in October 1993 as the principal coordination mechanism on policy matters related to the WBGS development program. More recently, the AHLC has assisted in coordinating the activities of the PA, Israel, and donors with the aim to resolve Palestinian fiscal difficulties through fair burden- and revenue-sharing and, more generally, to facilitate longer-term development. These objectives and plans are outlined in the Tripartite Action Plan on Revenues, Expenditures and Donor Funding for the Palestinian Authority (TAP), initially signed in April 1995 and revised in January 1996.

Holst Fund. Administered by the World Bank, the Holst Fund has received support from 25 donors. The Holst Fund, closely associated with the AHLC, has been a primary instrument for channeling donor support to fund the PA's recurrent budget and start-up expenses. More recently, the Holst Fund has served as a key funding instrument for employment-generation initiatives to offset the loss of Palestinian jobs in Israel. Between 1994 and July 1997, it disbursed a cumulative total of $236 million.

Ministerial Meetings. Two ministerial-level pledging conferences on assistance to the Palestinians have been held—one in October 1993 in Washington, DC, chaired by the US, and one in January 1996 in Paris, chaired by France. Both meetings featured elaborate pledging sessions.

(box continues on next page)

litical and economic developments as the transitional arrangements outlined in the Declaration of Principles were gradually implemented. In January 1994, the Holst Fund was established under World Bank administration to channel donor contributions toward recurrent expenditure support in the PA's start-up phase. Throughout 1994, considerable attention was given to the budget deficit and developing an accountable process for channeling assistance. By end-1994, annual disbursements had reached $497 million, with $253 million for short-term (budget and start-up) support, $167 million for public investment, and $77 million for technical assistance.

In 1995, planned implementation of many large-scale investment projects was delayed and much of the donor support continued to cover recurrent expendi-

---

(Box 10.1 continues)

Consultative Group on the West Bank and Gaza Strip (CG). The CG, chaired by the World Bank, brought together more than 30 active donors, meeting in December 1993, October 1995, and November 1996. The CG meetings, which are technical in nature, provide participants with the opportunity to discuss policies, investment priorities, proposed projects, and potential co-financing arrangements. The CG meetings have also been used to mobilize commitments to specific priority projects. At the fall 1997 meeting, the CG reviewed implementation of the 1997 Palestinian Public Investment Program and public investment funding needs for 1998 and beyond.

Joint Liaison Committee (JLC). In November 1994, the AHLC established the JLC (comprising the PA, Israel, and major donors) to provide a forum on assistance policy and practical matters related to enhancing donor effectiveness. Since then, the JLC has developed the capacity to formulate practical strategies to respond to donor or bilateral needs, and deal with policy matters concerning immediate project implementation.

Local Aid Coordination Committee (LACC). To accelerate the development effort, the AHLC devolved greater responsibility for aid coordination to WBGS donor representatives and established the LACC. The LACC is composed of the PA and approximately 30 donors, including Israel, who are represented locally. The LACC is chaired jointly by UNSCO, the World Bank's WBGS representative, and the Norwegian representative in the WBGS who also represents the chair of the AHLC. As one of its first actions, the LACC in December 1994 agreed on establishing 12 Sector Working Groups (SWGs) to improve operational coordination and sector planning. The effectiveness of the SWGs has been restrained due to the limited number of technical experts and decision-makers who are represented locally.

ture. At the outset, the PA had not been expected to require budgetary support beyond 1994. However, initial expectations had not taken into consideration how long it would take to set up a mechanism for the timely transfer of revenue clearances from Israel to the PA. Further, to smooth the unanticipated adverse effects of closures, donor support was channeled into works programs and labor-intensive rehabilitation projects to mitigate closure-related income losses. By end-1995, disbursements for the year amounted to $442 million, with $210 million for short-term support, $144 million for public investment, and $88 million for technical assistance.

In 1996, a similar pattern of disbursements favoring consumption over investment continued under repeated closures and lack of movement on large-scale public investment projects. Subtler tensions underlying Palestinian-Israeli political relations contributed to delays in implementing investment projects, and thereby the flow of donor funding. For example, a major factor behind the delay in beginning construction of the Gaza port has been Israel's insistence on a prior agreement detailing security arrangements that govern the transit of merchandise and passengers. Despite long-standing donor commitments to fund the port, as of mid-1997 construction had not begun. Similar factors affect completion of the Gaza airport, where a runway is already functional. By end-1996, disbursement for the year amounted to $528 million, with $267 million for short-term support, $183 million for public investment, and $78 million for technical assistance.

By end-March 1997, $2,714 million (about 80 percent of the cumulative pledges) had been committed by donors to specific uses. However, cumulative disbursements, at $1,527 million, were less than half the amount of funds pledged (Box 10.2). Not surprisingly, the greatest lag between commitments and disbursements was in the public investment category, while disbursements for short-term support and technical assistance have been more in line with commitments. Figure 10.1 shows that only $519 million had been disbursed for public investment, against commitments of $1,373 million. Conversely, disbursements for short-term support stood at $746 million compared to commitments of $900 million. Disbursements for technical assistance amounted to $262 million compared to commitments of $442 million.

In accounting for genuinely unanticipated factors that have slowed or otherwise affected donor disbursements, it is a useful exercise to select two sets of targets established on behalf of the donor community at different points in time for comparison with actual outcomes. One set of targets is in the Emergency Assistance Program for the Occupied Territories (EAP), prepared by the World Bank immediately after the October 1993 donor conference and endorsed by donors at the December 1993 meeting of the CG. The EAP was prepared in response to donor requests for the World Bank to provide the analytical framework and technical underpinning to make effective use of the assistance pledged by donors. Among its other elements, the EAP embodied a three-year (1994-96) expenditure program comprised of public investment projects, support for the private sector (chiefly through long-term finance), start-up expenditure support, and technical assistance. Figure 10.2 indicates EAP targets in comparison to actual disbursements.

A more recent set of targets for the delivery of donor assistance is associated with the January 1996 Ministerial (Donor) Conference on Assistance to the Palestinians. The Tripartite Action Plan (TAP), signed by the PA, Israel, and the AHLC chair on behalf of the donors, called for (i) improved PA fiscal performance and revenue collection; (ii) commitment by Israel to cooperate with the PA in revenue clearance and "do its utmost" to enhance trade flows in and out of the WBGS; and (iii) disbursement of donor funds to cover the PA recurrent deficit until end-

---

Box 10.2 *Donor Arithmetic: Pledges, Commitments, and Disbursement*

A pledge refers to a general indication of intent by a donor to provide financial support of a given amount within a time frame that may or may not be well defined. A commitment refers to a binding undertaking to provide funding of a given amount within a well-defined time frame for a specified purpose. Clearly, the exact point at which a pledge becomes a commitment is a matter of contextual judgment, but pledges are not necessarily translated into commitments the same year. A disbursement is defined as the donor having transferred funds to the implementing agency. Actual disbursement of funds from the implementing agency can involve further delays.

To date, the largest pledges have come from the EU and European Investment Bank ($658 million), the US ($500 million), Japan ($233 million), Saudi Arabia ($200 million), the Netherlands ($153 million), Norway ($150 million), Germany ($149 million) and the World Bank ($230 million). See Tables A.13-15 in the Annex for a complete breakdown of donor assistance by pledges, commitments, and disbursements for 45 donors.

Status of Total Donor Pledges, Commitments, and Disbursements
(January 1994 to March 1997) in million US$

Donor Assistance	Total Pledges	Total Commitments	Total Disbursements
Grants	2,652	2,349	1,461
Loans and Guarantees	785	365	66
Public Investment*		1,373	519
Short-term Support		900	746
Technical Assistance		442	262
Total	3,437	2,714	1,527

* *Note:* Public investment is defined as public investment projects, private sector support, capital assets supplied in-kind, and rehabilitation of capital assets under employment-generation programs.
Sources: MOPIC and World Bank estimates.

Figure 10.1 Donor Assistance (1994-March 1997)

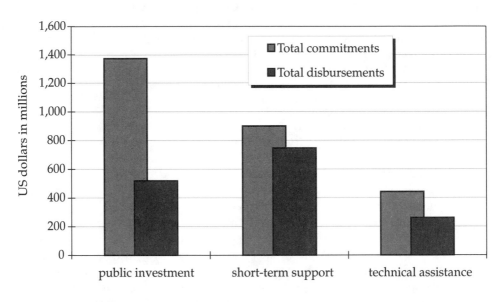

Source: MOPIC (1997).

Figure 10.2 EAP Targets vs. Actual Disbursements (Total Disbursements)

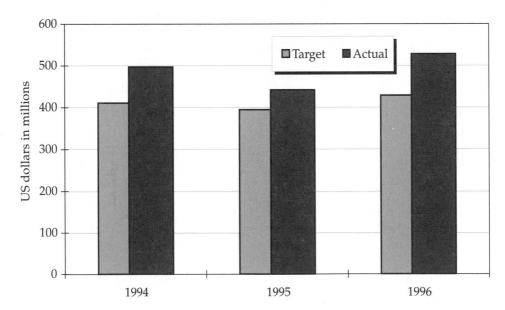

Source: MOPIC (1997).

1996, and to enable quick-disbursing job creation activities. The TAP undertook to disburse a total of $500 million during 1996 to ongoing and new activities (of which $75 million was to be directed toward recurrent budget support for the PA). Many of the new activities consisted of priority investments that formed a "core investment program," which had been deliberated and endorsed by donor representatives at the October 1995 CG meeting.

In aggregate terms, actual disbursements have easily kept pace with the EAP and TAP targets, despite more adverse circumstances than originally envisioned. With an estimated cost of closure in 1996 of $957 million (see Chapter 4), the magnitude of the shock approximately offsets revenues from tax clearances ($420 million) plus donor support ($528 million). Without donor support for employment-generation programs, closures would have had a more severe impact on unemployment and welfare than was experienced. Likewise, without donor budget contributions and IMF technical assistance, the PA would have been financially crippled. Therefore, donor assistance has not fallen short in the aggregate. However, in terms of composition, actual disbursements have been tilted more heavily in favor of short-term support than originally expected.

Have the Donors Delivered on Promises? Consumption Versus Investment

There was widespread agreement that social and economic development for Palestinians was a necessary element for further advances in the Palestinian-Israeli negotiations under the Oslo framework. In October 1993, the donors set twin goals: (i) to support continued negotiations for a comprehensive settlement throughout the transitional period; and (ii) to marshal substantial resources to meet immediate and longer-term development needs of Palestinians. It was expected that short-term assistance would have an immediate, visible impact on economic prospects and living standards, while longer-term assistance would lay the basis for sustained growth and labor absorption.

The donor effort has been criticized for falling short of fulfilling its promise, with delays in committing funds and sluggish performance in implementing projects being the rule rather than the exception. In reality, unforeseen events, including acts of violence and delays in peace process negotiations, have complicated implementation of donor assistance plans. Border closures, especially in the Gaza Strip, have severely slowed project implementation. Investment projects have been particularly difficult to implement under conditions of closure. There are delays resulting from closure-induced shortages in materials and impediments to the movement of local personnel. Closures consequences—increased unemployment, reduced production, and diminished trade flows—have directed attention toward emergency measures to the detriment of longer-term priorities.

Figure 10.3 compares the composition of disbursement with the targets set in the EAP. Investment support was below the target by almost half, while disbursements for short-term support exceeded the target by almost three times. The EAP foresaw start-up support needs of no more than $176 million in 1994 (the year the

PA was established), declining to $40 million in 1995 and $27 million in 1996, and confined in the latter years to incremental support for NGOs. Donors contributed well over $700 million for short-term support between the beginning of 1994 and end-March 1997.

Figure 10.3 EAP Targets vs. Actual Disbursements (by Catagory)

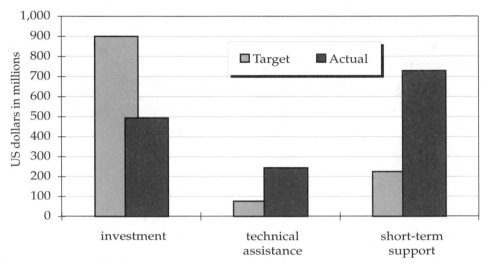

Source: MOPIC (1997).

Given the predominance of short-term support, compared with original expectations, it is not surprising to find claims that support for investment projects has been slow to arrive. However, it is not clear that higher-than-expected disbursements for short-term support was the direct or, indeed, sole cause of the lower-than-expected disbursements for investment projects. Weaknesses in institutional structures and rigidities in established procedures on both the donor and Palestinian sides have been a factor in delaying donor assistance for investment projects. For instance, investment support might have flowed faster with the earlier establishment of a local donor forum for collective examination and discussion of priority investment proposals and financing needs with Palestinian counterparts. If it had been more effective, such a forum could have played a role in pooling funding intentions for larger-scale, longer-term investment. It is likely that assistance would have flowed faster if a single Palestinian ministry or agency had been unambiguously designated from the outset to draw up and periodically update donor-funded investment priorities. Other functions to enhance coordination, such as matching priorities with donors' funding plans and monitoring donor contributions flows, are now done by the Ministry of Planning and International Cooperation. Even if more efficient Palestinian and donor coordination structures had been in place early on, the relative inexperience of implementing agencies, particularly in areas such as procurement and accountability requirements, was bound to entail some delay in funding flows.

The main reasons behind low disbursements for investment lie elsewhere. To a large extent, the overrun in short-term support needs relative to original targets has been the result of factors outside the control of Palestinian policy makers. Budgetary shortfalls have occurred mainly due to the loss of revenue and greater expenditure needs as a result of closures. Donors have tried to direct disbursements at consumption in order to smooth shocks to the economy. At the same time, the move toward consumption-oriented support has been accentuated by certain Palestinian policy decisions, notably concerning the rapid expansion of public sector employment (see Chapter 8).

Donors have tried to cushion the impact of negative shocks by shifting assistance to emergency efforts, such as job creation and public sector recurrent cost. Among other issues, the AHLC has focused on a succession of funding crises, dealing with two kinds of emergencies: funding shortages for Palestinian public sector salaries (both civilian and police), and financing employment-generation programs. Two events can be singled out to illustrate this point: (i) in June 1994, the AHLC redirected a considerable amount of already-committed funds to meet the urgent but temporary requirements for PA start-up and recurrent costs; and (ii) in November 1994, the AHLC decided to accord equal priority to maintaining living conditions as to fiscal problems, turning job-creation activities into a permanent feature of donor assistance.

The investment program has also had to face a host of difficulties. Investment projects have become more difficult to implement on the ground due to closure-related delays and hindrances. Long-term investment projects are almost always tied to ongoing or future negotiations, and hence are subject to controversy between the PA and Israel. Estimates regarding the pace of the peace process have often proven wrong, with agreements generally taking longer to negotiate than first anticipated.

Looking toward the future, it is not expected that much short-term support, especially for the PA's recurrent budget, will be required over the remainder of 1997 or in future years as revenue collection efforts are further consolidated. Current projections foresee a recurrent budget deficit of substantially less than the $52 million originally projected for 1997. In addition, about $10-$15 million is expected to be disbursed from the Holst Fund for employment-generation activities over the course of 1997, of which $3 million was disbursed during the first three months of the year. To ensure that donors help to lay the foundation for medium-term economic growth, focus should now shift to removing impediments that block implementation of public investment projects.

The post-Oslo experience suggests that more donor assistance should be directed toward investment for two key reasons. First, closure policy will likely remain as a permanent feature. Borders are now less porous than in the past due to changes in Israeli internal security arrangements. Security checks are now concentrated at the borders, while in the past under the ICA they were more diffuse.

This increases the cogency of projects that connect the WBGS to the rest of the world (such as operating the port and airport) and foster more efficient border operations for access to outside markets. Second, the partial loss of labor market opportunities in Israel is also a permanent feature. It is not feasible in the long run to compensate households for the reduction in income from employment in Israel through subsidies. Rather, the only way of generating future incomes in a sustainable way is to raise investment.

Without resolving key political issues, the donor community and private sector will be reluctant to supply the required investment capital. Arguably, donor efforts to assist WBGS economic development have been negated by the fallout from tense Palestinian-Israeli relations. Some clarity and resolution on where the peace process is going is therefore necessary to sustain the donor effort. This requires recognition of the intricate link between the evolving politics of the peace process and the economic means that donors apply to sustain the development process. The uncertainty surrounding political developments may also require donors to rethink their strategies in cases where the political situation does not improve. With high unemployment, falling incomes, very little productive investment, and significant fiscal pressures, the appropriate donor response may be to focus on basic public infrastructure rehabilitation, employment generation, welfare provisions, and basic human resource development until large-scale infrastructure projects and private sector support activities can be undertaken.

A related issue concerns the availability and terms of funding. In the near future, donors will have to take a collective decision on a renewal of funding commitments as the initial five-year pledge period (1994-98) draws to a close. In the interim, the CG meeting in late 1997 resulted in new pledges as a last push toward the final status in the peace process. Ideally, these donor pledges should closely reflect the PA's investment strategies as outlined in the Palestinian Development Plan. However, the terms and conditions of future donor assistance may be less generous than those of the 1993 original donor pledges. It is possible, for example, that an increasing share of donor assistance will take the form of loans (with varying degrees of concessionality) rather than grants as in the first round of pledges. This could impose an unforeseen financial burden in the medium to long term that needs to be taken into account by the PA when drawing on further donor assistance.

* * *

The need for recurrent budget and other short-term support over a much longer period and in larger amounts than originally envisioned has been mirrored in a delayed flow of support for investment. Due to donors' obliging response to short-term crises, the impact on living standards from large negative shocks has been partly mitigated. However, a unique opportunity to lay the foundations for sustained medium-term economic growth is being lost. It is not evident that disbursements for investment projects have been lower than expected solely because of the higher disbursements for short-term support. It could be argued that disbursements for investment projects would have been low even without the concurrent increase in disbursements for consumption-oriented activities. This argument hinges on the underlying impediments facing the implementation of investment projects. In any case, further analysis is required to determine the impact of donor assistance on economic development of the WBGS.

In the future, it is unlikely that the donor community will show the same willingness to provide short-term financial support; perhaps the need for such support will also be lower as the PA further consolidates its revenue collection effort. Rather, the post-Oslo experience suggests that more donor assistance should be directed toward investment. To generate sustained future increases in income, investment must rise. Without the resolution of key political issues, however, it will be difficult to overcome reticence among the donor community and the private sector toward supplying the required investment capital. Some clarity and resolution on where the peace process is going is therefore required to sustain the donor effort. The opportunity and challenge for donors now is to step in and guide the peace process more firmly. A related issue is whether donors will renew funding commitments as the initial five-year pledge period draws to a close. For its part, the PA needs to assess carefully the financial burden imposed on future generations if new funding is provided on less generous conditions than during the first round of pledges.

Looking beyond donor assistance, the real issue is how to support investment projects to ensure sustained growth and poverty alleviation without relying solely on public finance. The challenge will be to assist and encourage the private sector to undertake projects, with donors offering complementary finance or by offering political risk guarantees or insurance. Likewise, more attention should be given to building competence within the PA, thus ensuring a capable system of governance that fosters and complements private sector-driven growth.

Bibliographical Note: This chapter relies upon data provided by MOPIC (1997), the Tripartite Action Plan, UNSCO-World Bank (1996), UNSCO (1996c), and Hooper (1996).

Part III

Building the Enabling Environment for Long-term Growth

There is a pressing need for Palestinian policy makers to focus immediately on the underpinnings of sustainable economic growth. The resolution of politics is obviously necessary for long-term growth, but sustainable growth requires reform and the revitalization of a host of organizations that, under conditions of occupation, were managed on a day-to-day basis rather than with a long-term view.

An enabling environment for growth includes

- central and local government institutions that efficiently manage expenditures and raise revenue;
- a legal apparatus to enforce contracts and defend property rights;
- a well-regulated and confidence-inspiring financial sector;
- a flexible and fair labor market;
- good regulations that allow for efficient private provision of public goods and services; and
- well-functioning health and education systems that resourcefully utilize NGO activism.

If these fundamentals are in place, growth will occur if, when, and as, the political situation starts improving, and hopefully, as a political resolution is reached.

Three sectors that are essential for long-term growth stand out in their need for reform and modernization. These are education, health systems, and infrastructure. In each sector, it is essential to focus on a systems view—with partnerships between providers and beneficiaries, regulatory frameworks, enforcement mechanisms, and feedback loops.

Chapter 11

Improving the Education System

Sue Berryman

Introduction

Of the civilian sectors, education accounted for the largest share (19 percent) of total budgeted expenditures for 1996. Teachers in the basic and secondary educational levels totaled 21,600 in the 1995-96 academic year, constituting 4.3 percent of the labor force. The quality of policy-making and policy implementation in this sector is critical. Education absorbs a significant share of public investment and recurrent budget expenditures, and serves as an important instrument for economic growth and poverty alleviation.

This chapter examines the major challenges facing policy makers in the education sector, including access, quality, and efficiency. It also examines how the institutional infrastructure can build an education system that will evolve to best serve its beneficiaries. Except for a discussion on financing tertiary education, this chapter is restricted to pre-tertiary education (grades 1-12) and, therefore, to the Ministry of Education (MOE).

The Education System

Authority Over the Educational System

Authority over the WBGS education system is divided between the PA, UNRWA, and the private/NGO sector. The PA assumed control of all schools under Israeli jurisdiction (except East Jerusalem) by August 1994. When the status of Palestinian refugees is resolved, the PA will assume financial, policy, and operational responsibility for schools currently under UNRWA auspices.

Upon transfer of authority to the PA, the Ministry of Education and Higher Education (MEHE) was established and successfully negotiated the transition from the ICA. In 1996 the MEHE split into the MOE, responsible for pre-tertiary education, and the Ministry of Higher Education (MHE), responsible for post-secondary education. Table 11.1 shows the educational responsibilities that the PA assumed from the Israelis. It excludes schools in East Jerusalem, where jurisdiction is split between the Israeli government, private/NGOs (including the *Wakf*), and UNRWA. Table 11.2 presents the distribution of students among the various administrative auspices in 1995-96. It includes students in UNRWA and private/NGO schools in East Jerusalem, but excludes those in Israeli-controlled schools.

As Table 11.1 shows, private/NGO education exists at all levels, but is concentrated proportionally at levels that make good economic sense: preschool, vocational education, community colleges, and universities. Private/ NGO education has a particular history and meaning in WBGS; "private/ NGO" means that no public Palestinian agency has financed the education. However, from the point of view of students and their families, most private education was virtually free, since charitable organizations and donors funded most of the private/NGO education. Local and international NGOs provided education at all levels, and were essentially the sole providers at the preschool level. Prior to the Gulf War, about 60 percent of the community colleges and all universities were funded with contributions from other Arab nations that the PLO channeled through the Council on Higher Education. These transfers declined precipitously after the Gulf War, leaving Council-funded institutions in dire financial straits. After the Oslo II Agreement, international donor organizations picked up a substantial share of the costs for community colleges and universities. Although these institutions have responded by raising fees and taking other revenue-generating actions, financing post-secondary level education has yet to be organized rationally.

Table 11.1 Auspices for the WBGS Educational System: Number of Schools by Level (1993-94)

	Authority		
Level	**PA**	**UNRWA**	**Private/NGOs**
Preschool	0	0	453
Basic (Grades 1-10; ages 6-15)	739	254	70
Secondary (Grades 11-12; ages 16-17)	253	NA (close to 0)	41
Vocational Training Centers	NA (not 0)	3	NA (not 0)
Two-year Colleges	3	4	13
Universities / Four-year Colleges	0	2	8

Note: Figures for UNRWA and private/NGOs include Palestinian institutions in East Jerusalem while figures for the PA are limited to the RWB.
Source: PCBS (1995).

Table 11.2 *Number of Students by Auspices and Level in the WBGS* (1995-96)

Level	Total	Authority								
		PA			UNRWA			Private/NGO		
		Subtotal	Gaza Strip	West Bank	Subtotal	Gaza Strip	West Bank	Subtotal	Gaza Bank	West Strip
Kindergarten Primary	44,838	0	0	0	0	0	0	44,838	1,123	43,715
Basic (1-10)	606,802	395,411	106,829	288,582	175,306	129,494	45,812	36,085	2,890	33,195
Secondary (11-12)	50,054	45,618	19,381	26,237	0	0	0	4,436	742	3,694
Total	701,694	441,029	126,210	314,819	175,306	129,494	45,812	85,359	4,755	80,604

Note: Figures exclude East Jerusalem students enrolled in Israeli-controlled schools, but include those enrolled in UNRWA and private/NGO schools in East Jerusalem.

Sources: PCBS and MOE (1995-96), Table 6.23.

High Literacy Rates

Palestinians have relatively high literacy rates—84 percent for the population 15 years or older (Table 11.3). The rates differ between males and females (91 and 76 percent, respectively), but this difference is primarily attributable to literacy differences between older men and women. There is virtually no difference in literacy rates between the West Bank and Gaza Strip. The difference among the cities, refugee camps, and villages (87, 84, and 81 percent, respectively) is also primarily attributable to differences among older members of the population. In contrast, in 1995 the MENA region, as a whole, had an estimated adult literacy rate of only 57 percent.

Table 11.3 Comparative Indicators of Educational Attainment (in percentage)

Indicator	WBGS	MENA
Literacy Rate:		
Age 15-19	97	79
Age 15+	84	57
Primary School Enrollment:		
Males	91	104
Females	92	91
Preparatory School Enrollment:		
Males (Age 12-14)	90	NA
Females (Age 12-14)	92	NA
Secondary School Enrollment:		
Male + Female (Age 12-17)	NA	56
Males (Age 15-17)	68	NA
Females (Age 15-17)	64	NA

Sources: PCBS (1996a) and World Bank (1996d).

High Enrollment Rates

Gross enrollment rates are high, especially at the primary and preparatory, or lower secondary, levels (about 90 percent for the West Bank, Gaza Strip, refugee camps, cities, and villages). Enrollment rates drop to about 65 percent at grades 11-12. Males have higher enrollment rates than females at the upper secondary level in refugee camps and villages, but equal rates in the cities. In contrast, the MENA region has an average gross enrollment rate of 97 percent for primary school (ages 6-11) and 56 percent for lower and upper secondary schools (ages 12-17). Since upper-secondary enrollment rates are lower than the lower-secondary level in all countries, the WBGS is clearly achieving better gross enrollment rates at the post-primary level than MENA as a whole. Completion rates for 15-

19 year-olds were 93 percent for primary school and 63 percent for lower secondary school. Forty-four percent of the 20-24 year-olds completed upper secondary school, and 20 percent of the 25-34 year-olds held post-secondary degrees.

Quality of Education

Quality is defined as student performance relative to WBGS's curricular goals and relative to students in other nations with which WBGS must ultimately trade and compete. Available evidence indicates that the WBGS education system is not well organized to develop the foundation skills and higher-order cognitive thinking abilities that students will need to succeed.

Although there are no data for assessing the performance of WBGS students relative to curricular goals, Box 11.1 reports their performance relative to students in other countries. The secondary school exit examinations in mathematics and biology were also analyzed for Tunisia, Morocco, Iran, Lebanon, Jordan, and Egypt. West Bank schools use the Jordanian curriculum; Gazan schools, the Egyptian curriculum. The results for these six countries were compared to those for the French *baccalaureate* examinations. If the exit examinations reflect the content and performance expectations embodied by these countries' curricula, then the analyses tell us something about the knowledge and skills that WBGS students are expected to learn.

In mathematics, the MENA tests indicate a conception of school mathematics as a subject largely devoted to the recognition and repetition of definitions and theorems, and the performance of algorithms or other routine procedures. Tasks evaluating examinees' abilities in problem-solving were largely absent from the MENA mathematics tests; conversely, the French *baccalaureate,* in addition to the performance expectations typical of the MENA tests, assessed students' abilities to solve, predict, verify, generalize, and apply mathematical principles to real world problems.

In biology, all of the MENA tests evaluated a very large array of topics—many more than those evaluated in the French sample tests. Given their broad scope, it is not surprising that these tests expected very limited performance, concentrating on understanding and remembering simple facts, with some attention to the informed use of scientific principles to develop explanations. In contrast, the French *baccalaureate* did not assess mastery of simple concepts, but rather focused on complex data, thematic information, abstracting and deducting scientific principles, constructing and using models, designing investigations, and interpreting investigative data.

Avoiding Costly Policy Mistakes and Increasing Efficiency

As new ministries, the MOE and MHE can avoid the policy mistakes made by many MENA (and other) countries that have led to serious inefficiencies. An example of good policy is the joint MOE, MHE, and Ministry of Labor strategy for vocational/technical education. The plan will save money by eliminating duplicate programs and improving economies of scale. It anticipates establishing a single training system to be used by students (after they complete grades 10 or 12) and by adults, including experienced workers. Plans include a system of training centers, each organized around an occupational "family" or category. Each center will use modularized curricula, allowing a trainee to customize a program by selecting modules relevant to the trainee's needs.

Box 11.1 *International Assessment of Educational Progress*

In 1991, the International Assessment of Educational Progress measured the performance of 13-year-old students in science and mathematics. Jordan participated in this assessment in 1991. The same tests were administered to 13-year olds in the West Bank in 1992 and in UNRWA schools in Gaza Strip in 1993.

Of the 15 countries that assessed comprehensive samples of students (including Korea, Taiwan, Hungary, Switzerland, the Soviet Union, Israel, Canada, France, and the US), Jordan scored the lowest for average percent correct in both mathematics and science. Students in the West Bank and UNRWA students in Gaza Strip scored below Jordanian students. West Bank students in private/NGO schools performed significantly better than those in the schools under the ICA, who performed somewhat better than students in UNRWA's West Bank schools. Although both Jordan and the West Bank use the Jordanian curriculum, *Intifada*-related school closures for several years prior to the assessment undoubtedly depressed the scores of West Bank and Gaza students. Notably, Jordanian students scored poorly relative to other countries, especially in mathematics, without *Intifada*-related closures affecting the schools. These results indicate general weaknesses in the Jordanian curriculum and pedagogy.

More important are test results for cognitive processes, which assessed the grasp of concepts and facts and the use of knowledge and principles to solve complex problems. Problem-solving skills are particularly important in internationally competitive economies, where adaptation to continuous change and the need to manage unfamiliar situations are crucial. On average, students from all countries that participated in the international assessment performed less well on problem-solving tests than on the conceptual understanding and knowledge items. In mathematics, their average problem-solving score was about 90 percent of their average score for conceptual understanding; in science, the problem-solving score was 94 percent of the knowledge score. However, the performance gaps between knowledge versus problem-solving items were greater for both the Jordanian and West Bank students: about 80 percent in mathematics and about 75 percent in science.

Maintain Access at the Lowest Cost

The WBGS has respectable enrollment rates at all levels. However, very high fertility rates, especially in the Gaza Strip, will severely challenge the system's ability to maintain, let alone improve, access.

Meeting the rising demand for education will require substantial increases in school spaces and teachers. The cumulative percent increase in the number of school spaces from 1995 to 2020 for the total system for ages 6-11 is 96 percent. For 12-14 year-olds, it is 115 percent; for ages 15-17, 123 percent; and for 18 and above, 192 percent. The student population for grades 1-12 will double in this 25-year period, increasing 106 percent. If a doubling of enrollments translates into doubling the number of schools, the physical plant will have to increase from its 1,357 schools in 1993-94 to about 2,700 schools by the year 2020. Just meeting enrollment growth for grades 1-12 by the year 2000 will require an additional 330 schools (see Table A.12 in Annex). These enrollment projections demand a substantial investment budget for system costs.

The MOE has adopted a policy of single-shift schools; however, about 18 percent of its schools are currently double shift. Population pressures on the schools should trigger a reconsideration of the single-shift policy. Double-shift schools make more efficient use of the physical plant, and the WBGS has been able to run double-shift schools without compromising annual instructional time.

Maintain Diversified Funding and Provision of Education

The PA inherits a sector with a history of diversified funding and provision at all levels of education. The challenge is to continue to encourage that diversity, especially at post-secondary levels. In several MENA countries, all levels of the education system are seriously distorted and quality visibly compromised because governments have been reluctant to diversify funding and provision between the public and private/NGO sectors, especially at the expensive post-secondary level. Economic and political pressures could cause the PA to make similar mistakes. The donor community has reduced its support of the university sector. The decline in NGO funding and political tensions between the NGO sector and PA could result in displacing NGOs as providers and financiers. One of the several policy challenges confronting the MHE will be to craft a technically and politically sophisticated strategy that mixes public and private financing and that can easily accommodate greater private financing as the economic situation improves.

Do Not Use the Teaching Corps as a Public Sector Jobs Program

Currently the average student to teacher ratio is 46:1, with average class size in the high thirties at all levels. These are acceptable figures by international standards. Faced with high unemployment, the greatest danger is that the PA will use the civil service, including the teaching force, as a jobs program. The case of

Egypt shows how disastrous this policy can be. The Egyptian civil service is bloated and sclerotic. Overstaffing makes it impossible to compensate each civil servant adequately. With wages so low, civil servants often work two or three jobs and have little commitment to their civil service job. Teachers frequently supplement their incomes with well-paid private lessons, an income source that operates as a disincentive for quality teaching in the public schools.

A second efficiency issue involving teachers is weekly teaching loads. At the primary grades, WBGS teachers teach 26 classes of 45 minutes per week for a total weekly teaching load of 1,170 minutes. Relative to teaching loads in 19 other countries, this is a fairly light schedule. The WBGS plainly needs an inquiry to determine if net savings can be realized by increasing the teaching loads, increasing teacher salaries in compensation for the additional work, and reducing the rate of new hires to meet enrollment pressures.

Improving the Quality of the System

Sustainable growth of the Palestinian economy critically depends on an export-oriented development strategy (see Chapter 6). Palestinian wages are too high in comparison to China, India, or Indonesia for the economy to compete in unskilled labor-intensive production. The alternative is to develop the WBGS into a center of skilled labor and services that will supply Arab markets and produce goods and services to meet regional and international demand. Moving into the higher-wage regional and international market presents WBGS suppliers with a particular profile of customer demand. International customers expect a large, varied, and continuously improving basket of goods and services, fast delivery of orders, high and consistent quality, and low prices. In response, suppliers have to place a high premium on the diversification of goods and services, accelerated product and process innovation, speed, low cost, and quality. To meet these requirements, employers usually have to change the organization of work and hire workers with different and higher levels of skills.

Competing successfully in regional and international markets requires conducive economic policies, good infrastructure, political stability, and high levels (and low variance) of skills throughout the occupational structure. If Palestinians are competent across the range of occupations that are needed to support manufacturing and service opportunities, then their economy can become increasingly attractive as a commercial center for the Middle East. A model is Singapore, which, along with other economic policies, strategically used educational and training investments, especially in the low- and medium-skilled occupations, to produce spectacular economic growth.

The WBGS education system will have to change at the classroom level if young Palestinians are to acquire the foundation skills and higher-order cognitive abilities required to support this long-term economic development strategy. Higher-order cognitive skills include problem-solving, decision-making, integration, and knowing how to learn. These skills turn out to be particularly important in internationally competitive economies, which demand continuous change and the need to make judgments in unfamiliar situations.

Traditional pedagogy and its results fit the skill requirements of command and control, hierarchical organizations structured around the performance of narrow and repetitive tasks that allow for little discretion. As enterprises change in response to the demands of international customers, traditional pedagogy begins to fail, especially in creating the higher-order cognitive skills valued in new workplaces. There is an alternative paradigm for organizing teaching and learning that better fits the skill requirements of new workplaces. This paradigm places more responsibility on the student for learning; focuses on the processes by which answers are reached, not just on finding the right answers; uses context to give intuitive meaning to abstract ideas; and stresses experience in using principles effectively. Table 11.4 compares the two alternative organizations of work and the two pedagogic paradigms.

Qualitative reforms have a particular and difficult political economy, especially when compared with reforms that increase access to education. Increasing access requires adding inputs—building new schools, hiring more teachers, and purchasing more textbooks and equipment. This kind of reform usually enjoys broad political support, as the benefits are visible, broadly distributed, rapid, and fairly certain. However, as quality reforms take much longer, their results are less visible and much less certain. Implementing quality reforms places greater demands on the system's management capacity for a longer time period. It re-

Table 11.4 Matches Between Workplaces and Pedagogies

Traditional Arrangements		New Arrangements	
Workplace	Pedagogy	Workplace	Pedagogy
Passive order-taking in a hierarchical work organization; Heavy supervision to control workers	Teachers as experts convey knowledge to passive learners	Workers are expected to take responsibility for identifying and solving problems and for adapting to change by learning	Under teacher support and guidance, students assume responsibility for learning, in the process developing knowing-how-to-learn skills
Emphasis on limited responses to limited problems and on getting a task done	Emphasis on facts and getting right answers	Workers deal with non-routine problems that have to be analyzed and solved	Focus is on alternative ways to frame issues and problems
Focus on the specific task independent of organizational context or business strategy	What is to be learned is stripped of meaningful context	Workers are expected to make decisions that require understanding the broader context of their work and their company's priorities	Ideas, principles and facts are introduced, used, and understood in meaningful context

Source: Berryman (1996).

quires changes in the classroom behaviors of thousands of teachers, which implies adjustments to teacher training and incentives.

The first step in a reform package is to develop a long-term strategy that sets goals, priorities, and accountabilities. Against the demands of such a package, the institutional weaknesses in the WBGS educational system are revealed.

Improving the Institutional Structure of the Education System

The ICA acted as a passive caretaker and administrator for that part of the WBGS educational system under its control. To secure efficiencies and produce the type of quality education needed for successful international competition in high-value goods and services, the education system will have to change from a maintenance mode to a continuous improvement mode.

Figure 11.1 displays functions that can be used to assess the institutional status and challenges facing the MOE. Not surprisingly, the analysis shows that the performance of all functions is handicapped in various ways and to differing degrees and reveals an accountability framework that is organized around conformity to rules and regulations.

Figure 11.1 Relationships Between System Functions

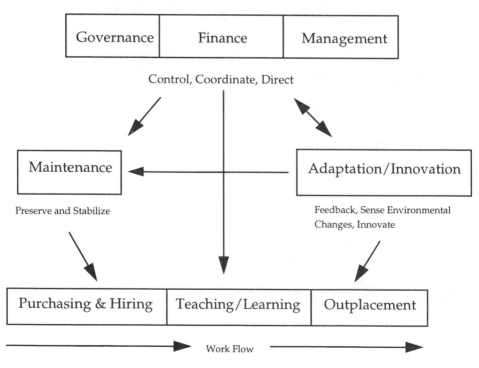

Source: Berryman (1996).

The primary function of the governors of the educational system is to establish goals. Curricular choices should emerge out of a national goal-setting process that develops consensus among the stakeholder groups. Given the recent transfer of authority, it is not surprising that the WBGS lacks clear goals for its educational system. Public debates and discussions about curricular goals were initiated with the new Curriculum Center, but an informed goal-setting process has not been conducted. Such a process requires trustworthy data for the education sector as well as the capacity to monitor progress toward achieving goals. Sound data are invaluable for building consensus, resolving disagreements, pinpointing major problems, selecting goals, and setting performance targets. Although information is presently being collected, some of the most relevant data are still missing, such as information on student learning achievements.

To organize resources effectively, set priorities, and measure the system's performance in relation to its goals, management needs a competent policy-making capacity, performance feedback mechanisms, and an accountability framework that focuses actors in the system on its goals. Although the MOE is beginning to develop this infrastructure, the top leadership has yet to collectively move out of a crisis management mode. Routines that ensure systematic, rather than ad hoc, policy-making have yet to be established. Until policy makers demand and use the policy-making infrastructure, the infrastructure itself will not be developed effectively.

Currently, the management framework seems to lack the feedback loops that monitor performance and trigger corrective actions when there are lapses between standards and performance. For example, the district offices have school inspectors to conduct evaluations, but teacher evaluations are not linked to training that improves their performance, and school evaluations are not linked to effective technical assistance services. The sector is therefore impaired in its capacity for adaptation and innovation. Feedback mechanisms include (i) management information (such as enrollment trends, number of teachers and their teaching specialties, expenditures, and completion of scheduled maintenance activities); (ii) education indicator data, especially data on student learning outcomes; and (iii) evaluations of managerial and educational initiatives (such as decentralizing selection management functions to the school level or introducing a new fourth grade curriculum). The MOE not only lacks data on student learning, but also lacks expertise in evaluating initiatives.

Accountability Framework Focused on Student Learning

The MOE should start to plan an accountability framework that focuses at least on student learning. The framework has to reflect the governors' key goals, which have yet to be established. However, since learning is the ultimate point of any educational system, it can be presumed that this will be one of the system's overarching objectives.

An accountability system requires performance objectives, measurable indicators of their achievement, a system of positive and negative incentives, and the political will to enforce sanctions. All players in the system—the MOE; ministerial under-secretaries and director-generals; ministerial, provincial, and local administrators; school directors; teachers; faculties of education; international organizations; donors; and NGOs—should be held accountable for meeting the performance objectives. The primary accountability for most actors should be for student learning, with special accountability criteria for functions such as finance or procurement. However, until national assessments of student learning become routine, an accountability framework organized around student learning obviously cannot be created.

Establishing a Financing Framework is a High Priority

The MOE has yet to establish modern budget planning processes and a trained staff to handle issues such as estimating the immediate and long-term financial impact of alternative cost-saving options or assessing the recurrent cost implications of proposed investments. The MOE and MHE should work closely on an overall financing framework for the sector. Bad financing decisions at the post-secondary level can create student disincentives and fiscal pressures that distort the compulsory and secondary levels and undermine their quality. Public finance for the tertiary level needs to be kept as limited and targeted as possible.

Improving Teacher Quality and Curriculum

Another challenge for the institutional infrastructure is to establish ways of acquiring and maintaining the quality of the human and physical assets required to produce learning. Major inputs include teachers, school buildings, curricular frameworks with associated textbooks and teacher guides, and equipment.

Improving the quality of the current teaching force should be one of the highest priorities for the MOE and international donor community. The MOE accurately views teacher quality as a very serious problem that will take years to solve. The current teaching force is seriously under-qualified, having received virtually no professional development under the ICA. Thus, teachers' skills and knowledge, which initially were not that strong, have not been refreshed and updated. There is also substantial out-of-field teaching. For example, the MOE estimates that about 37 percent of its science teachers have had no special training in science. Mathematics runs a close second to science in out-of-field teaching.

Teacher quality is a function of the selection standards for entering pre-service training, the quality of that training, and the quality of in-service professional development. For entry into teaching, the MOE should consider introducing national teacher licensing examinations that assess both content knowledge and pedagogic practice. The international literature shows that teachers' skills and knowledge are much better predictors of student learning than teachers' years of education. Good credentialling assessments, once developed, provide effective standard-setting guidelines for universities and community colleges that prepare future teachers. If too many graduates of particular pre-service programs fail the credentialling examinations, those programs will suffer enrollment declines.

Since the West Bank and Gaza Strip use different curricula and secondary school leaving examinations, curriculum and textbooks pose several problems. In the interest of creating a Palestinian identity, it is critical to integrate the curriculum for the two territories. The MOE's effort to integrate the territories' curricula around the newly revised Jordanian curriculum was met with political resistance from Gaza Strip. It is not efficient for the Palestinians to create their own curriculum and textbooks for subjects in which country-specific experiences are less relevant, such as mathematics and the sciences. However, solving the integration problem seems politically necessary. Given the political need to develop a Palestinian curriculum, the Curriculum Center has chosen to involve stakeholders in curricular decisions. It is important to address the issue of performance expectations that the new curriculum would set in light of optimal development of human capital, which is consistent with the strategy for economic development.

Setting priorities for school equipment is complicated. Simple equipment such as blackboards, maps, charts, globes, and sports equipment is relatively inexpensive, needs little maintenance, and could be funded by community and donor contributions. However, investments in more expensive resources, such as computer laboratories, science equipment, and libraries should be carefully analyzed in light of goals. Millions of dollars have been wasted in both developed and developing countries on these resources because one or more conditions for their effective use have not been met.

* * *

The education sector faces institutional challenges that will take years to solve and whose solutions have to be sequenced. The first step is the development of a long-term strategy that sets priorities and accountabilities. Medium-term priorities include developing systematic policy-making processes within the MOE; constructing a unified Palestinian curriculum that associates performance expectations with building skills and knowledge, for economic as well as democratic development; creating feedback mechanisms, especially student learning assessments; and broadly and intensely attacking the problem of teaching quality.

Bibliographical Note: This chapter is based on the background papers of Berryman (1996) and Abu-Duhou (1996). Data is drawn from PCBS (1995, 1996a) and World Bank (1996a). Other references include Valverde, Schmidt, and Bianchi (1996); Claudet (1996); US Department of Education, National Center for Education Statistics (1993); and Nelson and O'Brien (1993).

Chapter 12

Managing the Growth of the Health Sector

Mustafa Barghouthi, Jean Lennock, and Radwan A. Shaban

Introduction

The health status of the Palestinians is good in relation to prevailing income levels and countries at comparable levels of development. According to the PCBS demographic survey of 15,000 households, the mortality rate for infants less than one year old was 28 deaths per 1,000 live births in 1995 (25 per 1,000 in the West Bank and 32 per 1,000 in the Gaza Strip). Relatively low infant and child mortality rates are reflected in a fairly high life expectancy at birth (70 years for males and 73.5 years for females in both the West Bank and Gaza Strip). WBGS life expectancy is higher than most Middle East countries and comparable to upper middle-income economies, such as South Korea (Table 12.1). (Other studies document higher infant mortality and lower life expectancy in the WBGS.)

Table 12.1 Health Indicators

	West Bank	Gaza Strip	WBGS	Egypt	Jordan	Tunisia	Israel	South Korea
Life expectancy at birth (years)	71.7	71.7	71.7*	62	70	68	77	71
Infant mortality rate (per 1,000)	25*	32*	28*	52	32	40	8	12
Maternal mortality rate (per 100,000)	—	—	70-80	—	132	139	—	30
Total fertility rate	5.6	7.4	6.2	3.5	4.8	5.2	2.4	1.8
Access to piped water (percentage)	71.4	96.3	79.6	86	99	—	100	78
Access to public sewer (percentage)	19.2	48.7	28.9	—	70	72	70	100

* A study by Barghouthi and Lennock (1997) documents life expectancy at 66 years in the WBGS, and the infant mortality rate at 40-45 per 1,000 in Gaza Strip and 45-50 per 1,000 in the West Bank.
Sources: PCBS (1996a) and World Bank (1996d).

The reasonable health status in the WBGS is the result of an emphasis on primary care at the household level for the past two decades (Box 12.1). It has been achieved in spite of low investment in and poor quality of public infrastructure, including water supply, solid waste disposal, and sanitation facilities. The proliferation of non-profit NGOs contributed to health improvements by fulfilling health care needs not provided by the government or UNRWA.

While health conditions are favorable for the level of development in the WBGS, achievements in this area are fragile. Maintaining and improving health indicators is a serious challenge for the economy as a whole. The high population growth rate, epidemiological transition to diseases of high-income economies, and introduction of advanced medical technology imply a rapidly growing demand for

---

Box 12.1 Disease Patterns

Substantial improvement in mortality rates and life expectancy is largely a result of successful immunization programs that have controlled childhood communicable diseases. High levels of literacy and education have also contributed significantly to utilizing health care services, which improves health outcomes.

Seventy percent of child deaths result from infectious disease, predominantly to the respiratory system. Diarrhea is the second cause of death among children. The high prevalence of infectious diseases among children is related to overcrowding and poor environmental conditions. Only 28.9 percent of households had access to piped public sewers (19.2 percent in the West Bank and 48.7 percent in the Gaza Strip) (Table 12.1). Many sewers are poorly maintained and may be a major contributor to the spread of disease. Among adults, 37 percent of deaths resulted from cerebrovascular (strokes), coronary heart disease, and cancers. This reflects the progress of the epidemiological transition to the "modern" diseases common in high-income economies.

Maternal health is of special importance given that the WBGS has among the highest fertility rates in the world. The total fertility rate (children born to a woman through her reproductive years) is 5.61 in the West Bank and 7.44 in Gaza Strip, with a combined average of 6.24. MOH data suggest that maternal death is the third largest cause of death among women of reproductive age. According to the 1995 demographic survey, the maternal mortality rate was between 70 to 80 per 100,000. Hypertension caused by pregnancy (eclampsia), post-partum hemorrhage, and chronic diseases associated with pregnancy, are the leading causes of maternal mortality. The fraction of home births without professional attendance is 31.6 percent in the Gaza Strip and 40 percent in the West Bank.

Source: Barghouthi and Lennock (1997).

increasingly expensive health services which could have severe financial implications. On the delivery side, the health system needs to enhance its macro efficiency. This entails maximizing usage of excess capacity in various subsectors and improving the efficiency and quality of services provided at the individual facility level. For example, bed occupancy rates vary by region and by type of delivery institution. Border closures pose special difficulties for transforming the health care system, since its traditional premier institutions are located in East Jerusalem.

System of Delivering Health Services

Health care is provided by four major groups: the Ministry of Health (MOH), UNRWA for refugees, non-profit NGOs, and for-profit private sector practitioners and companies. The total recurrent expenditure on health was estimated at about $250 million in 1995, with the MOH spending 31 percent of the total, UNRWA 12 percent, NGO providers 17 percent, and the private sector 40 percent.

MOH Services: Building a Secondary and Tertiary Care Structure

In May 1994, the MOH took over the responsibility for health services in the Gaza Strip and Jericho and, at end-1994, in the RWB. The MOH provides selected primary care services such as prenatal care, vaccinations, and treatment for children under 3-years old free of charge to all Palestinians. Primary health care services are provided (free at point of delivery) through the MOH network of facilities to those enrolled in the government health insurance scheme (Table 12.2).

Most government primary health care clinics are staffed by a part-time general practitioner with nursing and ancillary staff. The general practitioner provides curative services (usually two days per week), while nurses and midwives provide a range of preventative services including prenatal care, well-baby clinics, and vaccination programs. Eighty-two percent of the doctors working in government clinics are general practitioners who rotate among clinics (Table 12.3).

The MOH provides secondary level services through nine hospitals in the West Bank (with 706 general beds) and five hospitals in the Gaza Strip (with 865 general beds). Tertiary level services and certain advanced diagnostic techniques are purchased by the MOH on behalf of insured patients from non-governmental hospitals in WBGS, and Israeli, Egyptian, and Jordanian hospitals. In 1995, $14 million was spent to purchase such treatment.

UNRWA Health Care: Basic Services under Extreme Stress

Health care services provided by UNRWA are largely limited to primary care. Facing extreme financial pressure, UNRWA's resources are seriously limited amidst a rapidly growing eligible population. UNRWA is expanding its health centers with support from the donor community to meet some of the increasing

Table 12.2 Health Institutions by Auspices

	MOH		UNRWA		NGOs
	1995 level	**new addition**	**1995 level**	**new addition**	**non-profit**
West Bank					
Primary care					
Primary care	178	6	22	13	176
Maternal & child clinics	9	—	0	—	—
Health rooms/posts	74	—	12	—	—
Secondary care					
General hospitals	9	1	1	0	10
General hospital beds	706	100	43	20	997
Maternity hospital beds	—	—	—	—	170
Psychiatric hospital beds	320	—	—	—	—
Gaza Strip					
Primary care					
Primary care	29	7	11	4	31
Maternal & child clinics	—	—	6	1	—
Health rooms/posts	—	—	1	—	—
Secondary care					
General hospitals	5	—	0	1	1
General hospital beds	865	—	50*	250	80
Maternity hospital beds	—	—	—	—	—
Psychiatric hospital beds	—	—	—	—	—

*contracted
Source: Barghouthi and Lennock (1997).

Table 12.3 Medical Workers in WBGS

	MOH (1995)	UNRWA (1995)	NGOs (1993)	**Total**
West Bank				
Doctors	451	52	392	895
Nurses	1,031	176	214	1,421
Technical	243	70	204	517
Gaza Strip				
Doctors	541	57	129	700
Nurses	912	184	124	1,220
Technical	252	70	96	415

Note: Table excludes the for-profit private sector.
Source: Barghouthi and Lennock (1997).

demand. A key challenge to UNRWA is its long-term future, given its anticipated integration with MOH services. This integration cannot be achieved until the status of refugees is settled in final status negotiations.

UNRWA directly provides free primary health services (including drugs) to the refugee population through its facilities. These health clinics provide a full range of preventative, curative, and community health care services. All health centers and posts provide special clinics for diabetes and hypertension. All health centers in the Gaza Strip and half of those in the West Bank provide dental services. Maternal and child health services are also provided free to non-refugees.

Most doctors employed by UNRWA are general practitioners. The number of clinics and doctors is extremely low relative to the target population, resulting in the lowest time per consultation among health subsectors. Typically, a doctor will see 101 patients per day. Thus, the quality of UNRWA medical care is perceived to be low in comparison to other health subsectors.

UNRWA's secondary and tertiary health services are very limited and usually contracted out to other hospitals with a co-payment from the patient. At these hospitals, refugees co-pay 25 percent of the cost of treatment. In Al-Makassed Hospital the co-payment is reduced to 10 percent if they are recognized hardship cases. Contracted hospitals include Al-Ahli in the Gaza Strip and Hebron, Itihad in Nablus, Palestine Red Crescent Society in Ramallah, and Augusta Victoria in East Jerusalem. UNRWA runs a 43-bed hospital in the West Bank, and is expected to run the 250-bed European hospital, under construction, in the Gaza Strip before eventually turning it over to the MOH.

Fragility and Decline of NGO Health Services

In the absence of adequate health services during the period of occupation, many NGOs started offering health care services as a not-for-profit activity. Prominent among these are the Palestine Red Crescent Societies (PRCS), Patients' Friend Societies, and the Union of Palestinian Medical Relief Committees. Their number expanded rapidly throughout the 1980s and particularly after the onset of the *Intifada*. Supported by external funding from Palestinians and others in the Gulf, the PLO, and international organizations, the NGOs succeeded in doubling the number of health care clinics with basic services during the *Intifada* years.

The NGO health subsector suffered a serious setback following the Gulf War, which effectively eliminated external support—private and PLO. The PA's establishment in 1994 caused donors to divert financial support from the NGOs to the MOH and UNRWA. As a result, the number of NGO clinics in the rural West Bank declined from 210 in 1992 to 128 in June 1996.

The NGOs have generally filled a need not satisfied either by the government or UNRWA, by providing curative services in primary health care clinics targeted to underserved communities. For example, NGO clinics have the highest number of specialty doctors of all providers. Specialty clinics in diabetes, obstetrics and gynecology, ophthalmology and dermatology are available in about 25 percent of NGO clinics in the West Bank. NGOs also provide secondary and tertiary care. The preeminent Palestinian tertiary center is East Jerusalem's Al-Makassed Hospital (the main referral hospital for the West Bank), with 250 beds, providing general and advanced surgery including cardiovascular, neurosurgery, plastic surgery, and gynecology.

Private Sector on the Rise

The private for-profit health sector runs private clinics and specialized private hospitals (particularly maternity hospitals), and provides technically advanced health services. Many solo private-sector health practitioners also work full-time in the government, UNRWA, or NGO sector. While its size is difficult to estimate, it appears that the private sector's role in service delivery has grown since the establishment of the PA. Large private health care companies have been formed and have started to buy out the operations of financially strapped NGO health providers. The PA supports the growth of private sector health since these companies provide health services to the MOH at a cost lower than Israeli providers or referring patients to Jordan and Egypt.

Improving Efficiency and Quality of Care

Over the past two decades, the health care system has been largely driven by an overall emphasis in primary care, due mainly to the significant involvement of grassroots NGOs and UNRWA. In recent years, the PA has placed more emphasis on expanding hospital capacity. This policy is intended to correct the limited investment in secondary and tertiary care under Israeli occupation and reduce costly reliance on Israeli hospitals. But the vacuum left by the declining role of NGOs could leave a significant fraction of the population—especially the poor—with reduced access to basic services.

The development of a rapidly growing unregulated private sector could exacerbate an emerging duality in the health care system: a low-quality system (accessible to all) focusing increasingly less on preventive care as the PA places increased emphasis on secondary and tertiary care; and a high-quality system focusing on curative treatment that caters mainly to richer segments of the population. These developments could ultimately result in deteriorating aggregate health indicators for the population. The need for primary care and preventive care remains high. For example, to address the epidemiological transition in a cost-effective manner, preventive approaches directed to non-communicable disease, such as cardiovascular disease and cancer, need to be developed and implemented so as to reduce the number of individuals who would require more expensive curative care.

In this context, the balance of public funds expended between primary and secondary or tertiary care requires careful evaluation. In the West Bank, the MOH currently spends one-third of its budget on primary care and two-thirds on hospital care (translating into $29 million on primary care and public health facilities and $70 million on hospital expansion and construction). In 1994-95, UNRWA spent 47 percent of its West Bank budget and 65 percent of its Gaza Strip budget on primary care, with the remainder allocated for hospital care. UNRWA's Gaza Strip operations appropriately emphasize primary care. But if previous health outcomes are to be maintained, the government's investment and recurrent budget should maintain previous emphasis on primary care facilities. With the decline in NGO funding, particularly in the West Bank, the MOH should emphasize the delivery of primary and public health.

An alternative approach to direct expansion of the government-run health system is to explore purchasing health services from the NGOs and private sector. This would increase overall macro efficiency of the system as it would make use of excess capacity in the NGO subsector, and incorporate previous experience and special knowledge of community needs. However, such collaboration between public and private sectors requires the development of appropriate regulatory and monitoring mechanisms that address financial performance. Examples include appropriate use of tax and customs exemptions, user evaluations, client surveys that are accessible to the press and public, and professional accreditation review. These instruments should be complemented by feedback mechanisms to help institutions upgrade their capacity and improve performance. During the transition phase, the creation of accountability mechanisms should not be heavily dependent on a rigid legal system. Formulating an NGO law is a governance challenge best done through the integration of appropriate stakeholders, so that the law is "owned," and transaction and enforcement costs are kept low.

A unified licensing system could be established for all health professionals and institutions both in the public and private sector (including NGOs) in the medium term. The MOH, in collaboration with professional associations, should be responsible for monitoring the quality and efficiency of services using consistent and transparent indicators. Wide publication of such indicators could provide information to help the market evaluate performance and make choices that stimulate quality-based competition among various providers. Collection of such transparent indicators and client surveys could help to professionalize NGOs by introducing objective performance-based measures. Investigative journalism and public citizen policing may be among the least costly and most effective enforcement instruments to ensure accountability.

Paying for Health Services

Estimates of the total expenditure on health range between 8 to 9 percent of GDP, or a little less than $100 per capita per year. In 1996, MOH expenditure accounted for about one-third of total health expenditure. Direct household expenditure accounted for about 40 percent. MOH's 1996 revenues were derived from the general tax revenues (63 percent), Government Health Insurance Scheme (27 percent) and co-payment and fees collected at facilities (10 percent).

The relative importance of insurance premiums to MOH expenditure has declined. This is largely related to the PA decision to lower premium levels significantly to encourage expansion of insurance coverage. Coverage increased from

20 percent in 1993 to 50 percent in 1996. Although enrollment rates have increased overall, certain categories such as contributions from workers in Israel have declined (Table 12.4). The resulting shortfall has been increasingly covered by PA general revenue. Given the worsening economic situation and rising unemployment, it is unlikely that total revenues from the health insurance program will rise significantly. Thus, any increasing recurrent costs related to expansion of the system would need to be covered by increasing general revenue allocations to the MOH.

*Table 12.4 Changes in the Cases Enrolled in Government Health
Insurance Scheme (1994-95)*

Category	Gaza Strip			West Bank		
	Jan. 1994	Dec. 1995	% change	Jan. 1994	May 1996	% change
Voluntary	9,000	18,624	107%	8,000	18,228	128%
Government Employees	8,000	17,748	122%	16,000	25,464	59%
Workers in Israel	23,000	16,000	-30%	46,000	10,376	-77%
Police Officers	0	18,000		0		
Social Welfare Cases	12,000	15,109	26%	12,000	15,123	26%
Ex-Prisoners	0	0		0	6,782	
Total	52,000	85,481	64%	82,000	75,973	-7%

Sources: Israeli Ministry of Health (1994); Palestinian MOH (1996a, 1996b); and information from Health Insurance Department.

Presently, the Government Health Insurance Scheme functions essentially as an earmarked tax-collection mechanism for health services (all funds collected are transferred to MOF) to supplement the general revenues. Other essential functions of an insurance agency or a third-party payer (such as contracting services with providers; designing, costing and evaluating benefits packages for the covered population; and fund management) are performed, to a limited extent, by various departments and committees within the MOH. Thus, linkages between revenue collection and resource allocation decisions appear to be relatively weak.

Certain groups, such as non-refugee poor or uninsured families, are facing greater financial difficulties in accessing health care. The existing insurance system is likely to present certain major obstacles to expanding coverage, maintaining solidarity, and protecting access for the poor. They include (i) the relatively low ceiling on monthly insurance premium payments ($22), which establishes a regressive system of revenue collection and limits the contributions from the well-to-do; (ii) the voluntary nature of participation in the social insurance system that allows the well-to-do and low-risk population groups to "opt out" of the system; and (iii) the high unemployment rate. The MOH requires better information on the characteristics of the insured and uninsured population in order to evaluate the redistribution effects of its financial policies. For example, at present there is no analysis available on the socio-economic profile of the uninsured population. Private insurance appears to be limited to richer Palestinians, with less than 2 percent of population covered.

Controlling Costs

Controlling the cost of the health care system is critical given the rapidly increasing demand for expensive health services. There are three broad areas of concern: (i) expenditure on pharmaceuticals is rapidly rising; (ii) expansion of hospital facilities and advanced medical technology may result in significant long-run recurrent operating costs; and (iii) limiting expensive treatment abroad, especially in Israeli hospitals, in favor of building the local capacity.

In examining the MOH expenditure categories, about 21.5 percent of total expenditure is spent on drugs and medication. Pharmaceuticals account for 36 percent of total health expenditure, as private providers rely excessively on prescribing drugs. To rationalize overall health expenditure, major pharmaceutical reform is essential, such as introducing standard protocols or essential drug lists.

The current hospital bed to population ratio is 1.2 per 1,000 in the WBGS (including East Jerusalem), for a total of 3,127 beds. There are plans for constructing new hospitals in Jericho, Nablus, and the Gaza Strip. Expanding existing hospitals (with donor assistance) would increase the number of beds by at least 1,190 for a total of 4,317, resulting in a ratio of 1.7 beds per 1,000. This expansion should reduce the cost of treatment abroad. However, at current operational costs and without improved quality, the expansion in hospital bed capacity will substantially increase operating costs by up to $19 million per annum (almost 20 percent of MOH's 1996 expenditure) according to one estimate.

The cost of patient treatment abroad must also be controlled. The MOH paid $14.1 million for treatment abroad in 1995, accounting for 18.2 percent of total MOH recurrent expenditure. Half the cases were referred to Al-Makassed Hospital in Jerusalem in 1995 and an additional number of cases were referred to the PRCS hospital in Cairo and the Arab Heart Surgical Center in Amman. The bulk of expenditure went to Israeli hospitals. Expenditure at the Israeli Hadassah Hospital amounted to $10.1 million or 71 percent of all expenditure on treatment abroad.

Impact of Closures on Palestinian Health System

The difficulties in movement resulting from permit and closure policies create challenges for managing and delivering health services. The training of health care professionals is undermined and training costs increase, as health professionals cannot easily move between the two regions. Communication between staff of the MOH in the Gaza Strip and the West Bank is difficult at best, which creates obstacles for devising the right policies for the whole Palestinian economy.

The most dramatic impact of the permit policy is the difficulty for Palestinians to access NGO hospitals in East Jerusalem. There are four Palestinian hospitals in East Jerusalem, with 546 beds, that provide essential secondary services. Al-Makassed Hospital is the main teaching hospital and the only tertiary-level hospital for Palestinians. Sixty percent of its patients are from the RWB. It provides services that are not available in other hospitals such as plastic and cardiothoracic surgery, and employs some of the most experienced medical staff. St. John's Hospital is the only ophthalmic hospital for West Bank residents and 85 percent of its patients come from the RWB. For the last 28 years, Augusta Victoria Hospital has been the main secondary health care facility for the refugee population of the West Bank. Problems such as serious burns, oncology problems, cardiovascular surgical problems, and pediatric surgical problems can only be treated at the Palestinian hospitals in East Jerusalem or at Israeli hospitals. West Bank medical staff of Jerusalem hospitals and RWBGS patients may be issued special permits to report to the Jerusalem medical facility. These permits are for a short duration, with uncertain renewability, and may not necessarily be issued for patients (see Box 4.1 in Chapter 4).

During closure, the entry of WBGS medical staff to Jerusalem is much more uncertain even with the proper Israeli-issued permits. Sometimes, medical staff may be allowed to enter but without their vehicles. The entry of patients is even more difficult. This places the health needs of the WBGS population at great risk. Bed occupancy and the number of outpatients decline substantially during closures, causing financial losses to these hospitals.

The separation between the West Bank and Gaza Strip, and difficult access to Jerusalem is likely to result in the proliferation of new hospitals and medical facilities throughout the RWBGS. This raises questions about the overall efficiency of delivering health care services by numerous small units. Hospital expansion is likely to have a negative impact on the financial viability of the Jerusalem hospitals that have served the Palestinians for decades. The evolving strategy for the health care system must weigh in economic terms the cost of irreversible investment that is built on the assumption of lack of access.

* * *

The WBGS health sector is rich in its diversity and institutional structure. Yet, this structure is facing serious challenges that should be addressed in a comprehensive framework. The NGO health providers have expanded the delivery system and satisfied many important needs. The Jerusalem hospitals have served the Palestinians when investment in expensive new hospitals for the RWBGS would not find funding or permission from the ICA. Yet, both the primary care NGO clinics and the Jerusalem hospitals are marginalized in the new environment, but for different reasons. The strengthening of government's role in delivering health services is essential, and it only makes economic sense for the for-profit private sector to increase its role in delivering health care. Yet, there is a danger in the new environment that some of the fundamental achievements of the Palestinian health system would be reversed. To preserve and strengthen existing health levels, it is essential to improve the overall governance of the health care system and ensure its financial sustainability.

Bibliographic Note: This chapter draws extensively on the background paper by Barghouthi and Lennock (1996), and information from World Bank (1993, 1996d, 1997) and PCBS (1996a and 1996b).

Chapter 13

Infrastructure for Growth

Ashoka Mody

Introduction

Compared to other countries at similar levels of income, the provision of infrastructure services is seriously deficient in the WBGS. In the 1990s, there has been virtually no expansion of infrastructure services. It has fallen behind in per capita terms. Years of neglect and under-investment have resulted in an inadequate and unreliable infrastructure. Large parts of the infrastructure stock are unused because of system losses or disrepair. The quality of services is poor and deteriorating. The provision of infrastructure and hence its prospects continue to be predominantly in Israeli hands.

A necessary, but modest, effort at rehabilitating the infrastructure began in 1993. But in 1995 and 1996, infrastructure investment amounted to only $50 to $60 million annually, translating to less than 2 percent of GDP. On average, developing countries invest 4 percent of GDP in infrastructure, with a high of 6 to 8 percent of GDP in rapidly growing economies. Clearly, the present levels are low by international standards and if not stepped up, will severely constrain economic growth. This chapter discusses infrastructure needs in transportation, electricity, communications, and water, along with some of the principles that should guide the development of these sectors.

Palestinian Infrastructure in an International Perspective

Transport

The WBGS road network is just over 2,000 km in length, with 750 km of main roads, 550 km of regional roads, and 850 km of local roads. Virtually all the major roads were constructed before 1967 and have received minimal or no maintenance. International transportation (ports and airports) are almost entirely under Israeli control. The exceptions are the bridges to Jordan and the Rafah crossing to Egypt (see Chapter 6).

Electricity

Over 95 percent of households have electricity connections. Those not connected tend to be located in remote communities. However, connection does not necessarily imply an adequate or steady supply of electricity. Presently, the WBGS has access to about 300 Mw of power, almost entirely supplied by the Israel Electric Company (IEC). Certain village communities not connected to the grid use local generators. Per capita supply is significantly lower than for other countries in the region (see Table 1.1 in Chapter 1). Effective supply to consumers is even smaller because of very large system losses that have apparently increased in the past few years as the assets have been allowed to depreciate.

Telecommunications

Restricted access to telecommunications presents a major limitation for growth. With 78,000 phones, there are just over three phones for every 100 persons. Due to the extreme shortage of conventional phones, 25,000 mobile phones are in use (about one mobile phone for 100 persons).

Prior to the peace process, telecommunication services were supplied by the Israeli company, Bezeq, and the ICA controlled the local access to service. Since 1993, the local loop is controlled by the PA's Ministry of Communications. However, most long-distance services, even within the Palestinian areas, and all international services, continue to be provided by Bezeq. The lack of phones is already proving a constraint to investment. In Ramallah, obtaining a phone connection is a major undertaking and has deterred investors. In Gaza City, the most modern hotel was operating with one phone line as of August 1996. If the vision of an information society is to be seriously pursued, and if trade in services is to take off, basic phone service needs a major boost.

Water

Over 90 percent of households are connected to a water supply, but the volume of the supply has been declining over the 1990s. Water consumption per head is much lower than in neighboring countries (less than 90 liters per capita per day in the WBGS compared to 140 and 280 liters in Jordan and Israel, respectively). Water quality has been steadily deteriorating. With depleting aquifers, seawater seepage in the Gaza Strip has rendered the water brackish. The entry of sewage, fertilizers, and other chemicals into the water system continually damages the water quality Water supply is substantially, and increasingly, dependent upon the Israeli company, Mekoroth, though not quite to the same extent as electricity. Israel restricts the digging of new wells by Palestinians. New sources within the WBGS can be tapped by Mekoroth, which then supplies distributors in the Palestinian areas. For example, in 1974 the Jerusalem Water Undertaking purchased virtually no water and produced about 1.3 MCM of water. By 1994, purchased water amounted to 5.0 MCM, almost all from Mekoroth, while water production had gone up to 2.6 MCM.

Sanitation

The most serious immediate problem is the state of sanitation services. The share of households connected to sewage networks is small by any standard, at 25 percent. Collection, treatment, and disposal of sewage are growing problems. The networks, where they exist, are under great strain and are liable to burst frequently, risking people's health and causing severe disruption to the movement of goods and people as roads are flooded.

Beyond Rehabilitation: Strategic Investments and Sector Organization

Since rehabilitation has such high economic returns, efforts to restore existing infrastructure stocks must be a part of any long-term strategy for infrastructure development. As emergency restoration is brought to a close and normal operations resume, the present rehabilitation would convert into routine but essential maintenance, which has similarly high economic returns.

Effort must begin, in parallel, to undertake new investments. On average, developing countries spend 4 percent of GDP on basic infrastructure investments (transportation, electricity, communications, and water). This is over and above the regular maintenance expenditures. In the rapidly growing East Asian economies infrastructure investments of 6 to 8 percent of GDP have been common. If the average for developing countries is accepted as the target for ongoing infrastructure investments in the WBGS, and if an additional one percent of GDP is allocated to continued rehabilitation to make up for past neglect, then infrastructure investments (between 4 and 5 percent of GDP) would need to rise to between $140 and $175 million a year. Such expenditures, while reasonable for most economies, would represent a quantum leap from the current level of $50 to $60 million.

To prioritize the investments, special features of the WBGS and its vision of economic development need to be taken into account.

- The relatively small size of the economy makes it heavily dependent on international commerce. The historical and religious significance of the region makes it a major tourist attraction. As a consequence, trade and tourism are likely to be dominant economic activities. Moving goods and people within the territories requires a network of roads and moving across international borders requires land, sea, and air links (see Chapter 6).
- WBGS is heavily dependent on Israel for infrastructure services. Diversifying the sources of services, through internal development and by creating the ability to purchase them from other countries in the region, will permit cheaper and more reliable services in the long run. Certain internal investments may appear sub-optimal when viewed by themselves. However, diversification benefits not only the WBGS but also Israel as the multi-sourcing capability can reduce the huge transactions costs associated with bilateral negotiations on mechanisms of delivery.
- An unusually high level of human capital could be leveraged by using modern information technologies. Such technologies would not only support domestic transactions, but also would enhance international linkages and develop trade in a variety of services.

• A chronic water shortage is aggravated by a growing population and rising incomes. Waste water transport, collection, treatment, and disposal require substantial new investments.

An efficient strategy would be to move from more modest to more ambitious investments. Infrastructure investments are sometimes thought to give the "big push" to accelerate growth. Not only is that strategy often wasteful, but the resources simply do not exist to implement any grandiose plans.

Transport: Moving Goods and People

Linking the Gaza Strip and West Bank with a "Safe Passageway"

The economies of the Gaza Strip and West Bank are almost completely disassociated due to the lack of transportation links. For many Palestinian policy makers a passageway has the highest priority among transportation projects. While the Declaration of Principles requires the establishment of safe passage of persons and transportation, no progress has been made on implementation despite its urgency. Discussions about possible options have drifted over the past few years. An early feasibility study is required of the various options floated. Should the connection be elevated or not as it passes through Israeli territory? Should it be a motorway or a high-speed rail? What should be the connection points on both sides? Other questions of a contractual nature have been raised. Will ownership of the passageway be Israeli because it passes over Israeli territory? Should its management be in private hands, possibly with a joint Palestinian-Israeli company? What security mechanisms would be acceptable to minimize the risk of closure disruptions? While this project is under discussion, safe passage for authorized persons and vehicles through existing, heavily secured Israeli roads is likely to be permitted.

Mobility within the WBGS

Under the Emergency Assistance Program, road rehabilitation was initiated and is expected to continue for the coming years. The focus of the rehabilitation has been on internal village roads and rural access roads. Inter-urban road rehabilitation and investment are only beginning.

Planning for inter-urban roads within the West Bank is conditioned by the guidelines established by the Oslo II Agreement. Under the Interim Agreement, zone A is under the political jurisdiction and security control of the PA. In zone B, the PA has administrative jurisdiction but security control is in the hands of Israeli authorities. In zone C, which is presently the large bulk of the land area, Israeli authorities have both administrative and security control. For this reason, early efforts have been devoted to rehabilitating roads within areas of Palestinian control, focusing on internal village and rural access roads. Planning for inter-urban transportation requires a level of coordination between the Palestinian and Israeli authorities that has not yet materialized.

The Interim Agreement also contains a "principle of graduality," which requires the periodic transfer of areas from zone B to zone A and from zone C to zone B until full Palestinian authority—final status—is achieved. This mechanism and the associated forums could be used to determine coordination procedures on a West Bank road network that would permit the PA to commence serious network planning. Candidate projects include (i) reinforcing and broadening from one to two lanes a 136-km north-south link connecting the cities of Nablus, Ramallah, Jerusalem, Bethlehem, and Hebron; and (ii) an east-west link from the Israeli border, passing through Tulkarem and Nablus to Jordan across the Damiah Bridge.

Electricity: Powering Homes and Businesses

Evidence indicates that electricity consumption is low relative to income levels and has apparently been falling. To fulfill a large demand from businesses and households for efficient, secure, and reliable electricity networks, a progressive strategy is required to

- restore existing distribution networks;
- construct new networks to support the development of regional distribution utilities;
- build new transmission networks linking the regions, and an associated dispatch capacity;
- build new generation capacity; and
- invest in international interconnections.

An institutional strategy is required to underpin these investment plans. In keeping with modern trends, the sector needs to be "unbundled" into the distribution, transmission, and generation segments.

Virtually all power consumed in the WBGS is supplied by the IEC. In the Gaza Strip, the power is supplied to the Palestinian Electricity Authority (PEA), which is responsible for distributing the electricity. In the West Bank, the IEC negotiates power supply with individual municipalities, except in the case of the Jerusalem Electricity Distribution Company (JEDCo.), a shareholder-owned utility, which serves Jerusalem, Jericho, Bethlehem, Ramallah, and Al Bireh. Power is supplied by the IEC at a flat rate of about $0.07 per kilowatt-hour. This steep rate reflects the technical complexity of supply to small, dispersed communities and reveals the weak bargaining position of the Palestinians, who have virtually no alternatives.

With rapidly growing demand and very limited investments in past years, the investment requirements in the power sector are considerable (Table 13.1). Rehabilitation focused principally on local distribution networks is expected to require upward to $40 million per year for the next three years. Substantial new investments in transmission and generation are required and will need to be spread over the next three to five years.

Table 13.1 Investments in the Power Sector

Project	Description	Estimated Cost
Distribution network rehabilitation	Replace and upgrade substations, introduce automatic regulators, additional switching devices, and new interconnections between locations to optimize supply management	Over three years: Gaza Strip: $30 million West Bank: $100 million Continuing investment thereafter of $30 to $50 million per year
Regional distribution networks	Add new capacity to optimize networks and support: (a) three planned, regional utilities in the north, center, and south of the West Bank and (b) a network for the Gaza Strip	Gaza Strip: $50 million West Bank: $100 million
National transmission capacity	Capacity to link and dispatch power sources to regional distribution networks	$150 million
Independent power generation	New generation capacity	Gaza Strip: $250 million West Bank: (still a concept) $400 million (estimate)
International interconnections	Egypt-Gaza Strip Gaza Strip–East Jerusalem–Hebron West Bank–Jordan	$150 million

Sources: PEA (1996) and PA (1995).

Distribution: Rehabilitation and Investment through Regional Utilities

The PEA estimates the immediate rehabilitation needs of the distribution system at $100 million in the West Bank and $30 million in the Gaza Strip. The distribution networks have been managed by the municipalities, and assets have deteriorated over time. New substations are required in the Nablus, Hebron, and JEDCo. areas, and various substations need to be upgraded. In addition, automatic voltage regulation to prevent large drops in voltage is needed. New interconnections within the existing jurisdictions are required to manage distribution more efficiently. As with roads, such rehabilitation would need to convert to ongoing, regular maintenance to prevent future asset depreciation.

Presently, the electricity network is designed principally to receive power from Israel. Power at low voltage is supplied to individual municipalities, resulting in substantial system losses. The municipalities are technically isolated from each other, so effective load management is not possible. Consolidating municipalities into regional utilities will permit greater technical efficiencies and increase administrative and managerial efficiency. Moreover, utilities of a certain critical size are much more likely to attract private investments than are small municipal networks.

Based on geographical conditions and demand projections, one proposal suggests creating one utility for the Gaza Strip and three West Bank "regional" utilities in the north, center, and south. These utilities would be responsible for sourcing electricity, dispatching and transmitting, and distribution to households and businesses. Such utilities would require constructing new transmission facilities to link the principal locations in their respective regions. This will require the right-of-way to lay the lines. As with the development of the road network, obtaining and establishing the rights-of-way will require Israeli permission to cross zonal boundaries within the West Bank.

The challenge ahead lies in managing the interests of municipal governments, for whom electric power distribution has been a lucrative business in the past. These interests could be met by making the municipalities shareholders in their utility, along with rotating the membership of the utility's board. Once such a structure is in place, and when an independent, commercially operated distribution utility becomes a reasonable prospect, then private investment will become attractive. Strategic private investment by an internationally experienced operator combined with public shareholding should be possible to implement.

Transmission and Dispatch

A national grid will be required to link various power sources of the IEC to independent power generators in the WBGS, and to receive power from international interconnections. The manager of the grid will ensure that power is efficiently distributed according to prevailing supply and demand conditions at particular times in the day. A Palestinian Grid Company—possibly under private ownership—will be required to undertake the necessary investments and manage transmission and dispatch operations.

Power Generation Capacity

Should a small economy such as that of the WBGS invest in its own power generation capacity? Is the demand large enough to support an efficiently sized plant? The numbers suggest a positive answer. The WBGS has access to about 300 Mw of power through the IEC in Israel. A study by the consulting firm, Kennedy and Donkin, shows a huge potential demand, which is evident even from the basic figures presented in Table 1.1 in Chapter 1. If power consumption in the WBGS is to reach Egyptian levels in per capita terms, generation capacity would increase to 450 Mw. Hence, an extra 150 Mw could be used immediately. Population and income growth over the next five years will likely require 250 Mw or more of added capacity, if peace allows rapid growth.

A reasonable strategy appears to be one of procuring power from multiple sources. The supplies from the IEC will continue, though at lower levels. New generating capacity should be created within the WBGS. In the longer term, interconnections to networks in Egypt and Jordan could provide an extra source of power. Links to other sources could increase the efficiency with which capacity is used and, equally importantly, create a measure of competition between the different sources, allowing the Palestinians to procure power at lower costs.

The PEA presently is negotiating the development of a power generating plant in the Gaza Strip under a 20-year build-operate-transfer contract with a private sponsor. In the first phase, two gas turbines of 40 Mw each will provide 80 Mw of power. These will be augmented with additional gas turbines and a steam turbine to create a combined-cycle, 215-Mw plant. The goal was to have the first phase completed by February 1997 and the second phase by March 1998.

Contract negotiations for the Gaza power plant are still underway. The present state of discussions, however, indicate some noteworthy features. First, the cost of the power is to be $0.047 per kilowatt-hour, compared to $0.07 paid to the IEC. If realized, the price of power compares favorably with the power being procured in the Philippines, which has the most extensive private power program in the developing world. Second, a more intriguing feature of the contract is the lack of a commitment to buy the full (or substantial) capacity of the plant. All private power contracts in developing countries have the so-called "take-or-pay" feature—or more accurately, the "take-or-pay anyway" requirement. Private sponsors and lenders require a commitment that even if the power is not required, payment will be made to pay back the lenders and provide some equity return. For the Gaza plant, the take-or-pay requirement does not presently exist, allowing for the possibility that no payment need be made if the power is not needed. Furthermore, it is likely that the private sponsors will be able to sell excess capacity to the IEC.

Two hurdles need to be crossed before the Gaza power plant is a reality. First, permission is required from Israeli authorities for the construction of the plant. Second, as in other countries, the government has taken on the obligation of providing the sponsors with the land. The chosen site of the plant, near the proposed Gaza port, is private property and cash compensation would make the costs prohibitive. It is expected that the owners of the preferred site would be compensated with government land of equal value.

International Interconnections

Interconnections of networks in Egypt, the Gaza Strip, Israel, the West Bank, and Jordan are expected to bring significant benefits, which include

- the capacity to exchange power on a daily, weekly, monthly, or seasonal basis because of different load patterns in different areas, thereby reducing overall demand for reserves and hence generation capacity;
- the consumer benefits from greater continuity in services (reduced load shedding) and the ability to recover more rapidly from disturbances to the network; and
- greater interconnection, for technical reasons, which reduces network losses.

Interconnections linking the WBGS to Israel, Egypt, and Jordan are still at an early stage of conceptualization. While a *prima facie* case exists for the interconnections, detailed technical planning, identifying sites for interconnection, and performing feasibility studies of alternative options are required. But obtaining the right-of-way is of critical importance. The Gaza Strip-West Bank link could, in principle, use the same right-of-way as the safe passageway. Once established, this interconnected network could further integrate into more ambitious schemes planned for the Middle East.

Telecommunications

The fundamental requirement for an information economy is a substantial and efficiently functioning telecommunications network. It is often tempting to compare the WBGS with Singapore and Hong Kong, as model small economies, based on international trade and investment, and supported by a world-class communications infrastructure. While that vision is presently a distant one, an immediately relevant lesson is the need to invest in modern telecommunications. Once in place, several creative opportunities that build on such a network are likely to arise, with little or no government involvement. Since telecommunications is extremely attractive to private investors, the PA's primary objective should be to ensure efficient new entry by multiple providers.

The economics of telecommunication networks is quite different for the local loop, domestic long-distance services, and international services. Beyond this basic network is an overlay of services that typically requires additional investment in hardware and software.

Until the mid-1980s, the entire communications network was regarded as a "natural monopoly" and hence thought to be best provided by a single operator. The advent of wireless technologies (permitting transmission using microwaves, radio waves, and satellites) has led to increased competition in both long-distance and international communications.

The local loop has remained a monopoly in most countries, but the trend is toward increasing competition. Even in the local loop competition can occur because radio-based technologies and cable networks offer an alternative conduit. Most importantly, regulators are no longer able to keep pace with changing technologies and the innovative opportunities they offer. As a consequence, a policy of open entry to all segments of the network (with due vigilance for preventing fly-by-night operators) is increasingly becoming the benchmark.

Infrastructure investments must be guided by the vision of an open network, where a *prima facie* basis exists for allowing all new entrants to establish new networks or lease lines to provide services. Only then would it be possible for the WBGS to exploit the several new opportunities afforded by international developments in technologies and organizational structures. In particular, links to international consortia offering global services will provide alternative channels to the rest of the world, reducing the dependence on Israel.

There are two hurdles for achieving rapid telecommunications expansion. Early resolution of these considerations must be a priority for peace negotiators and Palestinian policy makers. First, all policy options are directly or indirectly constrained by Israeli regulations. Even domestic long-distance services are provided by Bezeq. For international services, Bezeq provides the only gateway, on onerous terms. For any progress, and especially to attract private, competitive suppliers, greater operational flexibility and choices will be required. Second, a certain degree of confusion presently prevails on the policy of new entry into the sector. While telecommunications legislation appears to provide the openness required, discussions are ongoing to award an exclusive franchise to a single company for a 10-year period (with a non-exclusive franchise for an additional 15 years). The lack of clarity in this regard is damaging not only for urgently needed investment in the sector, but also may ultimately have wider adverse implications. The private company expecting to receive the exclusive license, Paltel, has raised $70 million through a public share offering, but does not yet have the license to operate.

Water: A History of Shortage

The scarcest resource, and one for which there are the fewest immediate solutions, is water. Sources of water supply are under Israeli control and the development of new supplies requires extensive negotiations. As a consequence, dependence on Israeli sources, principally through Mekoroth, is high and increasing.

The Palestinian Water Authority (PWA) has been established to determine strategy and policy in the sector. Since any discussion of the basic problem of long-term water supply appears to be on hold, PWA's focus has been on (i) continued rehabilitation of existing networks; (ii) restoring management capacity to deliver water through an innovative management contract for water supply in the Gaza Strip; (iii) laying the basis for creating regional water utilities, parallel to regional electric utilities; (iv) planning modest desalination plants; and (v) planning and implementing investments in sewage collection and treatment.

As in other sectors, rehabilitation needs are enormous. Some rehabilitation has occurred under existing programs and will continue under multilateral initiatives (such as the World Bank-coordinated Municipal Development Project) and with bilateral assistance. The rates of return to such rehabilitation are estimated to be very large.

The institutional structure to channel these expenditures and future investments is being considered. A step in that direction is the amalgamation of municipal authority to deliver water and sanitation services in the Gaza Strip. A management contract has been awarded to an international operator for a four-year period, during which time significant new capacity is expected to be built, both in physical distribution and managerial strengths. The contract was awarded through an international competitive bidding process with payment linked to performance, which imposes tight incentives on the contractor.

The consolidation of municipal authorities into regional utilities is planned for the West Bank (as with electric power) for the north, center, and south. The economic logic for such consolidation is the same as for the electric power sector. A similar institutional structure that makes the municipalities shareholders and board members is being proposed.

New planned investments include small desalination plants in the Gaza Strip, where brackish water needs to be rendered potable. The major new investments will likely occur not in water supply but in waste water and sewage treatment, where they are urgently needed. Over the next three to five years, these investments could amount to a few hundred million dollars.

Regulating Private Infrastructure

The entire Palestinian commonwealth and a global network of private sector investors are available to provide the raw materials for new partnerships that can enable growth. Global trends indicate that private actors can get into increasingly broader fields of public interest if the proper regulatory system can be put in place. Efficient governance systems of this sort are decentralized, with an emphasis on competitively contracting out infrastructure to private companies and non-government citizen groups. The provision of public goods is safeguarded by mechanisms that foster accountability and contested markets.

Infrastructure partnerships consist of users and providers of services where users can exercise varying degrees of voice or exit. Many OECD countries have recently corporatized, privatized, or simulated market dynamics for core government activities through the funder-provider models. In New Zealand, most central services have been eliminated as the public sector competitively bids out government agencies as business units. For example, road construction was outsourced by the Ministry of Transportation with compensation tied to performance. In Laos, a weak public sector limited its role to steward and regulator, working in partnership with the private sector.

In the absence of full-blown regulatory agencies, a mature legislature, or an independent judiciary, client surveys provide sound regulatory and enforcement mechanisms. They can introduce information and accountability mechanisms to help government regulate private-public utilities and quasi-public NGOs. Simulated market mechanisms, which can help to ensure peak performance and fair pricing despite monopoly conditions, include renewing contract bids every several years, performance evaluation through user surveys, referendums with broadly published findings, establishing price caps that are readjusted over time, and enacting various commissions to assure quality control relative to health and environmental standards. One or two start-up pilot projects of this nature could begin to introduce these lessons within well-defined areas, such as power generation, telecommunications, water supply, and perhaps later in the social services domain. With the right incentives, the governance framework can improve regulation and enforcement.

The increasingly popular method to ensure fair pricing in monopoly conditions is price caps. Instead of restricting the rate of return of a provider with market power, prices are capped at a pre-specified level based upon a study of cost accounting, pricing, and willingness to pay. Where prices are capped, the provider has the incentive to operate as efficiently as possible. In practice, periodic revisions in the level of the cap require a measurement of the rate of return to the provider.

Among the important and precedent-setting initiatives of the past three years has been the harnessing of private enterprise for public utility provision, such as the PEA's effort to negotiate a 20-year build-operate-transfer contract with a private sponsor for the Gaza power generating plant. One of its noteworthy features is the reduced cost of power generation.

The challenge of price regulation, however, will increase over time. For many sectors, including telecommunications and electric power, the basic determination of tariff structures needs to be undertaken. The benefits of an umbrella structure, such as a US-style regulatory commission, are worth considering. The commission would serve two functions. It would establish common principles of regulation across sectors and insulate the regulatory process from political interference. Political insulation occurs as the commissioners, appointed for fixed terms, are responsible ultimately to the legislature.

Beyond this, institutional innovations and mechanisms need to be conceived and put in place for planning, regulation, project implementation, and coordination. Some economies may be realized by coordinating the activities of regional electricity and water utilities. There are likely to be economies in joint billing and collection, saving both on software development and collections costs as well as in joint network planning, such as laying of pipes and cables, and maintenance. Creating incentives for performance, which is already being adopted for the Gaza Strip bulk water supply management contract, ties compensation to performance. But most municipalities do not know the maintenance and asset depreciation costs they incur. The scarcity factor in the supply of water is an even more refined concept that plays no role in current pricing.

*   *   *

While significant opportunities exist for growth, so do many challenges. In 1995, a program of much needed infrastructure rehabilitation did commence, but only at a level of 1 to 2 percent of the GDP. To compensate for years of asset depreciation and to meet the needs of future growth, a significant increase in infrastructure investment is needed to reach the average for developing countries—about 4 percent of GDP.

The key challenge will be to build increasingly sophisticated institutions to ensure efficient investment in infrastructure. Building institutional capacity will require coordinating the activities of agencies and ministries with overlapping jurisdiction—an inevitable necessity in complex infrastructure projects. A lack of coordination among donors is liable to create sub-optimal investments while fostering divisions within the PA. The financial role of the PA and donors will need to evolve from full responsibility to being a catalyst. Related challenges include the ability to negotiate contracts with the private sector in a transparent manner, diversifying the sources of infrastructure services, and measuring the impact of stepped-up investments on the environment. Since few options exist to mitigate external hazards, additional instruments such as shared guarantees that distribute risk among donors may be effective in obtaining acceptable levels of risk for investors and commercial bankers. The initial steps have been made and significant international experience exists from which Palestinian policy makers can draw.

Infrastructure development, economic growth, and the peace process can powerfully reinforce each other. The ability to expand infrastructure is conditioned by the continued legacy of Israeli occupation. While the easing of this legacy and its associated restraints is permitting some new investment, further relaxation of the limitations needs to occur to stimulate growth.

Bibliographic Note: The chapter is based on Mody (1995). It also used information from Lahmeyer International and Verbund-Plan (1995), World Bank (1994c); International Yearbooks of Telecommunications Statistics, Electricity Statistics, Road Statistics; and the KPMG report on telecommunications.

Annex

Contents

Table A.1 *Production*

West Bank and Gaza Strip

in millions of US$	1980	1981	1982	1983	1984	1985	1986	1987	1988	1989	1990	1991	1992	1993
GDP at market prices	1 249	1 157	1 219	1 283	1 225	1 161	1 788	1 991	1 828	1 859	2 238	2 161	2 686	2 557
GDP at factor costs	1 058	948	1 009	1 042	989	945	1 544	1 703	1 826	1 720	2 126	2 011	2 449	2 521
Agriculture	312	279	264	244	184	188	475	317	520	347	449	328	477	344
Construction	191	172	186	200	175	161	247	310	295	295	334	312	406	411
Industry	78	69	73	81	77	76	129	156	146	137	167	174	211	215
Public service community	171	153	160	188	205	165	183	214	218	233	272	286	297	302
Others	307	274	326	330	347	356	509	706	648	708	904	910	1,058	1,248
GDP at factor costs (%)	1.00	1.00	1.00	1.00	1.00	1.00	1.00	1.00	1.00	1.00	1.00	1.00	1.00	1.00
Agriculture	0.29	0.29	0.26	0.23	0.19	0.20	0.31	0.19	0.28	0.20	0.21	0.16	0.19	0.14
Construction	0.18	0.18	0.18	0.19	0.18	0.17	0.16	0.18	0.16	0.17	0.16	0.16	0.17	0.16
Industry	0.07	0.07	0.07	0.08	0.08	0.08	0.08	0.09	0.08	0.08	0.08	0.09	0.09	0.09
Public service community	0.16	0.16	0.16	0.18	0.21	0.17	0.12	0.13	0.12	0.14	0.13	0.14	0.12	0.12
Others	0.29	0.29	0.32	0.32	0.35	0.38	0.33	0.41	0.35	0.41	0.43	0.45	0.43	0.50
Net factor income	242	274	311	389	343	227	354	523	675	663	769	708	898	552
GNP at market prices	1 491	1 431	1 530	1 673	1 568	1 388	2 143	2 514	2 503	2 522	3 007	2 869	3 584	3 109
Memo items														
Share of GDP/GNP	0.84	0.81	0.80	0.77	0.78	0.84	0.83	0.79	0.73	0.74	0.74	0.75	0.75	0.82
GDP per capita (in US$)	1 045	951	981	999	925	851	1 271	1 363	1 208	1 193	1 367	1 252	1 477	1 345
GNP per capita (in US$)	1 247	1 177	1 231	1 302	1 185	1 017	1 523	1 721	1 654	1 618	1 837	1 662	1 970	1 636

(table continues on next page)

(Table A.I continues)

Gaza Strip

in millions of US$	1980	1981	1982	1983	1984	1985	1986	1987	1988	1989	1990	1991	1992	1993
GNP at market prices	439	492	494	574	494	415	590	788	663	763	882	872	990	907
GDP at market prices	332	365	357	390	333	319	429	553	399	544	589	603	691	726
GDP at factor costs (%)	1.00	1.00	1.00	1.00	1.00	1.00	1.00	1.00	1.00	1.00	1.00	1.00	1.00	1.00
Agriculture	0.21	0.20	0.16	0.16	0.14	0.19	0.21	0.18	0.20	0.18	0.18	0.18	0.16	0.14
Construction	0.23	0.23	0.23	0.23	0.22	0.19	0.22	0.22	0.23	0.22	0.19	0.18	0.21	0.22
Industry	0.09	0.09	0.09	0.10	0.10	0.09	0.11	0.14	0.11	0.11	0.12	0.13	0.12	0.12
Public service community	0.22	0.22	0.23	0.25	0.31	0.28	0.21	0.20	0.22	0.22	0.23	0.23	0.21	0.20
Others	0.26	0.26	0.28	0.26	0.23	0.25	0.26	0.27	0.24	0.27	0.28	0.28	0.29	0.31
GDP per capita (in US$)	711	760	730	770	636	588	764	948	657	862	884	858	925	922
GNP per capita (in US$)	940	1 024	1 010	1 131	943	766	1 052	1 352	1 091	1 209	1 324	1 241	1 325	1 152

West Bank

in millions of US$	1980	1981	1982	1983	1984	1985	1986	1987	1988	1989	1990	1991	1992	1993
GNP at market prices	1 052	939	1 036	1 099	1 074	973	1 553	1 726	1 840	1 759	2 125	1 997	2 594	2 202
GDP at market prices	917	792	862	893	892	843	1 360	1 438	1 429	1 315	1 649	1 558	1 995	1 831
GDP at factor costs (%)	1.00	1.00	1.00	1.00	1.00	1.00	1.00	1.00	1.00	1.00	1.00	1.00	1.00	1.00
Agriculture	0.34	0.34	0.30	0.26	0.20	0.20	0.34	0.19	0.31	0.21	0.22	0.16	0.21	0.13
Construction	0.16	0.16	0.17	0.17	0.16	0.16	0.14	0.17	0.14	0.15	0.14	0.15	0.15	0.14
Industry	0.07	0.07	0.07	0.07	0.07	0.08	0.08	0.08	0.07	0.07	0.06	0.07	0.07	0.07
Public service community	0.14	0.14	0.13	0.15	0.17	0.14	0.09	0.10	0.09	0.10	0.10	0.11	0.09	0.09
Others	0.30	0.30	0.34	0.34	0.39	0.42	0.35	0.46	0.39	0.47	0.47	0.52	0.48	0.56
GDP per capita (in US$)	1 259	1 076	1 143	1 149	1 115	1 024	1 607	1 639	1 577	1 418	1 698	1 522	1 861	1 644
GNP per capita (in US$)	1 444	1 276	1 373	1 413	1 343	1 183	1 836	1 966	2 031	1 897	2 188	1 951	2 420	1 978

Source: ICBS and World Bank estimates.

Table A.2 Expenditures

West Bank and Gaza Strip

as shares of GDP	1980	1981	1982	1983	1984	1985	1986	1987	1988	1989	1990	1991	1992	1993
Consumption	1.01	1.08	1.03	1.10	1.12	1.14	1.04	1.10	1.17	1.13	1.14	1.25	1.18	1.18
Private	0.91	0.97	0.92	0.97	0.97	1.03	0.96	1.00	1.06	1.02	1.02	1.14	1.08	1.07
Public	0.10	0.11	0.11	0.13	0.14	0.11	0.09	0.10	0.11	0.11	0.11	0.11	0.10	0.11
Investment	0.29	0.26	0.29	0.26	0.25	0.24	0.28	0.27	0.23	0.26	0.27	0.29	0.30	0.24
Private	0.29	0.24	0.24	0.22	0.21	0.22	0.20	0.24	0.16	0.25	0.22	0.27	0.25	0.21
Public	0.00	0.04	0.04	0.04	0.05	0.04	0.03	0.05	0.03	0.02	0.02	0.03	0.03	0.05
Variation stocks	0.00	-0.02	0.01	-0.01	-0.01	-0.02	0.04	-0.01	0.03	-0.01	0.02	-0.02	0.02	-0.02
Resource balance	-0.30	-0.34	-0.32	-0.35	-0.37	-0.38	-0.32	-0.37	-0.40	-0.39	-0.40	-0.54	-0.48	-0.43
Memo item (*Real prices, index base 1980*)														
Private consumption per capita	1.00	1.02	1.03	1.01	1.01	0.98	1.10	1.14	0.98	0.99	1.07	1.12	1.19	1.12

(table continues on next page)

(*Table A.2 continues*)

Gaza Strip

as shares of GDP	1980	1981	1982	1983	1984	1985	1986	1987	1988	1989	1990	1991	1992	1993
Consumption	1.07	1.03	1.06	1.13	1.27	1.33	1.33	1.20	1.57	1.16	1.25	1.38	1.28	1.18
Private	0.94	0.90	0.93	0.99	1.09	1.21	1.22	1.09	1.39	1.02	1.12	1.24	1.16	1.06
Public	0.13	0.13	0.14	0.14	0.18	0.12	0.11	0.11	0.18	0.14	0.14	0.15	0.13	0.12
Investment	0.29	0.32	0.31	0.30	0.30	0.26	0.27	0.29	0.05	0.29	0.26	0.25	0.32	0.32
Private	0.29	0.29	0.28	0.25	0.25	0.23	0.23	0.25	0.00	0.26	0.24	0.23	0.28	0.23
Public	0.00	0.03	0.04	0.04	0.05	0.03	0.04	0.05	0.05	0.03	0.02	0.02	0.04	0.09
Variation stocks	0.00	0.00	0.00	0.00	0.00	0.00	0.00	0.00	0.00	0.00	0.00	0.00	0.00	0.00
Resource balance	-0.36	-0.34	-0.37	-0.42	-0.56	-0.59	-0.59	-0.50	-0.62	-0.45	-0.52	-0.63	-0.60	-0.50
Memo item (*Real prices, index base 1980*)														
Private consumption per capita	1.00	0.99	0.99	0.99	1.01	1.00	1.06	1.10	0.87	0.91	0.93	1.04	1.03	1.05

(*table continues on next page*)

(*Table A.2 continues*)

West Bank

as shares of GDP	1980	1981	1982	1983	1984	1985	1986	1987	1988	1989	1990	1991	1992	1993
Consumption	0.99	1.11	1.02	1.08	1.06	1.07	0.96	1.06	1.06	1.12	1.09	1.21	1.14	1.18
Private	0.90	1.00	0.91	0.96	0.93	0.96	0.87	0.97	0.97	1.02	0.99	1.11	1.05	1.08
Public	0.08	0.11	0.11	0.12	0.13	0.11	0.08	0.10	0.09	0.10	0.10	0.10	0.10	0.10
Investment	0.29	0.23	0.28	0.24	0.24	0.24	0.28	0.26	0.28	0.25	0.27	0.30	0.29	0.21
Private	0.29	0.21	0.22	0.20	0.19	0.22	0.20	0.23	0.21	0.24	0.22	0.29	0.24	0.20
Public	0.00	0.04	0.04	0.05	0.05	0.04	0.03	0.05	0.03	0.02	0.02	0.03	0.03	0.04
Variation stocks	0.00	-0.03	0.02	-0.01	-0.01	-0.02	0.05	-0.02	0.04	-0.01	0.03	-0.03	0.03	-0.02
Resource balance	-0.28	-0.34	-0.30	-0.32	-0.30	-0.31	-0.23	-0.32	-0.34	-0.37	-0.36	-0.50	-0.44	-0.40
Memo item (*Real prices, index base 1980*)														
Private consumption per capita	1.00	1.03	1.04	1.01	1.02	0.98	1.12	1.16	1.04	1.03	1.15	1.17	1.27	1.18

Source: Statistical Abstract of Israel, 1981-94, ICBS.

200

Table A.3 Trade

West Bank and Gaza Strip

in millions of US$	1980	1981	1982	1983	1984	1985	1986	1987	1988	1989	1990	1991	1992	1993
Export of GNFS*	375	436	422	416	318	305	421	439	259	202	278	303	365	245
Merchandises	343	403	391	382	289	272	380	385	209	156	228	246	299	236
Non-factor services	32	33	32	34	29	33	41	54	50	46	50	57	66	9
Import of GNFS	749	829	813	871	770	750	992	1 178	988	929	1 179	1 470	1 647	1 333
Merchandises	665	737	729	785	686	668	890	1 051	676	632	843	1 139	1 232	1 138
Non-factor services	84	92	85	86	84	82	102	127	312	297	336	331	415	195
Resource balance	-374	-393	-391	-455	-452	-445	-571	-740	-729	-727	-901	-1 167	-1 282	-1 088
Trade balance	-321	-334	-338	-403	-397	-396	-510	-666	-467	-476	-615	-893	-933	-902
NFS balance	-53	-59	-53	-51	-55	-50	-61	-74	-262	-251	-286	-274	-349	-186
as shares of GDP														
Export of GNFS	0.30	0.38	0.35	0.32	0.26	0.26	0.24	0.22	0.14	0.11	0.12	0.14	0.14	0.10
Merchandises	0.27	0.35	0.32	0.30	0.24	0.23	0.21	0.19	0.11	0.08	0.10	0.11	0.11	0.09
Non-factor services	0.03	0.03	0.03	0.03	0.02	0.03	0.02	0.03	0.03	0.02	0.02	0.03	0.02	0.00
Import of GNFS	0.60	0.72	0.67	0.68	0.63	0.65	0.55	0.59	0.54	0.50	0.53	0.68	0.61	0.52
Merchandises	0.53	0.64	0.60	0.61	0.56	0.58	0.50	0.53	0.37	0.34	0.38	0.53	0.46	0.45
Non-factor services	0.07	0.08	0.07	0.07	0.07	0.07	0.06	0.06	0.17	0.16	0.15	0.15	0.15	0.08
Resource balance	-0.30	-0.34	-0.32	-0.35	-0.37	-0.38	-0.32	-0.37	-0.40	-0.39	-0.40	-0.54	-0.48	-0.43
Trade balance	-0.26	-0.29	-0.28	-0.31	-0.32	-0.34	-0.29	-0.33	-0.26	-0.26	-0.27	-0.41	-0.35	-0.35
NFS balance	-0.04	-0.05	-0.04	-0.04	-0.04	-0.04	-0.03	-0.04	-0.14	-0.14	-0.13	-0.13	-0.13	-0.07

(table continues on next page)

(*Table A.3 continues*)

Gaza Strip

in millions of US$	1980	1981	1982	1983	1984	1985	1986	1987	1988	1989	1990	1991	1992	1993
Export of GNFS	165	210	202	194	116	119	157	180	88	51	76	96	106	65
Merchandises	154	198	190	181	105	106	140	157	67	31	48	71	77	63
Non-factor services	11	12	12	13	11	13	17	23	21	20	28	25	29	2
Import of GNFS	286	335	335	359	304	307	412	454	337	295	380	478	520	426
Merchandises	261	310	310	332	279	281	378	412	223	200	269	355	366	353
Non-factor services	25	26	25	26	25	25	34	42	114	95	111	123	154	72

West Bank

in millions of US$	1980	1981	1982	1983	1984	1985	1986	1987	1988	1989	1990	1991	1992	1993
Export of GNFS	209	226	220	222	202	186	264	259	171	151	202	207	259	180
Merchandises	189	205	201	201	185	166	240	228	142	125	180	175	222	173
Non-factor services	20	21	20	21	18	19	24	31	29	26	22	32	37	7
Import of GNFS	463	494	478	512	466	443	580	724	651	634	799	992	1127	907
Merchandises	404	428	419	453	407	387	512	639	453	432	574	784	866	785
Non-factor services	60	67	60	59	59	57	68	85	198	202	225	208	261	123

* GNFS = goods and non-factor services
Source: Based on Statistical Abstract of Israel, 1981-94, ICBS.

Table A.4 Income from Abroad

West Bank and Gaza Strip

in millions of US$	1980	1981	1982	1983	1984	1985	1986	1987	1988	1989	1990	1991	1992	1993
Net factor income	242	274	311	389	343	227	354	523	675	663	769	708	898	552
Receipts	372	407	459	560	490	368	526	714	692	682	794	737	930	586
Payments	130	133	149	171	147	141	172	191	17	19	25	29	32	34
Net current transfers	111	112	107	104	93	71	77	128	-64	-54	-21	278	11	14
Receipts	167	174	172	183	165	108	122	188	18	9	3	278	11	14
Payments	56	62	65	79	73	38	45	60	82	63	24	0	0	0
Net capital inflows	-21	-7	26	38	-16	-147	-139	-89	-118	-118	-153	-181	-373	-522
Memo items (NIS/US$)														
Average exchange rate	0.01	0.01	0.02	0.06	0.29	1.18	1.49	1.59	1.60	1.92	2.02	2.28	2.46	2.83
as shares of GDP														
Net factor income	0.19	0.24	0.25	0.30	0.28	0.20	0.20	0.26	0.37	0.36	0.34	0.33	0.33	0.22
Receipts	0.30	0.35	0.38	0.44	0.40	0.32	0.29	0.36	0.38	0.37	0.35	0.34	0.35	0.23
Payments	0.10	0.12	0.12	0.13	0.12	0.12	0.10	0.10	0.01	0.01	0.01	0.01	0.01	0.01
Net current transfers	0.09	0.10	0.09	0.08	0.08	0.06	0.04	0.06	-0.04	-0.03	-0.01	0.13	0.00	0.01
Receipts	0.13	0.15	0.14	0.14	0.14	0.09	0.07	0.09	0.01	0.00	0.00	0.13	0.00	0.01
Payments	0.05	0.05	0.05	0.06	0.06	0.03	0.02	0.03	0.04	0.03	0.01	0.00	0.00	0.00
Net capital inflows	-0.02	-0.01	0.02	0.03	-0.01	-0.13	-0.08	-0.04	-0.06	-0.06	-0.07	-0.08	-0.14	-0.20

(table continues on next page)

(Table A.4 continues)

Gaza Strip

in millions of US$	1980	1981	1982	1983	1984	1985	1986	1987	1988	1989	1990	1991	1992	1993
Net factor income	107	127	137	183	161	97	161	235	264	219	293	269	299	181
Receipts	152	176	190	252	221	154	234	310	270	226	302	278	303	193
Payments	45	49	53	68	61	57	72	74	6	7	9	9	4	12
Net current transfers	51	54	51	46	45	39	43	56	-30	-23	-12	100	4	5
Receipts	75	82	79	80	77	54	61	81	0	0	0	100	4	5
Payments	24	28	28	35	31	15	18	25	30	23	12	0	0	0
Net capital inflows	37	56	55	65	18	-51	-51	17	-15	-48	-23	-14	-111	-175

West Bank

in millions of US$	1980	1981	1982	1983	1984	1985	1986	1987	1988	1989	1990	1991	1992	1993
Net factor income	135	147	174	206	183	131	193	288	411	444	476	439	599	371
Receipts	219	231	269	308	269	214	292	405	422	456	492	459	627	393
Payments	84	84	96	103	86	83	99	117	11	12	16	20	28	22
Net current transfers	60	58	56	58	48	32	34	72	-52	-40	-12	178	7	9
Receipts	92	92	93	102	89	54	61	106	0	0	0	178	7	9
Payments	32	35	37	44	41	23	26	34	52	40	12	0	0	0
Net capital inflows	-59	-63	-29	-26	-33	-95	-89	-106	-121	-79	-133	-167	-262	-347

Source: Based on Statistical Abstract of Israel, 1981-94, ICSB.

Table A.5. Fiscal Accounts

in millions of US$	West Bank and Gaza Strip									
	1987	1988	1989	1990	1991	1992	1993	1994	1995	1996
Revenue	216	230	241	271	225	328	279	269	511	684
Domestic revenue										
Tax revenue	122	139	142	164	130	233	170	132	144	179
Non-tax revenues	95	91	99	107	95	95	109	112	100	86
Revenues clearances	0	0	0	0	0	0	0	25	266	420
Current expenditure	179	203	199	234	207	252	258	334	578	779
Wage bill civil service	0	0	0	0	0	0	0	44	194	247
Wage bill police service	0	0	0	0	0	0	0	30	110	156
Other current expenditures	179	203	199	234	207	252	258	260	274	426
Interest payments	0	0	0	0	0	0	0	0	0	3
Current balance	37	27	42	37	18	76	21	-65	-67	-95
(excluding employment-generation programs)										
Employment-generation programs	0	0	0	0	0	0	0	0	0	49

(table continues on next page)

(Table A.5 continues)

in millions of US$	1987	1988	1989	1990	1991	1992	1993	1994	1995	1996
Current balance (excl. employment generation program)	37	27	42	37	18	76	21	-65	-67	-144
Capital expenditures	54	26	26	37	32	59	126	45	189	160
Overall balance	-17	1	17	0	-15	16	-104	-110	-256	-304
Financing	0	0	0	0	0	0	104	118	325	293
Domestic financing	0	0	0	0	0	0	0	8	0	0
Foreign financing	0	0	0	0	0	0	0	109	325	293
of current expenditure	0	0	0	0	0	0	0	109	136	84
of employment generation program	0	0	0	0	0	0	0	0	0	49
of capital expenditures	0	0	0	0	0	0	0	0	189	160
Residual discrepancy (financing gap or surplus)	17	-1	-17	0	15	-16	0	-8	-69	11

(table continues on next page)

(Table A.5 continues)

as shares of GDP	1987	1988	1989	1990	1991	1992	1993
Revenue	0.11	0.13	0.13	0.12	0.10	0.12	0.11
Domestic revenue							
Tax revenue	0.06	0.08	0.08	0.07	0.06	0.09	0.07
Non-tax revenues	0.05	0.05	0.05	0.05	0.04	0.04	0.04
Revenues clearances	0.00	0.00	0.00	0.00	0.00	0.00	0.00
Current expenditure	0.09	0.11	0.11	0.10	0.10	0.09	0.10
Wage bill civil service	0.00	0.00	0.00	0.00	0.00	0.00	0.00
Wage bill police service	0.00	0.00	0.00	0.00	0.00	0.00	0.00
Other current expenditures	0.09	0.11	0.11	0.10	0.10	0.09	0.10
Interest payments	0.00	0.00	0.00	0.00	0.00	0.00	0.00

Sources: ICA from 1987-93; IMF/PA from 1993-96.

Table A.6 Fiscal Operations of Palestinian Authority, May 1994 - December 1996

in millions of US$ unless otherwise indicated	1994 May-Sep [1]	1994 Q IV [2]	1994 Total	1995 Q I	1995 Q II	1995 Q III
Revenue	20.95	30.74	**51.69**	63.10	104.28	124.10
Domestic revenue	10.09	16.28	**26.37**	30.40	37.78	47.30
Tax revenue	3.53	9.23 [2a]	**12.76**	22.40	26.53	29.30
Non-tax revenue	6.56	7.05	**13.61**	8.00	11.25	18.00
Revenue clearances	10.86	14.46 [2b]	**25.32**	32.70 [3a]	66.50 [4a]	76.80 [5a]
Current expenditure	52.63	63.97	**116.60**	103.10	106.70	127.30
Wage bill civil service	22.17	21.39	**43.56**	43.30	47.90	48.70
Wage bill police service	13.66	16.33	**29.99**	23.70	19.50 [4b]	25.90
Non-wage budgetary expenditure						
Other current expenditure	16.80	26.25	**43.05**	36.10 [3b]	39.30 [4c]	52.70 [5b]
Current balance (excluding employment-generation programs)	-31.68	-33.23	**-64.91**	-40.00	-2.42	-3.20
Employment-generation programs (foreign-financed)		0	**0.00**	0	0	0
Current balance (including employment-generation programs)	-31.68	-33.23	**-64.91**	-40.00	-2.42	-3.20
Capital expenditure		0	**0.00**	20.00	25.20	33.20
Overall balance	-31.68	-33.23	**-64.91**	-60.00	-27.62	-36.40
Financing	5.28	67.64	**72.92**	75.50	29.20	44.10
Foreign financing	5.28	59.44 [2c]	**64.72**	73.30	63.30 [4d]	66.10
Of current expenditure	5.28	59.44	**64.72**	53.30	38.10	32.90
Of employment gen. prog.	0	0		0	0	0
Of capital expenditure	0	0		20.00	25.20	33.20
Domestic financing	0.00	8.20	**8.20**	2.20	-34.10	-22.00
Residual discrepancy	26.40	-34.41	**-8.01**	-15.50 [3c]	-1.58	-7.70
Memorandum items						
Revenue (% of GDP)			**1.6**			
Current expenditure (% of GDP)			**3.7**			
of which: Wage expenditure			**2.3**			
Current balance (% of GDP)			**-2.1**			
GDP (US$ millions)			**3,160**			
Exchange rate (NIS/US$)	3.01	3.02	**3.01**	3.01	2.98	3.01

(table continues on next page)

(Table A.6 continues)

in millions of US$ unless otherwise indicated	1995 Q IV [6]	1995 Total	1996 Q I [7]	1996 Q II [8]	1996 Q III [9]	1996 QIV [10]	1996 Total
Revenue	133.40	**424.88**	160.30	148.30	186.10	189.50	**684.20**
Domestic revenue	43.00	**158.48**	57.50	60.70	69.60	76.80	**264.60**
Tax revenue	30.00	**108.23**	40.30	40.50	47.40	50.60	**178.80**
Non-tax revenue	13.00	**50.25**	17.20	20.20	22.20	26.20	**85.80**
Revenue clearances	90.40	**266.40**	102.80	87.60	116.50	112.70	**419.60**
Current expenditure	154.80	**491.90**	166.40	195.40	201.30	216.10	**779.20**
Wage bill civil service	53.90	**193.80**	58.80	58.30	61.50	67.90	**246.50**
Wage bill police service	41.40 [6a]	**110.50**	32.20	36.10	42.30	45.40	**156.00**
Non-wage budgetary expenditure			72.40 [7a]	78.00 [8a]	91.50 [9a]	102.80 [10a]	**344.70**
Other current expenditure	59.50 [6b]	**187.60**	3.00	23.00 [8b]	6.00 [9b]	0.00 [10b]	**32.00**
Current balance (excluding-employment generation programs)	-21.40	**-67.02**	-6.10	-47.10	-15.20	-26.60	**-95.00**
Employment-generation programs (foreign-financed)	0	**0.00**	1.70	17.70	22.40	7.40	**49.20**
Current balance (including employment-generation programs)	-21.40	**-67.02**	-7.80	-64.80	-37.60	-34.00	**-144.20**
Capital expenditure	110.90	**189.30**	11.00	42.00	58.00	49.00	**160.00**
Overall balance	-132.30	**-256.32**	-18.80	-106.80	-95.60	-83.00	**-304.20**
Financing							
Foreign financing	121.80 [6c]	**324.50**	12.70	128.30	79.40	72.40	**292.80**
Of current expenditure	10.90	**135.20**	0	68.70	-1.00	16.00	**83.70**
Of employment gen. prog.	0	**0.00**	1.70	17.70	22.40	7.40	**49.20**
Of capital expenditure	110.90	**189.30**	11.00	42.00	58.00	49.00	**160.00**
Domestic financing	[6d]		[7b]	[8c]	[9c]	[10c]	
Residual discrepancy						83.00	
Memorandum items							
Revenue (% of GDP)		11.1					19.8
Current expenditure (% of GDP)		12.8					22.6
of which: Wage expenditure		7.9					11.7
Current balance (% of GDP)		-1.7					-2.8
GDP (US$ millions)		3,837					3,451
Exchange rate (NIS/US$)	3.03	**3.01**	3.12	3.22	3.18	3.19	**3.18**

Notes to Table A.6

1. Gaza and Jericho only.

2. Includes revenue and expenditures of the Gaza Strip and Jericho, and newly inherited spheres in the West Bank as specified under "early empowerment" which took effect in December 1994.

2a. In the West Bank, tax collection by the PA started in December 1994 and covered only income tax and VAT on domestic production.

2b. Gaza/Jericho component includes retroactive amounts of VAT for the period May-October 1994 as well as amounts remitted on account of petroleum excises, and a disbursement order of US$1.5 million issued on December 3, 1994, but actually drawn on January 3, 1995.

2c. Includes financing prior to the November 30, 1994 AHLC meeting when new donor funding agreed in the "Understanding" signed at the meeting.

3a. Includes US$18.54 million transferred to the Bank of Palestine. These deposits were held as a reserve to cover the outstanding overdraft of the Ministry of Finance to domestic commercial banks.

3b, 4c, 5b, 6b. A reduction in the amounts is shown vis-a-vis earlier estimates. This is due to a change in previous assumptions regarding the disposition of petroleum excise clearances. It had previously been assumed that these revenues were reflected one-for-one in expenditures during the same year.

3c. Minus sign indicates surplus.

4a. Includes petroleum excise clearances transferred to an extra-budgetary account not controlled by the Ministry of Finance at Bank Leumi (US$6.5 million). Also includes US$17.1 million transferred to the Bank of Palestine. These deposits were held as a reserve against outstanding overdrafts of the Ministry of Finance to domestic commercial banks.

4b. Wages of police inside Gaza/Jericho for the month of June were paid in the third quarter and wages for May were paid in the fourth quarter.

4d. Includes disbursement of new donor financing pledged in Paris on April 27, 1995 under the Tripartite Action Plan.

5a. Second and third quarter VAT clearances include clearances for the West Bank for the first quarter of the year.

6. Includes eight additional spheres in the West Bank.

6a. Includes one month's delayed police wages from the second quarter.

6c. Includes a lump sum transfer (US$4 million) by Israel to cover part of the wage costs associated with the eight spheres.

6d. Data on the net claims of the PA on the banking system are incomplete.

7. Estimates of revenue include excise tax collections transferred to bank accounts outside the control of the Ministry of Finance. Estimates of expenditure may underestimate the PA's actual spending levels as the estimates do not include expenditure financed from excise tax collections.

7a. Includes expenditure on emergency programs associated with the border closures.

7b. Data on the net claims of the PA on the banking system are incomplete.

8. Estimates of revenue include excise tax collections transferred to bank accounts outside the control of the Ministry of Finance. Estimates of expenditure may underestimate the PA's actual spending levels as the estimates do not include expenditure financed from excise tax collections.

8a. Includes expenditure on emergency programs associated with the border closures and additional unbudgeted expenditures that are not included in the 1996 draft budget.

8b. Closure-related expenditures from accounts not directly controlled by the Ministry of Finance.

8c. Data on the net claims of the PA on the banking system are incomplete.

9. Estimates of revenue include excise tax collections transferred to bank accounts outside the control of the Ministry of Finance. Estimates of expenditure may underestimate the PA's actual spending levels as the estimates do not include expenditure financed from excise tax collections.

9a. Includes expenditure on emergency programs associated with the border closures and additional unbudgeted expenditures that are not included in the 1996 draft budget.

9b. Closure-related expenditures from accounts not directly controlled by the Ministry of Finance.

9c. Data on the net claims of the PA on the banking system are incomplete.

10. Estimates of revenue include excise tax collections transferred to bank accounts outside the control of the Ministry of Finance. Estimates of expenditure may underestimate the PA's actual spending levels as the estimates do not include expenditure financed from excise tax collections.

10a. Includes expenditure on emergency programs associated with the border closures and additional unbudgeted expenditures that are not included in the 1996 draft budget.

10b. Closure-related expenditures from accounts not directly controlled by the Ministry of Finance.

10c. Data on the net claims of the PA on the banking system are incomplete.

Table A.7: Revenues of the Palestinian Authority, 1996

in millions of US$	1996 Q I		1996 Q II		1996 Q III		1996 Q IV	
	in US$	% of total	in US$	% of total	in US$	% of total	in US$	% of total
TOTAL REVENUE	160.40	100	148.40	100	186.10	100	189.50	100
Domestic tax revenues	40.30	25	40.50	27	47.40	25	50.70	27
Income tax	12.10	8	13.00	9	10.40	5	16.40	9
VAT	14.80	9	12.70	9	18.00	9	20.30	11
Customs duties	4.50	3	4.50	3	9.50	5	4.60	2
Property tax	0.20	0	0.50	0	0.10	0	0.10	0
Excises	8.70	5	9.30	6	9.40	5	9.30	5
Other	0.00	0	0.00	0	0.00	0	0.00	0
Revenue clearances	102.90	64	87.70	59	116.50	64	112.70	59
Customs duties	13.90	9	21.80	15	25.50	14	25.20	13
VAT	55.80	35	40.40	27	62.30	34	58.30	31
Petroleum excise	25.30	16	23.40	16	26.00	14	25.70	14
Income tax	1.70	1	0.40	0	0.50	0	1.40	1
Health fees	2.10	1	0.80	1	1.20	1	2.10	1
Other	4.10	3	0.90	1	1.00	1	0.00	0
Non-tax revenues	17.20	11	20.20	14	22.20	11	26.10	14
Transportation fees	5.60	3	5.40	4	3.90	1	7.70	4
Health insurance	3.40	2	3.30	2	2.50	2	3.40	2
Health fees	2.10	1	1.90	1	2.60	2	2.80	1
Other non-tax revenues	6.10	4	9.60	6	13.20	7	12.20	6

(table continues on next page)

Table A.7 continues

in millions of US$	Q I to Q II		Q II to Q III		Q III to Q IV	
	change in US$	% change	change in US$	% change	change in US$	% change
TOTAL REVENUE	-12.0	-7	37.7	25	3.4	2
Domestic tax revenues	0.2	0	6.9	17	3.3	7
Income tax	1.4	12	-3.1	-23	6.0	58
VAT	-2.1	-14	5.3	42	2.3	13
Customs duties	0.0	0	5.0	111	-4.9	-52
Property tax	0.3	150	-0.4	-80	0.0	0
Excises	0.6	7	0.1	1	-0.1	-1
Other	0.0	0	0.0	0	0.0	0
Revenue clearances	-15.2	-15	28.8	33	-3.8	-3
Customs duties	7.9	57	3.7	17	-0.3	-1
VAT	-15.4	-28	21.9	54	-4.0	-6
Petroleum excise	-1.9	-8	2.6	11	-0.3	-1
Income tax	-1.3	-76	0.1	25	0.9	180
Health fees	-1.3	-62	0.4	50	0.9	75
Other	-3.2	-78	0.1	11	-1.0	-100
Non-tax revenues	3.0	17	2.0	10	3.9	18
Transportation fees	-0.2	-4	-1.5	-28	3.8	97
Health insurance	-0.1	-3	-0.8	-24	0.9	36
Health fees	-0.2	-10	0.7	37	0.2	8
Other non-tax revenues	3.5	57	3.6	38	-1.0	-8

Table A.8 Size of WBGS Civil Service and Police Force

	Civilian Employees			Police Force			Total Public Sector Employees
	Gaza / Jericho	West Bank	Total	Gaza / Jericho	West Bank	Total	
December 1993	7,376	15,403	22,779				22,779
December 1994	8,500	17,000	25,500	14,000	0	14,000	39,500
January 1995	12,160	16,700	28,860	16,000	0	16,000	44,860
February 1995	11,800	16,800	28,600	18,000	0	18,000	46,600
March 1995	12,500	17,000	29,500	18,000	0	18,000	47,500
June 1995	13,000	17,100	30,100	18,000	0	18,000	48,100
August 1995	13,400	17,300	30,700	19,000	0	19,000	49,700
September 1995 [1]			33,100			19,500	52,600
			31,900			20,700	52,600
December 1995 [2]			34,800			24,000	58,800
March 1996 [2]			36,700			26,700	63,400
June 1996 [2]			38,400			30,200	68,600
September 1996 [2]			38,900			32,600	71,500
December 1996			41,020			34,027	75,047

1. Disaggregation into Gaza/Jericho and West Bank not available; different figures cited in different IMF reports.
2. Disaggregation into Gaza/Jericho and West Bank not available.

Table A.9: Size of Palestinian Population, Labor Force and Employment

in thousands	1980	1981	1982	1983	1984	1985	1986	1987	1988	1989	1990	1991	1992	1993	1994	1995	1996
Total population without Jerusalem [1]	1,196	1,216	1,243	1,285	1,323	1,365	1,407	1,461	1,514	1,559	1,637	1,726	1,819	1,901	2,015	2,151	2,280
Total population with Jerusalem [2]	-	-	-	-	-	-	-	-	-	-	-	-	2,019	2,110	2,238	2,390	2,535
Gaza Strip	467	480	489	507	524	542	561	583	608	631	666	703	747	788	843	905	963
West Bank without Jerusalem	728	736	754	777	800	823	846	878	906	927	971	1,024	1,072	1,113	1,172	1,246	1,317
East Jerusalem [2]	-	-	-	-	-	-	-	-	-	-	-	-	200	210	223	239	254
Pop aged 15+ without Jerusalem [3]	652	658	661	692	712	734	731	752	766	787	823	856	882	927	1,026	1,135	1,203
Population aged 15+ with Jerusalem	-	-	-	-	-	-	-	-	-	-	-	-	982	1,032	1,144	1,266	1,343
Gaza Strip	248	253	252	268	272	287	285	291	301	311	326	339	351	369	404	450	479
West Bank without Jerusalem	403	405	409	424	440	448	446	461	465	476	497	517	532	557	621	685	724
East Jerusalem	-	-	-	-	-	-	-	-	-	-	-	-	99	105	118	131	140
Total labor force without Jerusalem [4]	255	253	269	277	291	296	318	336	342	343	365	372	398	405	428	438	464
Total labor force with Jerusalem	-	-	-	-	-	-	-	-	-	-	-	-	445	452	481	482	518
Gaza Strip	114	117	118	121	124	130	135	144	143	143	154	159	170	172	173	176	187
West Bank without Jerusalem	141	137	151	156	167	166	183	192	199	200	212	212	229	233	254	262	277
East Jerusalem [5]	-	-	-	-	-	-	-	-	-	-	-	-	46	47	53	44	54
Total employment without Jerusalem [6]	252	252	262	273	283	286	309	329	333	331	352	344	382	378	385	349	324
Total employment with Jerusalem	-	-	-	-	-	-	-	-	-	-	-	-	426	422	430	387	364
Gaza Strip	114	117	114	120	123	128	133	142	140	140	148	153	164	164	167	121	114
West Bank without Jerusalem	139	136	148	153	161	158	176	187	193	191	204	190	218	214	218	228	210
East Jerusalem [5]	-	-	-	-	-	-	-	-	-	-	-	-	44	44	46	39	41

Notes to Table A.9

1. To adjust the population number for 1980-91 to the most recent results provided by PCBS, the total population for 1980-91was recalculated taking 1992 as the base year (PCBS, Demographic Survey, December 1994) minus the population of East Jerusalem, and using the same annual growth rates as those observed by ICBS for 1980-92 for Gaza Strip and West Bank, individually.

2. The population of East Jerusalem, about 254,387 in 1996 (according to PCBS, Small Area Population Revised Estimates for 1996) was estimated for 1992-95 using the same annual growth rate as that observed in the West Bank during that period.

3. The population aged 15+ was estimated using the same ratio (*i.e.*, population aged 15+/total pop) as ICBS used for 1980-93. The ratio was estimated by World Bank staff for 1994 and by PCBS (Labour Force Survey, press release) for 1995-96.

4. Total labor force was estimated using 1995 as the base year (PCBS, Labor Force Survey). ICBS annual growth rates for Gaza Strip and West Bank separately were used to derive annual labor force for 1980-94. For 1996, the labor force growth rate was assumed to equal the population growth rate.

5. Labor force of East Jerusalem was estimated using the same participation rate (LF/pop aged 15+) as observed by the World Bank.

6. Total employed was estimated as the same proportion of the total labor force as observed by ICBS for 1980-93. The ratio was estimated by World Bank staff for 1994 and by PCBS (Labour Force Survey, press release) for 1995-96.

Table A.10 Distribution of Labor Force and Employment

West Bank and Gaza Strip

	1980	1981	1982	1983	1984	1985	1986	1987	1988	1989	1990	1991	1992	1993	1994	1995	1996
Unemployment rate (%)	0.01	0.01	0.03	0.01	0.03	0.03	0.03	0.02	0.03	0.04	0.04	0.07	0.04	0.06	0.10	0.20	0.30
Adjusted unemployment rate [1]	0.05	0.01	0.03	0.01	0.03	0.07	0.05	0.02	0.13	0.11	0.07	0.12	0.08	0.10	0.14	0.25	0.35
Employment by sector	1.00	1.00	1.00	1.00	1.00	1.00	1.00	1.00	1.00	1.00	1.00	1.00	1.00	1.00	1.00	1.00	1.00
Agriculture	0.27	0.25	0.26	0.25	0.23	0.23	0.24	0.22	0.26	0.23	0.26	0.25	0.25	0.23	0.21	0.13	0.16
Industry	0.17	0.16	0.15	0.16	0.16	0.16	0.17	0.17	0.16	0.16	0.14	0.15	0.15	0.15	0.14	0.17	0.17
Construction	0.09	0.10	0.10	0.10	0.10	0.11	0.11	0.11	0.10	0.12	0.11	0.10	0.11	0.15	0.14	0.21	0.12
Others	0.47	0.49	0.49	0.49	0.50	0.50	0.49	0.51	0.48	0.50	0.50	0.50	0.48	0.47	0.51	0.49	0.55
Employment in Israel [2] (% of total employed)	0.30	0.30	0.30	0.32	0.32	0.31	0.31	0.33	0.33	0.32	0.31	0.28	0.30	0.22	0.17	0.09	0.08
Employment in Israel by sector	1.00	1.00	1.00	1.00	1.00	1.00	1.00	1.00	1.00	1.00	1.00	1.00	1.00	1.00	1.00	1.00	1.00
Agriculture	0.14	0.13	0.13	0.12	0.14	0.16	0.16	0.15	0.15	0.14	0.12	0.12	0.09	0.10	0.15	0.17	0.17
Industry	0.21	0.18	0.18	0.19	0.18	0.18	0.18	0.18	0.15	0.13	0.10	0.08	0.06	0.06	0.08	0.10	0.10
Construction	0.47	0.51	0.53	0.50	0.48	0.48	0.48	0.46	0.50	0.53	0.60	0.68	0.74	0.73	0.64	0.63	0.63
Others	0.18	0.18	0.17	0.19	0.19	0.19	0.19	0.22	0.20	0.20	0.18	0.12	0.11	0.11	0.13	0.09	0.09
Wage index	0	0	0	122	116	106	122	0	0	133	131	130	127	135	78	0	0
Wage index workers in Israel	0	0	0	123	107	99	123	0	180	182	174	184	185	202	113	115	0
Average hours worked in WBGS	43	44	44	43	43	43	43	43	32	34	36	38	39	40	40	42	0
Average hours worked in Israel	45	46	46	45	44	45	45	44	33	35	37	37	39	35	18	19	0

217

(table continues on next page)

Gaza Strip

	1980	1981	1982	1983	1984	1985	1986	1987	1988	1989	1990	1991	1992	1993	1994	1995	1996
Unemployment rate (%)	0.00	0.00	0.03	0.01	0.01	0.01	0.01	0.01	0.02	0.02	0.04	0.04	0.03	0.04	0.04	0.31	0.39
Adjusted unemployment rate	0.03	0.00	0.03	0.01	0.01	0.05	0.05	0.01	0.14	0.12	0.10	0.09	0.08	0.09	0.08	0.36	0.45
Employment by sector	1.00	1.00	1.00	1.00	1.00	1.00	1.00	1.00	1.00	1.00	1.00	1.00	1.00	1.00	1.00	1.00	1.00
Agriculture	0.19	0.18	0.19	0.19	0.17	0.18	0.17	0.16	0.19	0.18	0.20	0.22	0.21	0.20	0.16	0.11	0.11
Industry	0.19	0.17	0.15	0.15	0.17	0.16	0.18	0.18	0.16	0.14	0.11	0.13	0.13	0.13	0.10	0.15	0.16
Construction	0.07	0.08	0.09	0.08	0.09	0.08	0.08	0.08	0.08	0.13	0.11	0.10	0.12	0.15	0.11	0.18	0.09
Others	0.55	0.57	0.59	0.57	0.58	0.57	0.57	0.58	0.57	0.56	0.57	0.56	0.54	0.52	0.63	0.56	0.64
% of employment in Israel	0.30	0.31	0.32	0.33	0.33	0.33	0.33	0.32	0.32	0.28	0.29	0.27	0.26	0.19	0.12	0.13	0.11

West Bank

	1980	1981	1982	1983	1984	1985	1986	1987	1988	1989	1990	1991	1992	1993	1994	1995	1996
Unemployment rate (%)	0.02	0.01	0.02	0.02	0.04	0.05	0.04	0.03	0.03	0.04	0.04	0.10	0.05	0.08	0.14	0.13	0.24
Adjusted unemployment rate	0.06	0.01	0.02	0.02	0.04	0.08	0.06	0.03	0.13	0.11	0.06	0.14	0.07	0.11	0.19	0.17	0.28
Employment by sector	1.00	1.00	1.00	1.00	1.00	1.00	1.00	1.00	1.00	1.00	1.00	1.00	1.00	1.00	1.00	1.00	1.00
Agriculture	0.33	0.31	0.32	0.30	0.29	0.27	0.29	0.26	0.31	0.26	0.30	0.28	0.29	0.25	0.25	0.13	0.19
Industry	0.15	0.16	0.16	0.16	0.16	0.16	0.16	0.17	0.16	0.17	0.16	0.17	0.17	0.17	0.17	0.18	0.18
Construction	0.11	0.12	0.11	0.11	0.11	0.12	0.13	0.12	0.11	0.11	0.11	0.11	0.11	0.15	0.17	0.23	0.13
Others	0.41	0.42	0.41	0.43	0.44	0.44	0.43	0.45	0.42	0.45	0.44	0.45	0.43	0.44	0.41	0.45	0.50
% of employment in Israel	0.29	0.29	0.29	0.31	0.31	0.30	0.29	0.34	0.33	0.34	0.32	0.29	0.33	0.25	0.21	0.07	0.06

1. Ratio: (total unemployed + temporarily absent) / total employed persons.
2. ICBS for 1980–93; PCBS since 1994.

Table A.11 Demographic Indicators for the WBGS in 1996

	Gaza Strip	West Bank	WBGS
Population (in thousands) [1]	843	1 395	2 238
Male	425	703	1 128
Female	418	693	1 111
Sex ratio (males per 100 females) [2]	103.8	105.6	104.96
Age distribution [2]			
Percentage aged 0-4	21.1	17.9	19
Percentage aged 5-14	29.2	27.1	27.9
Percentage aged 15-24	19	21.1	20.4
Percentage aged 15-64	46.9	51.3	49.7
Percentage aged 60+	4.5	5.6	5.2
Percentage aged 65+	2.8	3.7	3.4
Percentage women aged 15-49	40.82	44.83	43.37
Median age [2]	14	16	16
Dependancy ratio [2]	113.2	95.1	101.3
Population growth rate (%) [1]	8.2	6.7	7.2
Crude birth rate (per 1000) [1]	52.4	41.2	45.4
Crude death rate (per 1000) [1]	6.5	6.9	6.7
Natural growth rate [1]	4.6	3.4	3.9
Infant mortality rate [1]	35	38	37
Life expectancy at birth [1]			
Both sexes	68.2	67.5	67.8
Male	68.2	67.5	67.8
Female	68.2	67.5	67.8
Age specific fertility rate (per 1000) [3]			
15-19	144	98	114
20-24	340	274	297
25-29	347	274	300
30-34	289	239	246
35-39	231	160	183
40-44	123	71	90
45-49	5	7	6
Total fertility rate [3]	7.44	5.61	6.24

Sources:
1. Demographic Survey, 1994.
2. Demographic Survey, March 1996, pp. 188-89.
3. Demographic Survey, March 1996, p. 132.

Table A.12 Projected Gross Enrollments in Schools by Authority, Level, and Age for the WBGS, 1995-2020

Level (age)	Year	Authority								
		Palestinian Authority			UNRWA			Private		
		Subtotal	Gaza Strip	West Bank	Subtotal	Gaza Strip	West Bank	Subtotal	Gaza Strip	West Bank
		(in thousands)								
Primary	**1995**	217	54	162	101	73	28	17	2	15
(6-11)	**2000**	279	70	209	130	94	36	21	2	19
	2005	329	82	246	154	111	43	25	3	23
	2010	351	88	263	164	118	46	27	3	24
	2015	404	101	303	189	136	53	31	3	28
	2020	425	107	319	199	143	55	33	3	29
Preparatory	**1995**	92	21	72	46	33	14	5	0	5
(12-14)	**2000**	111	25	86	56	39	17	7	0	6
	2005	143	32	111	72	51	22	8	0	8
	2010	161	36	125	81	57	24	9	1	9
	2015	176	39	136	89	62	26	10	1	10
	2020	199	45	155	101	70	30	12	1	11
Secondary	**1995**	92	39	53	1	1	0	7	1	6
(15-17)	**2000**	107	45	62	2	2	0	8	1	7
	2005	130	55	75	2	2	0	9	1	8
	2010	167	71	96	2	2	0	12	2	10
	2015	172	73	99	3	3	0	12	2	11
	2020	205	87	118	3	3	0	15	2	13
Total for	**1995**	401	114	287	149	107	42	29	3	26
Pre-Tertiary	**2000**	497	140	357	188	135	53	36	4	32
Levels	**2005**	602	170	432	228	163	64	43	5	39
	2010	680	195	484	248	178	70	49	5	43
	2015	752	214	538	280	201	79	54	6	48
	2020	830	239	592	302	217	86	59	6	53

Note: Figures do not include Jerusalem.
Sources: PCBS (1995), Tables 7.23 and 7.24, pp. 138-39; World Bank Population Projections; PCBS (1996a), Table 3.1.3.9, p. 89.

Table A.13 Total Donor Assistance to WBGS, 1994-96

in million of US$	Total Pledges (1994-98)	Pledges	Total 1994-96 Commitments	Disbursements
Algeria	10.00	7.00	4.00	4.00
Arab Fund (AFSED)	100.00	110.00	110.00	0.00
Australia	13.01	13.01	13.01	12.64
Austria	20.00	13.00	9.36	6.57
Belgium	20.51	20.51	17.20	8.80
Brunei	6.00	6.00	6.00	6.00
Canada	33.89	33.98	33.98	26.65
Cyprus	2.20	2.20	2.20	0.00
Czech Republic	3.00	3.00	3.00	0.00
Denmark	61.47	61.47	61.47	37.83
Egypt	6.30	6.30	6.36	5.54
European Union	300.00	310.72	310.72	177.42
European Invest. Bank	300.00	130.00	150.50	0.00
Finland	15.78	15.78	16.86	6.68
France	65.00	65.00	54.37	24.53
Germany	92.98	92.98	92.98	58.38
Greece	16.10	16.10	16.10	15.50
Iceland	1.30	0.90	0.00	0.00
India	2.00	2.00	1.00	0.00
Indonesia	5.00	4.00	2.00	0.00
IFC	70.00	48.75	18.75	0.00
Ireland	5.00	4.72	4.32	2.77
Israel	74.50	44.50	25.00	10.50
Italy	80.00	62.00	69.50	28.30
Japan	256.13	256.13	209.00	192.52
Jordan	12.61	12.61	12.61	8.83
Kuwait	25.00	25.00	22.00	22.00
Luxembourg	5.91	5.91	5.91	0.60
Netherlands	120.65	120.65	113.83	36.86
Norway	150.00	140.57	140.57	109.48
Qatar	2.56	2.50	2.50	2.50
Republic of Korea	13.54	3.54	3.14	0.60
Romania	2.88	2.88	2.88	1.80
Russia	0.00	0.00	0.00	0.00
Saudi Arabia	200.00	215.00	205.00	82.50
Spain	51.47	51.47	51.47	49.98
Sweden	69.53	69.53	66.87	43.69
Switzerland	70.17	70.17	70.17	49.74
Turkey	52.00	52.86	2.86	2.86
UNDP[1]				0.00
UNRWA[1]				0.00
United Arab Emirates	25.00	15.00	15.00	15.00
United Kingdom[2]		0.00		19.08
United States	500.00	232.16	232.16	225.80
World Bank	140.00	140.00	140.00	51.93
TOTAL	$3 ,001.49	$2 ,489.89	$2, 324.62	$1, 347.87

1. To be treated as conduit or channel of assistance.
2. The United Kingdom does not provide annual commitments.

Table A.14 Annual Donor Assistance to WBGS, 1994-96

in millions of US$	1994			1995			1996		
	Pledges	Commitments	Disbursements	Pledges	Commitments	Disbursements	Pledges	Commitments	Disbursements
Algeria	4.00	4.00	4.00	3.00	0.00	0.00	0.00	0.00	0.00
Arab Fund (AFSED)	30.00	30.00	0.00	10.00	10.00	0.00	70.00	70.00	0.00
Australia	4.84	4.84	6.06	4.67	4.67	4.66	3.50	3.50	1.91
Austria	4.48	3.59	3.59	5.14	2.39	2.39	3.38	3.38	0.60
Belgium	3.49	3.49	3.49	10.96	7.65	4.45	6.06	6.06	0.86
Brunei	1.00	1.00	1.00	5.00	5.00	5.00	0.00	0.00	0.00
Canada	13.73	13.73	7.74	13.59	13.59	10.08	6.66	6.66	8.83
Cyprus							2.20	2.20	0.00
Czech Republic							3.00	3.00	0.00
Denmark	42.98	42.98	15.33	0.34	0.34	16.33	18.15	18.15	6.17
Egypt	5.30	5.33	5.33	0.00	0.03	0.03	1.00	1.00	0.18
European Union	101.94	101.94	46.09	80.10	80.10	59.30	128.68	128.68	72.04
European Investment Bank	0.00	0.00	0.00	32.50	32.50	0.00	97.50	118.00	0.00
Finland	2.81	2.81	2.50	3.87	3.87	1.94	9.10	10.18	2.24
France	24.00	16.00	15.10	24.00	19.47	5.67	17.00	18.90	3.76
Germany	24.07	24.07	10.68	27.85	27.85	19.49	41.06	41.06	28.21
Greece	15.00	15.00	15.00	0.10	0.10	0.00	1.00	1.00	0.50
Iceland	0.50	0.00	0.00	0.40	0.00	0.00	0.00	0.00	0.00
India	0.50	0.00	0.00	0.50	0.00	0.00	1.00	1.00	0.00
Indonesia	1.00	0.00	0.00	1.00	0.00	0.00	2.00	2.00	0.00
IFC	18.75	18.75	0.00	30.00	0.00	0.00	0.00	0.00	0.00
Ireland	1.00	0.60	0.52	1.12	1.12	1.15	2.60	2.60	1.10
Israel	15.00	6.50	6.50	15.00	4.00	4.00	14.50	14.50	0.00

(table continues on following page)

222

(Table A.14 continues)

in millions of US$	1994			1995			1996		
	Pledges	Commitments	Disbursements	Pledges	Commitments	Disbursements	Pledges	Commitments	Disbursements
Italy	18.50	18.40	11.65	18.50	21.10	6.65	25.00	30.00	10.00
Japan	100.00	89.83	89.83	100.00	63.04	63.04	56.13	56.13	39.65
Jordan	8.83	8.83	8.83	3.78	3.78	0.00	0.00	0.00	0.00
Kuwait	25.00	22.00	8.00	0.00	0.00	14.00	0.00	0.00	0.00
Luxembourg	0.00	0.00	0.00	0.13	0.13	0.13	5.78	5.78	0.47
Netherlands	31.92	31.92	16.55	18.13	11.30	9.59	70.61	70.61	10.72
Norway	34.42	34.42	30.07	43.15	43.15	34.29	63.00	63.00	45.13
Qatar	2.50	2.50	0.00	0.00	0.00	2.50	0.00	0.00	0.00
Republic of Korea	0.26	0.06	0.00	0.28	0.08	0.60	3.00	3.00	0.00
Romania	1.80	1.80	1.80	1.08	1.08	0.00	0.00	0.00	0.00
Russia	0.00	0.00	0.00	0.00	0.00	0.00	0.00	0.00	0.00
Saudi Arabia	100.00	100.00	30.00	100.00	90.00	37.50	15.00	15.00	15.00
Spain	11.94	11.94	10.65	25.33	25.33	17.53	14.20	14.20	21.80
Sweden	10.50	10.50	3.07	20.49	17.82	10.99	38.55	38.55	29.63
Switzerland	31.44	31.44	19.90	14.43	14.43	14.31	24.30	24.30	15.53
Turkey	2.00	2.00	2.00	25.00	0.00	0.00	25.86	0.86	0.86
UNDP[1]									
UNRWA[1]									
United Arab Emirates	5.00	5.00	5.00	10.00	10.00	10.00	0.00	0.00	0.00
United Kingdom[2]			9.62			7.14			2.32
United States	90.43	90.43	87.23	74.10	74.10	69.40	67.64	67.64	69.18
World Bank	30.00	30.00	2.60	20.00	20.00	22.17	90.00	90.00	27.17
TOTAL	818.90	785.68	479.70	743.54	608.02	454.32	927.45	930.93	413.85

1. To be treated as conduit or channel of assistance.
2. The United Kingdom does not provide annual commitments.

223

Table A.15 Donor Assistance by Category and Year, 1994-96

	Category					
	Public investment	Technical assistance	Transitional & budgetary support	Employment generation	Other	Total
in millions of US$						
1994						
Commitment 281.570	136.292	198.874	27.601	98.926	**$743.23**
Disbursement 143.365	76.983	171.942	12.847	91.628	**$496.75**
1995						
Commitment 273.288	100.034	132.303	10.591	110.684	**$626.90**
Disbursement 123.388	88.491	118.578	13.122	98.172	**$441.71**
1996						
Commitment 419.240	104.829	168.947	38.794	165.552	**$897.32**
Disbursement 152.208	78.094	158.293	36.080	103.247	**$527.92**
1994-1996						
Commitment 974.098	341.155	500.124	76.986	375.162	**$2,267.52**
Disbursement 418.961	243.568	448.813	62.049	293.047	**$1,466.43**
Ratio 43.0	71.3	89.7	80.5	78.1	64.6

Bibliography

Background Papers

Abu Dagga, Husam. "Gaza's High Value-Added Crops." 1996.

Abu-Duhou, Ibtisam. "Education for Development in Palestine." 1996.

Abu-Ghaida, Dina. "Palestinian Entrepreneurs in the Diaspora." July 1996.

Al-Qudsi, Sulayman S. and Radwan A. Shaban. "The Economic Returns to Schooling in the West Bank and Gaza Strip - Revisited." August 1996.

Arnon, Arie. "Links Between the Israeli and Palestinian Economies." June 1996.

Askalan, Hanan. "Information Infrastructure and Technology Status in West Bank and Gaza." September 1996.

Barghouthi, Mustafa and Jean Lennock. "Health in the West Bank and Gaza Strip." 1997.

Berryman, Sue. "The Education Story." 1996.

Birzeit University Women's Studies Center. "Gender Segmentation in Palestinian Economic Life." 1997.

———. "Country Economic Memorandum on Palestine Gender Gaps in Palestinian Economic and Social Life."

Brynen, Rex. "Recent Political Developments." 1997.

Claudet, Sophie. "The Changing Role of Palestinian NGOs Since the Establishment of the Palestinian Authority (1994-96)." 1996.

Hamed, Osama. "The Palestinian Banking System: Reality and Potential." December 1996.

Hooper, Rick. "Donor Aid and Donor Coordination." 1996.

Mody, Ashoka. "West Bank and Gaza: Infrastructure, Institutions, and Growth." August 1996.

Panagariya, Arvind and Ishac Diwan. "Trade Policy Options for the West Bank and Gaza Strip." January 1997.

Pissarides, Chris. "Unnecessary Labor Adjustment: The West Bank and Gaza under Border Closure." 1996.

Shaban, Radwan A. "Living Standards in the West Bank and Gaza Strip During the Transition." 1997. Jerusalem: Palestine Economic Policy Research Institute.

Silsby, Susan. "Governance: NGOs Private Sector and Public Sector in the Occupied Territory." June 1996.

Wijnbergen, Sweder van. "Macroeconomic and Financial Sector Issues in the West Bank and Gaza Strip." 1996.

References

Abdallah, Samir. 1994. "The Palestinian Public Sector." *The Economic Research Forum Newsletter.* Vol. 2. No. 2.

Abdulhadi, Rami. 1992. *Prospects for Sustained Economic Development in the Occupied Palestinian Territory: Construction and Housing,* UNCTAD.

Abed, George T. and Abdelali Tazi. 1994. "Laying the Foundation: a Fiscal System for Palestinian Autonomy." *Finance and Development.* Vol. 31. No. 3.

Abed, George T. 1996. "The Prospects for Long-run Sustainable Growth." Paper prepared for conference on The Palestinian Economy: Towards a Vision, Birzeit University, June 9-12. Arab Economists Association, Ramallah, West Bank.

Abou-Shokor, Abdel-Fattah. 1996. "Human Resources in Palestine Present and Future." Paper prepared for conference on The Palestinian Economy: Towards a Vision, Birzeit University, June 9-12. Arab Economists Association, Ramallah, West Bank.

Al-Botmeh, Samia and Edward Sayre. 1996. "Employment Generation Schemes in the West Bank and Gaza Strip." Jerusalem: Palestine Economic Policy Research Institute, July.

Ad Hoc Liaison Committee Secretariat. 1996. Donor Matrix, update, November.

Arab Economists Association. 1996. "The Conclusions of the Conference and Opening Speeches." Papers presented at conference on The Palestinian Economy: Towards a Vision, Birzeit University, June 9-12. Ramallah, West Bank.

Arab Economists Association (and Palestinian Trade Promotion Organization). 1997. "Financing Female Farmers." *Palestine Economic Pulse.* Vol. II, No.1. Ramallah, West Bank, January-February.

Arnon, Arie and Jimmy Wienblatt. 1994. "The Potential for Trade Between Israel, The Palestinians, and Jordan." Discussion Paper No. 94.10. Bank of Israel Research Department, Jerusalem.

Asfour, Edmond. 1996. "Respective Roles of Private, Public, and NGO Sectors." Paper prepared for conference on The Palestinian Economy: Towards a Vision, Birzeit University, June 9-12. Arab Economists Association, Ramallah, West Bank.

Balaj, Barbara, Ishac Diwan et Bernard Philippe. 1996. "Aide exterieure aux Palestiniens: ce qui n'a pas fonctionne." *Politique Etrangere*, pp. 753-67.

Barro, Robert J. and Jong Wha Lee. 1996. "International Measures of Schooling Years and Schooling Quality." *American Economic Review.* Vol. 86, pp. 218-23, May.

Center for Policy Research and Studies. 1997. *Public Opinion Polls*, 1993-1997, Nablus.

Clark, John D. and Barbara S. Balaj. 1994. "The West Bank and Gaza in Transition: The Role of NGOs in the Peace Process." World Bank, Washington, DC, December.

Dabbagh, Ossama. 1996. "Trade Prospects for Palestine." Paper prepared for conference on The Palestinian Economy: Towards a Vision, Birzeit University, June 9-12. Arab Economists Association, Ramallah, West Bank.

Data, Horizon, and Economic Cooperation Foundation. 1996. "Total Cumulating of Rules of Origin in Exporting to the EU from Israel, Jordan, Egypt & the PNA." Israeli-Palestinian-Jordanian Industrial Cooperation, June.

Ebel, Robert D. 1995. "West Bank & Gaza Strip: Intergovernmental Relations and Municipal Finance." World Bank Memorandum (Back-to-Office Report), March.

El-Jafari, Mahmoud. 1995. "Potential Merchandise Trade of The West Bank and Gaza Strip." Paper prepared for conference on Liberalization of Trade and Foreign Investment, Istanbul, sponsored by Economic Research Forum for the Arab Countries, Iran and Turkey, September 16-18.

Foreign Investment Advisory Service. 1995. "West Bank and Gaza Creating a Framework for Foreign Direct Investment." International Finance Corporation and The World Bank, Washington, DC, June.

Gotlieb, Daniel. 1996. "On the Economic Implications of the Peace Process for Israel." Bank of Israel, November.

Government Finance Statistics Yearbook. 1995.

Halevi, Nadav and Ephraim Kleinman. 1994. "Middle East Regional Trade Study: Israel's Trade and Payments Regimes." Paper prepared for a conference on Middle East Regional Trade, by the Institute for Economic and Social Policy, Harvard University, August 10-11.

Hamed, Osama A. 1997. "Monetary Policy Without National Currency." Draft. Jerusalem: Palestine Economic Policy Research Institute.

Hamed, Osama A. and Radwan A. Shaban. 1993. "One-Sided Customs and Monetary Union: The Case of the West Bank and Gaza Strip under Israeli Occupation." In Stanley Fischer, Dani Rodrik and Elias Tuma, eds., *The Economics of Middle East Peace: Views from the Region*. Cambridge: Massachusetts Institute Technology.

———. 1995. "Banking Regulation in the West Bank and Gaza Strip." MAS report submitted to Palestinian Monetary Authority.

Human Rights Watch-Middle East. 1996 "Israel's Closure of the West Bank and Gaza Strip." New York, July.

International Monetary Fund. 1994. "Taxation in Israel, the West Bank and the Gaza Strip: Policy and Administration for the Transition." Washington, DC. April.

———. 1994. "The West Bank and the Gaza Strip: Proposals for Establishing a Public Expenditure Management System." Washington, DC. April.

———. 1994. "The West Bank and the Gaza Strip: Improving Fiscal Administration in the Gaza Strip and Jericho Areas." Washington, DC. October.

———. 1995. "The West Bank and the Gaza Strip: Consolidating Improvements in Fiscal Administration." Washington, DC. March.

———. 1995. "The West Bank and the Gaza Strip: Tariff, Trade, and Customs Administration Issues." Washington, DC. September.

———. 1996. "The West Bank and the Gaza Strip: Improving Fiscal Management." Washington, DC. March.

———. 1997. "The West Bank and the Gaza Strip: Pension Reform Issues for the Palestinian Authority." Washington, DC. January.

International Yearbooks of Telecommunications Statistics, Electricity Statistics, Road Statistics.

Israeli Central Bureau of Statistics. 1995. Statistical Abstract of Israel, no. 46.

Israeli Ministry of Health. 1994. *Health in Judea, Samaria, and Gaza 1967-94.*

Iyyada, Reem Abu, Jane Hannon and Ard El Insan (Terre des Hommes). July 1996. "Food Security: A Study to Assess the Impact of the Closure on Household Food Security."

Jawhary, Muna. 1995. *The Palestinian-Israeli Trade Arrangements: Searching for Fair Revenue-Sharing.* Jerusalem: Palestine Economic Policy Research Institute, September.

Kanafani, Nu'man. 1996. *Trade Relations Between Palestine and Israel: Free Trade Area or Customs Union?* Jerusalem: Palestine Economic Policy Research Institute, December.

Kassis, Nabeel. 1996. "Permanent Status Agreements and Economic Development." Paper prepared for conference on The Palestinian Economy: Towards a Vision, Birzeit University, June 9-12. Arab Economists Association, Ramallah, West Bank.

Khadr, Ali M. 1996. "The Economics of Peace in the Middle East: Has Donor Assistance to the Palestinian Territories Been Slow to Flow?" Paper prepared for the European Economic Association Congress, August.

Khano, Mark and Edward Sayre. 1997. *The Palestinian Tourism Sector: Present State and Future Prospects.* Jerusalem: Palestine Economic Policy Research Institute.

Lahmeyer International and Verbund-Plan. 1995.

MAS Policy Notes. 1996a. "Palestinian-Israeli Trade Relations (1): Free Trade Area or Customs Union?" Issue No.1. Jerusalem: Palestine Economic Policy Research Institute, August.

———. 1996b. "Palestinian-Israeli Trade Relations (2): Trade Policy Options for the West Bank and Gaza Strip." Issue No. 2. Jerusalem: Palestine Economic Policy Research Institute, September.

———. 1996c. "The Legal Framework for Business in the West Bank and Gaza Strip." Issue No. 3. Jerusalem: Palestine Economic Policy Research Institute, September.

————. 1996d. "Standards of Living in the West Bank and Gaza Strip." Issue No. 4. Jerusalem: Palestine Economic Policy Research Institute, September.

————. 1996e. "The Palestinian Banking System: Reality and Potential." Issue No. 5. Jerusalem: Palestine Economic Policy Research Institute, November.

————. 1996f. "Gaps in Palestinian Economic and Social Life - Determinants and Trends in the Status of Palestinian Women: Fertility, Labor and Social Support." Issue No. 6. Jerusalem: Palestine Economic Policy Research Institute, November.

————. 1996g. "A Preliminary Evaluation of the Tax System in West Bank and Gaza Strip." Issue No. 7. Jerusalem: Palestine Economic Policy Research Institute, December.

Mattin, and Palestinian Trade Promotion Organization. 1996. "Set of Case Studies of the Impact of Spring 1996 Closure on Firms in the West Bank and Gaza Strip." Commissioned by Development Alternatives International.

Ministry of Planning and International Cooperation (MOPIC). 1997. First Quarterly Monitoring Report of Donor Assistance, June.

Mayo, Stephen K. 1995. "Housing Sector Performance and Housing Strategy in Gaza and the West Bank." Urban Development Division, The World Bank, June, unpublished manuscript.

Mustafa, Mohammed. 1996. "The Palestinian Diaspora." Paper prepared for conference on The Palestinian Economy: Towards a Vision, Birzeit University, June 9-12. Arab Economists Association, Ramallah, West Bank.

Naqib, Fadle Al. 1996. "A Preliminary Evaluation of the Tax System in the West Bank and Gaza Strip." Jerusalem: Palestine Economic Policy Research Institute.

National Center for Educational Research and Development (NCERD). 1993. "Student Achievement in Jordan and the West Bank: A Comparative Perspective," March.

Nelson, F. Howard and T. O'Brien. 1993. *How US Teachers Measure Up Internationally.* American Federation of Teachers, AFL-CIO, Washington, DC, July.

Palestinian Central Bureau of Statistics. 1994. *Demography of the Palestinian Population in the West Bank and Gaza Strip,* Current Status Report No. 1, December. Ramallah, West Bank.

————. 1995. *Education Statistics in the West Bank and Gaza Strip.* Current Status Report 5, Ramallah, West Bank, August.

————. 1996a. Demographic Survey in the West Bank and Gaza Strip, Preliminary Results, Ramallah, West Bank, March.

————. 1996b. Expenditure Consumption Surveys, October-September 1996 and April-May 1996. Ramallah, West Bank.

————. 1996c. Labor Force Survey Report Series: No. 1, April; and No. 2, Ramallah, West Bank, August.

————. 1996d. *Labour Force Survey: Main Findings (September-October 1995) Round.* Ramallah, West Bank, April.

————. 1996e. *Labour Force Survey: Main Findings (April-May 1996) Round.* Ramallah, West Bank, August.

Palestinian Ministry of Health. 1996. *Financial Report 1995*, Gaza.

Pannier, Dominique. 1996. "West Bank and Gaza Civil Service Study, Presentation and Technical Assistance Supervision." World Bank Memorandum, Washington, DC, July.

Pannier, Dominique and Ngy Hanna. 1996. "West Bank and Gaza—Public Sector Adjustment Program and Institutional Development Trust Fund." World Bank Memorandum, Washington, DC, July.

Shaban, Radwan A. 1993. "Palestinian Labour Mobility." *International Labour Review*, 1993, Vol. 134, no. 5-6, pp. 655-72.

————. 1995. "Role of Private Sector in Development of Palestine." Paper presented at seminar on the Reconstruction and Development of Palestine, November 7-9. Jerusalem: Palestine Economic Policy Research Institute, November.

————. 1996. *Toward a Vision of Palestinian Economic Development.* Jerusalem: Palestine Economic Policy Research Institute, September.

Shaban, Radwan A. and Samia Al-Botmeh. 1995. *Poverty in the West Bank and Gaza Strip.* Jerusalem: Palestine Economic Policy Research Institute, November.

Shabaneh, Luay. 1996. "Palestinian Labor Market and Wages." Palestine Central Bureau of Statistics, March.

Thomas, Vinod and Yan Wang. 1993. *The Lessons of East Asia: Government Policy and Productivity Growth. Is East Asia an Exception?* Washington, DC: World Bank.

United Nations. 1996. "Local Aid Coordination in the West Bank and Gaza Strip." Presentation to Informal Ad Hoc Liaison Committee Meeting. Washington, DC.

United Nations Office of the Special Coordinator in the Occupied Territories (UNSCO). 1996a. "Aggregate Trends in the West Bank and Gaza Strip Economy." Gaza, October.

UNSCO. 1996b. "Economic and Social Conditions in the West Bank and Gaza Strip." Quarterly Report, Autumn.

———. 1996c. *Putting Peace to Work.* October.

———. 1997. Quarterly Report, Spring.

UNSCO-World Bank. 1996. *Partners in Peace.* July.

United Nations Relief and Works Agency (UNRWA) and National Center for Human Resources Development (NCHRD). 1994. "Comparative Math & Science Achievement Across the UNRWA Fields of Gaza Strip, Lebanon, Syria, Jordan & the West Bank."

US Department of Education. 1993. *The Condition of Education.* National Center for Education Statistics, Washington, DC.

Valverde, G. A., W. H. Schmidt, and L. J. Bianchi. 1996. "An Exploratory Analysis of the Content and Expectations for Student Performance in Selected Mathematics and Biology School-Leaving Examinations from the Middle East and North Africa." World Bank, Washington, DC, July.

Volcker, Paul A. 1996. "Trade Arrangements in the Middle East & North Africa - Report of the Middle East Economic Strategy Group." Council on Foreign Relations, New York, November.

World Bank. 1993. *Developing the Occupied Territories: An Investment in Peace.* Volumes 1-6. Washington, DC.

———. 1993. *The East Asian Miracle: Public Policy and Economic Growth.* Policy Research Report. Washington, DC: World Bank and Oxford University Press.

———. 1994a. "The West Bank and Gaza: The Next Two Years and Beyond." Country Operations Division, Country Department II. Middle East and North Africa Region, (White Cover Second Draft), Washington, DC, June.

———. 1994b. "West Bank-Gaza Strip Reconnaissance of the Issues: Municipal Finance and Management" Draft Report. Washington, DC, October.

———. 1994c. *World Development Report 1994*.

———. 1995a. "From Scarcity to Security: Averting a Water Crisis in the Middle East and North Africa," Washington, DC, December.

———. 1995b. *World Development Report 1995: Workers in an Integrating World*. New York: Oxford University Press.

———. 1996a. "The Demographic Survey in the West Bank and Gaza Strip," Preliminary Report, World Development Report, Washington, DC, March.

———. 1996b. *Report on Palestinian Civil Service*, October.

———. 1996c. "Palestinian Housing Initiative. " Staff Appraisal Report, Washington, DC.

———. 1996d. *World Development Report 1996*.

———. 1997. "Medium-term Development Strategy and Public Financing Priorities for the Health Sector in West Bank and Gaza," Draft, Washington, DC.

Zuaiter, Ahmad F. and Hassan M. Abdou. 1996. "Palestine: The Competitive Positioning of a Nation." Final report, independent study, Harvard Business School, May.

Agreements

Agreement on the Gaza Strip and the Jericho Area, between the Government of the State of Israel and the Palestinian Liberation Organization, May 4 , 1994, Cairo.

Agreement on the Preparatory Transfer of Powers and Responsibilities, between the Government of the State of Israel and the Palestinian Liberation Organization, August 29, 1994, Erez.

Declaration of Principles on Interim Self-Government Arrangements, between the Government of the State of Israel and the Palestinian Liberation Organization, September 13, 1993, Washington, DC.

The Israeli-Palestinian Interim Agreement on the West Bank and the Gaza Strip, between the Government of the State of Israel and the Palestinian Liberation Organization, September 28, 1995, Washington, DC.

Protocol Concerning the Redeployment in Hebron, between the Government of the State of Israel and the Palestinian Liberation Organization, January 17, 1997, Jerusalem.

Protocol on Economic Relations—Annex IV of the Gaza-Jericho Agreement, between the Government of the State of Israel and the Palestinian Liberation Organization, April 29, 1994, Paris.

Index